PATERNOSTER BIBLICAL AND THEOLOGICAL MONOGRAPHS

Confronting the Will-to-Power

A Reconsideration of
the Theology of Reinhold Niebuhr

PATERNOSTER BIBLICAL AND THEOLOGICAL MONOGRAPHS

A complete listing of all titles in this series will be found at the close of this book.

SERIES PREFACE

At the present time we are experiencing a veritable explosion in the field of biblical and theological research with more and more academic theses of high quality being produced by younger scholars from all over the world. One of the considerations taken into account by the examiners of doctoral theses is that, if they are to be worthy of the award of a degree, then they should contain material that needs to be read by other scholars; if so, it follows that the facilities must exist for them to be made accessible. In some cases (perhaps more often than is always realised) it will be most appropriate for the distinctive contribution of the thesis to be harvested in journal articles; in others there may be the possibility of a revision that will produce a book of wider appeal than simply to professional scholars. But many theses of outstanding quality can and should be published more or less as they stand for the benefit of other scholars and interested persons.

Hitherto it has not been easy for authors to find publishers willing to publish works that, while highly significant as works of scholarship, cannot be expected to become 'best-sellers' with a large circulation. Fortunately the development of printing technology now makes it relatively easy for publishers to produce specialist works without the commercial risks that would have prevented them doing so in the past.

The Paternoster Press is one of the first publishers to make use of this new technology. Its aim is quite simply to assist biblical and theological scholarship by the publication of theses and other monographs of high quality at affordable prices.

Different publishers serve different constituencies. The Paternoster Press stands in the tradition of evangelical Christianity and exists to serve that constituency, though not in any narrow way. What is offered, therefore, in this series, is the best of scholarship by evangelical Christians.

Since the inception of this series in 1997 the scope of the works published has broadened considerably. The opportunity is now being taken to initiate parallel series which will cater in a more focussed way for the history and theology of the evangelical movement and for other interests. Alongside this series we now have *Studies in Evangelical History and Thought* and *Studies in Baptist History and Thought*. This development will leave the present series with a sufficiently wide field in biblical studies and theology.

PATERNOSTER BIBLICAL AND THEOLOGICAL MONOGRAPHS

Confronting the Will-to-Power

A Reconsideration of the Theology of Reinhold Niebuhr

Mark F. W. Lovatt

Wipf & Stock
PUBLISHERS
Eugene, Oregon

Wipf and Stock Publishers
199 W 8th Ave, Suite 3
Eugene, OR 97401

Confronting the Will-to-Power
A Reconsideration of the Theology of Reinhold Niebuhr
By Lovatt, Mark F. W.
Copyright©2001 Paternoster
ISBN 13: 978-1-59752-923-5
ISBN: 1-59752-923-0
Publication date 10/18/2006
Previously published by Paternoster, 2001

This Edition reprinted by Wipf and Stock Publishers
by arrangement with Paternoster

Paternoster
9 Holdom Avenue
Bletchley
Milton Keyes, MK1 1QR
Great Britain

Contents

FOREWORD .... **IX**

ACKNOWLEDGEMENTS .... **XIII**

PREFACE .... **XV**

ABBREVIATIONS .... **XVII**

CHAPTER 1: THE INFLUENCE OF HISTORICAL EVENTS UPON THE THEOLOGICAL DEVELOPMENT OF REINHOLD NIEBUHR ... 1

   Introduction... 1
   The United States of America at the start of the Twentieth Century 2
   The Effects of History upon Niebuhr's Theology....................................... 4
      1. The First World War: the first challenge to Niebuhr's early theology...........5
      2. The impact of the industrial situation on Niebuhr's theology......................5
      3. The impact of Russia on Niebuhr's theology..7
      4. The impact of Fascism on Niebuhr's theology 8
   Conclusion 9

CHAPTER 2: PHILOSOPHICAL AND THEOLOGICAL SCHOOLS OF THOUGHT SIGNIFICANT FOR THE DEVELOPMENT OF NIEBUHR'S THEOLOGY 11

   NIEBUHR'S CONCEPT OF LIBERAL PROTESTANTISM 11
      Introduction... 11
      A Definition of Liberal Protestantism.. 12
      Conclusion 14
   THE INFLUENCE OF MARXISM ON REINHOLD NIEBUHR 14
      Introduction... 14
      Marxism and Niebuhr's Theological Development............................. 16
      Aspects of Marxism Retained by Niebuhr... 23
      Conclusion 24
   THE INFLUENCE OF SØREN KIERKEGAARD UPON REINHOLD NIEBUHR 24
      Introduction... 24
      The Theology of Kierkegaard... 24
      Kierkegaard and Niebuhr... 30
      Conclusion 34
   THE INFLUENCE OF ROMANTICISM ON REINHOLD NIEBUHR 34
      Introduction... 34
      Niebuhr's Concept of Romanticism... 34

The Will to Power in the Philosophy of Nietzsche 35
Niebuhr and the Will-to-Power 39
Tragedy in Romanticism 42
Niebuhr's Concept of Tragedy 45
Conclusion 47
THE INFLUENCE OF WILLIAM JAMES ON REINHOLD NIEBUHR 48
Introduction 48
Modernism and the Problem of Power 48
James and Niebuhr: Matters of Style 50
The Philosophy of Pragmatism 51
   1. Pragmatism as method 51
   2. Ontology and Epistemology 54
   3. Anthropology and Epistemology 56
   4. God, Freedom and Evil 59
Conclusion 61
REINHOLD NIEBUHR AND NEO-ORTHODOXY: A DEBATE WITH KARL BARTH
.... 62
Introduction 62
Niebuhr as a Neo-orthodox Theologian 63
Niebuhr in Opposition to Barth 63
Key Issues: Evil, Sin and Salvation 65
Conclusion 70

CHAPTER 3: THE VARIOUS DOCTRINAL MOTIFS IN NIEBUHR'S THEOLOGY 73

COSMOLOGY 73
Introduction 73
Two realms of Being: Creator and Creation 73
   Creation as the work of God 74
   Considerations 76
Two Orders of Reality: Immanence and Transcendence 79
   Immanence and Transcendence 79
   Considerations 80
Two realms of Power: the Kingdom of God and Kingdom of the world . 85
   Considerations 88
ANTHROPOLOGY AND SIN 89
Introduction 89
Humanity 'Created in the Image of God' 90
Anxiety: the source of sin and the will-to-power 93
Security and the will-to-power 98
The will-to-power as the identity of sin 99
Original sin as pretence 101
Sin and the tragic human state 107
Considerations 110

SALVATION AND THE POWER OF GOD	113
Introduction	113
The task of salvation: Sinful humanity before a holy God	113
1. The human situation	113
2. The 'Prophetic Question': Can God be merciful as well as just?	114
The basis of salvation: Niebuhr's Christology	117
The means of salvation: The work of Christ on the Cross	119
1. The Cross of Christ: The revelation of God's justice and mercy	119
2. Christ and Power	121
The grace of God: wisdom and power	126
1. Grace as the wisdom of God	126
2. Grace as the power of God.	130
The event of salvation: life in the power of God	135
Galatians 2.20 in *NDM II*, Chapter IV part III	135
Taking up the revelation of Christ	137
Considerations	138
EPISTEMOLOGY PART 1: THE NATURE OF REASON	142
Introduction	142
Niebuhr's view of reason	143
The possibilities and limitations of reason	143
The test of tolerance	148
Considerations	149
EPISTEMOLOGY PART 2: REACHING THE WILL-TO-POWER EFFECTIVELY	151
Introduction	151
Three roles for epistemology	152
1. The revelation of profound truth	152
2. Bringing divine encounter	153
3. Making use of the will-to-power	155
Setting up the tension of impossible ideal	158
Myth, symbol and paradox	161
1. Myth	161
2. Symbol	165
3. Paradox	166
Considerations	168
CHRISTIAN REALISM	170
Introduction	170
Christian Realism	172
1. Social Realism	172
2. Human possibilities	173
Power and justice	175
Love, justice and pacifism	178
Considerations	180

CHAPTER 4: CONCLUSION **187**
    Introduction 187
    Consequences for the study of Niebuhr's theology 187
    Niebuhr's method: a Pragmatic approach to theology 189
    Niebuhr's theology as a response to problem of evil. 192
        1. Niebuhr's Pragmatic approach 194
        2. Niebuhr establishes the problem of evil as humanity's problem 196

APPENDIX 1: THE COSMOLOGICAL CHART **201**

BIBLIOGRAPHY **203**
    PUBLISHED WORKS BY REINHOLD NIEBUHR 203
    COLLECTIONS OF REINHOLD NIEBUHR'S SHORTER WRITINGS 203
    ARTICLE BY REINHOLD NIEBUHR CITED IN THE THESIS 204
    SECONDARY SOURCES ON REINHOLD NIEBUHR 204
    OTHER WORKS 205
    JOURNAL ARTICLES AND THESES 212

INDEX **213**

FOREWORD

John Heywood Thomas

I am pleased to contribute the Foreword to this book both because of the author and because of the subject. Dr. Lovatt was one of the students admitted in my penultimate year as Professor of Christian Theology and Head of the Department in the University of Nottingham. I have very clear memories of the undergraduate he was then and a very vivid recollection of his energetic enthusiasm. It was therefore a pleasing coincidence that my successor, Prof. The Rev. Canon A. C. Thiselton, invited me to act as the supervisor for Mr. Lovatt's doctoral research on Niebuhr. The fruits of those labours are evidenced not only in the successful submission of his dissertation but equally in the transformation of that work into this book. Transformation it has been; for, though careful readers will find echoes of the academic skill and industry that mark a thesis, the author is here seen to be addressing the wider theological public.

My second reason for readily agreeing to contribute this Foreword is my long-standing and very personal interest in Niebuhr. It is almost half a century since I met Reinhold Niebuhr: it is an experience that I shall never forget. I had gone to Union Theological Seminary, New York in the summer of 1953 armed with an introduction from the Niebuhrs' friend, the late Prof. Dorothy Emmet with whom I had several discussions when she delivered her Stanton Lectures in Cambridge. To my dismay I learnt that Niebuhr had suffered a stroke and was unable to lecture or indeed to make any public appearance. It was with delight as well as surprised relief, then, that one day in late Autumn I received an invitation to have tea with Niebuhr. We talked of a variety of things because I had been rather vociferous in my criticism of his colleague, Paul Tillich; but most of the conversation centred on the legacy that Kierkegaard had bequeathed theology. Two themes of that conversation are ingrained in my memory. Kierkegaard, said Niebuhr, had exposed as faults in Hegel tendencies which were the besetting sins of much philosophy. The trouble with Hegel had clearly been that he had treated the whole gamut of life and thought objectively. Though the conversation went on in an interesting enough fashion I did not think that I had been confronted with any remarkable insight. Then I suddenly heard Niebuhr say that, of course, Hegel's view of Christianity was really too subjective. At first I thought that he was mistakenly saying 'subjective' when he meant 'objective'. My second thought was that this was really typical of Niebuhr's rather cavalier attitude to scholarship and that, like Emerson, he believed that 'consistency is the logic of fools'. However, I soon realised that he meant exactly what he said and that it was an important point. It reminded me of a remark Kierkegaard makes in his Journal, that both Schleiermacher and Hegel reduce faith to mere subjectivity. Belonging though I did to the generation of students of theology who had been brought up on the 'commandment' – 'Thou shalt love the lord thy Dodd and thy Niebuhr as thyself' – I had nevertheless not been aware of the intellectual perspicacity and the profundity of general understanding which marked out Niebuhr as one of the greatest minds of the Twentieth Century. That meeting left me with a quite indelible impression of the sheer power of his intellect. This was very much in my mind when some months later as I was addressing a ministers' study group in Harlem I quoted some remarks from *The Nature and Destiny of Man* and added that, in my opinion, Niebuhr was the greatest theologian in America. Instantly there was a sonorous chorus of 'Amen, brother!'.

What I have sought to do whether in efforts of interpretation or as essays in theological creativity has been inspired by, rather than founded in, Niebuhr's work. So my perspective on Dr. Lovatt's book is very likely to correspond with that of the majority of the theological public. It is interesting to reflect that in neither Britain nor indeed America has there been a Niebuhr school of theologians; but this by no means implies that theologians have been unaware of him or without debt to him. For that reason it is important to see Niebuhr for what he was – a superb example of how theology can spring from the practicalities of daily Christian living and return to fructify that life of faith. In his 'Intellectual Autobiography' (Kegley and Bretall, *The Theology of Reinhold Niebuhr*, pp. 4 ff.) Niebuhr speaks of the 'boredom with epistemology' which made him 'foreswear graduate study and the academic career to which it pointed and to accept a parish...in Detroit'. It was, he says, the growth of Detroit as a city which 'determined (his) development more than any books which (he) may have read'. How the social realities forced him to reconsider the moralistic liberalist version of Christianity is a story that is well enough known; but there is an even more significant and revealing item of the young pastor's experience mentioned in the same context. Writing of his ministry to two ladies on their deathbeds he extols one, 'a nice old soul' from whom he 'relearned the essentials of the Christian faith'. Then he makes the telling comment – 'I appreciated that the ultimate problem of human existence is the peril of sin and death'. It is this which, I think, makes Dr. Lovatt's book so interesting and significant. While he wants to see Niebuhr and see him whole he argues that there is a perspective from which one must view his theology and that this is that of theodicy. What makes this thesis so persuasive to me is that when theodicy is seriously undertaken as a theological enterprise the theologian will sooner or later learn, as Job did, that the problem – whether it be that of suffering or of moral evil – is not solved by any intellectual theory. Undergirding any theoretical solution to the very real intellectual problem is the peculiar mystery of Job's confession 'Though he slay me yet will I trust in him'. Niebuhr would not have been surprised at the contemporary sentimentality which latches on to the dilemma though it has long absented itself from the passion of perplexed faith.

There is one other interesting feature of Dr. Lovatt's book. A considerable amount of ink has been spilt on the subject of Niebuhr's 'realism'. For myself, I must confess that I had never seen any reference to it when several years ago I suggested to one of my research students working on Niebuhr that this was the best way to encapsulate the vital but mercurial character of Niebuhr's theology. I cannot now remember when Mr. Lovatt and I discussed Niebuhr's realism but I do recall that I urged him to examine exactly what it signified. The result is a painstakingly thorough illumination of Niebuhr's mental outlook as an essentially theological response to Pragmatism. Too often in the past this term has been used to describe superficial aspects of Niebuhr's outlook – an acknowledgement, in fact, of Niebuhr's involvement in public affairs. Theological though his perspective was he had remarkably been a political analyst whose views were regularly sought by C.B.S. News, the unions and indeed politicians. Despite the fact that such superb studies as Robin W. Lovin's *Reinhold Niebuhr and Christian Realism* have summed up the reaction of a whole generation and have greatly helped our understanding of Niebuhr, Dr. Lovatt's book has brought fresh illumination to the subject. In particular, as I have indicated, he has done historians of thought as well as theologians a service by showing the contribution made to Niebuhr's thinking by William James' 'pragmatism'. In the last year or two there has been renewed interest in James as a philosopher and the generally experiential roots of his metaphysics have been recognised together with the very powerful mystical element which controls all his philosophical work. By his careful analysis of James' influence Dr. Lovatt gives us a new understanding of Niebuhr's views on epistemology and metaphysics. Rather than reducing Niebuhr's 'realism' to some recognition of the mixed nature of the Christian church or of the deficiencies of pacifism as a social policy or some hard-headed view of the realities of political power Dr. Lovatt has neatly put all these things in the context of a philosophical outlook. In doing that he has also managed not to play down in any way the dramatically powerful impact of Niebuhr's experience of Detroit struggles (a picture that is reminiscent of the young Barth of Safenwil with the Bible in one hand and the newspaper in the other).

I have reserved to the last what is perhaps my most commendatory comment on Dr. Lovatt's book: it is a remarkably faithful exposition of a great thinker. It is only as it enters on a critique that it fully reveals what is for the author the high ground from which he surveys his subject. Only then does Dr. Lovatt reveal that he views the theology as deficient. Securing that fidelity of interpretation was for me, as the supervisor of the research, as great a problem as it was – vice versa – for him; but so completely has it been achieved that the book shows great appreciation as well as criticism. Very often in theological debate one feels that what is missing is this kind of careful exposition. The theologian is committed to a truthful exercise and so should avoid tilting at windmills and fighting men of straw. I am reminded of a comment that was made about C. D. Broad, that unlike most philosophers one never knew from his exposition whether he agreed with the philosophical position under discussion. To compare him with that most perceptive and tidy of philosophers is one of the highest compliments one can pay Dr. Lovatt.

J. Heywood Thomas

Acknowledgements

I have many people to thank for the completion of this volume. First and foremost, the University of Nottingham, particularly the Theology department. My supervisors Professor A. C. Thiselton and Professor Emeritus John Heywood Thomas have been exemplary in their availability, personal interest and commitment to my studies, and I regard it as a privilege to have worked under them. I would also like to thank Mary Elmer for the way she has helped me with numerous small tasks over the years. The department as a whole has been most welcoming and helpful in providing me with the resources needed to complete this work. I would also like to thank the Graduate School for the use of the Graduate Room facilities.

Second, my grateful thanks to the Whitefield Institute, Oxford, under the direction of Dr. David Cook. As my main grant-making body the Institute was crucial for the successful completion of my PhD, which formed the main substance of this work.

I would also like to thank my many friends who have taken an active interest in my work throughout the six years the thesis took to write, particularly my friends Duncan and Joy Miller, who shared their home and lives with me in the last year of my research, and Dr. David and Catherine Parris and their children Jonathan and Hannah. Finally, my parents, John and Noël Lovatt, who provided all kinds of support – moral, financial, practical – through the course of all my studies.

Finally, I am keenly aware that it is only by the grace of God that this volume was completed. It was by the provision of God in every area of life – friendships, finance, accommodation, academic resources – that this project has been possible. Without such providence this course of study never would have been completed. 'Thanks be to God – through Jesus Christ our Lord.'

Preface

This study concerns the theology of Reinhold Niebuhr, in particular a contribution he has to make to the long-standing doctrinal issue of the problem of evil. Initial research into the problem of evil indicated that the main problem in the equation is in fact humanity itself. This leads us to the question of Why? What is it about us which consistently emerges in destructive activity against our fellow humans and the world around us? Niebuhr's study of human nature in *The Nature and Destiny of Man* emerged as a substantial contribution towards answering this difficult question. His perceptive analysis of the human situation regarding anxiety, security and power discussed in Chapter Three of this work seemed to make sense, and to match the activity seen all around us on a day-to-day basis. Discussions of this issue with people, Christian and otherwise, have consistently produced a recognition that there is something very valuable in this interpretation of human behaviour. It is hoped that it will be similarly useful for those who read this work.

Ultimately, though, the existence of evil must be discussed in relation to God, not just humanity. Evil does raise issues regarding God and our relationship with him – and this is so whether the matter is considered abstractly or as a result of direct personal suffering. It is not enough to simply 'get on with it' and try and fix the problems without confronting the deeper issues those situations raise about ourselves and our God. It seems also, however, that the understanding of God which too often underlies both the Christian and atheistic approach to the problem is fundamentally flawed and relies too uncritically upon unstated humanist assumptions regarding God and humanity which are at odds with the biblical message. This is discussed more thoroughly in Chapter Four. One of the intentions of this volume is to point out and challenge those assumptions in order to establish a better perception of these things than we have at present.

Concerning Niebuhr, then, it is argued here that his theology is to be understood at its deepest level, not in terms of political theology, or a Neo-orthodox response to liberalism, or a Pragmatic attempt to generate human vitality, but as an attempt to provide an effective Christian answer to the existence of evil. The manifestation of this problem of evil Niebuhr identifies using the Nietzschean term 'the will-to-power', a human trait of aggressive domination and manipulation which conditions all human behaviour. This, it is argued, is the quality of humanity that Niebuhr is directly and deeply concerned with, and which he seeks to respond to with his well-known Christian Realism, and less famous doctrines of anthropology, sin and salvation, Christology and epistemology.

It is hoped that this book provides food for thought, not only for those interested in Niebuhr's theology, or the doctrine of sin, but for those concerned with formulating an effect response, both practical and intelligent, to the existence of evil in God's Creation.

Mark Lovatt
Nottingham, April 2001

Abbreviations

BT	*Beyond Tragedy*
CLCD	*The Children of Light and the Children of Darkness*
CPP	*Christianity and Power Politics*
CRPP	*Christian Realism and Political Problems*
CRSW	*The Contribution of Religion to Social Work*
DCNR	*Does Civilisation Need Religion?*
DST	*Discerning the Signs of the Times*
FH	*Faith and History*
IAH	*The Irony of American History*
ICE	*An Interpretation of Christian Ethics*
Leaves	*Leaves from the Notebook of a Tamed Cynic*
MMIS	*Moral Man and Immoral Society*
MNC	*Man's Nature and His Communities*
NDM I	*The Nature and Destiny of Man, Volume I*
NDM II	*The Nature and Destiny of Man, Volume II*
REE	*Reflections at the End of an Era*
SDH	*The Self and the Dramas of History*
SNE	*The Structure of Nations and Empires*
KB	Kegley and Bretall, eds., *Reinhold Niebuhr: His Religious, Social, and Political Thought*

CHAPTER 1

The Influence of Historical Events upon the Theological Development of Reinhold Niebuhr

Introduction

Every theologian can be expected to be concerned with contemporary society and current events, and seek to relate Christian insight to the world in such a way as to ensure its positive reception and effectiveness. This was true of Niebuhr to such a degree that his actual method of doing theology consisted of correlating Christianity with culture to bring Christian truth to bear on the situations which unfolded during his lifetime. This produced a theology which was 'empirical':[1] piecemeal and unsystematic, yet consistently and powerfully relevant to his contemporaries. As Emil Brunner notes, one of Niebuhr's outstanding achievements was that he engaged successfully with the secular world, and that those in positions of power in America listened carefully to what he had to say. 'With him theology broke out into the world'.[2]

Niebuhr not only related theology to the world around him: his very theology developed and emerged as he engaged with situations which arose in both America and Europe. The fact that his writings appeared in so many newspapers, magazines and journals reflects this constant activity of using Christian concepts to unravel complex and difficult situations and provide a useful and relevant answer. The negative consequence of this approach was that his theology was in some respects too narrow in its scope, risking irrelevance in societies which do not share western culture, and due to its lack of system, was weak in areas which, though not immediately useful, are necessary for a solid and well-developed theology. However, his chosen agenda was to engage passionately in the areas he was concerned with, and this he did consistently well.

To understand Niebuhr's theology, then, it is necessary to consider the historical situations which arose during the formative period of his theology,

---

[1] A description used by Robert L. Calhoun in 'Review of Niebuhr, Reinhold, The Nature and Destiny of Man, Vol I: Human Nature', *The Journal of Religion*, 21 (1941), 473-80 (pp. 477-8).

[2] Emil Brunner, 'Some Remarks on Reinhold Niebuhr's Work as a Christian Thinker', in *KB*, pp. 27-33 (p. 29).

the first half of the twentieth century. The First World War, followed by the Depression, the rise of Fascism in Europe and the Second World War, formed the crucible within which the Nineteenth Century liberalism, humanism and optimism characterising the opening century were tested and largely discredited. Niebuhr's theological inheritance, particularly in the form of the Social Gospel, was severely tested, finding itself unable to explain or to give a solution to the problems of the new era. It was necessary to construct a new, more realistic, some might say more Christian theology on the ruins of the old. In Europe Karl Barth undertook the task, while amongst others, the Niebuhr brothers did so in America.[3]

Since the realities of the twentieth century, and the hopes and illusions it shattered, formed the context for the development of Niebuhr's thought, it is necessary to look at events and processes emerging in the phenomena of his time in order to understand better the work he undertook. In the next chapter we will consider a selection of theological and philosophical schools which were of particular significance in the formation of his thought. Here, we will examine a number of social and historical factors which influenced his development as a theologian.

The United States of America at the start of the Twentieth Century

The twentieth century began in America with a wave of hope and expectation that the new century would be the fulfilment of the dream of creating a community of love and justice, the Kingdom of God. The possibility of creating a godly, even ideal society had played a vital role in the history of the United States, reaching its climax in the high expectations at the turn of the century. The concept of the Kingdom of God finds it origins in the founding fathers of America themselves, who were a religious, largely Protestant people seeking to escape religious persecution and conflict in Europe. Despite their religious diversity, the first wave of settlers shared a common belief in biblical authority and the value of the Protestant tradition. This powerful Protestant identity distinguished early American society, with a strong alliance between Church and culture (but not State) and the idea that the American way of life was the most Christian of societies.[4]

The first period of settlement up to the first Great Awakening of 1735 was more centred round the sovereignty of God and of living a life in

---

[3] Lovin, R. W., *Reinhold Niebuhr and Christian Realism*, (Cambridge: CUP, 1995), pp. 41-5.

[4] Robert T. Handy, 'The American Scene', in *Twentieth Century Christianity: A Survey of Modern Religious Trends by Leading Churchmen*, ed. by Stephen Neill (London: Collins, 1961), pp. 191-229 (pp. 194-95, 200).

relation to him rather than the active construction of a Christian society.⁵ Perhaps their experience of 'Christian' institutions in Europe established a deep-seated aversion to recreating them in their new country. With the period of the Great Awakenings, firstly with Jonathan Edwards from the 1730's and later with Charles Finney in the 1820's, the idea of a more active approach began to take hold. The power of the natural 'will-to-live' in the believer could be put to good use in constructing a Christian society based on God's will and the principles revealed in the Scriptures. Of particular importance would be the law of love so prominent in Jesus' own teachings. From these foundations, a new society of democracy for all, based on a community of love could be established.

This intention produced a long and powerful drive to Christianise America, beginning with the revivals, developing into the social Christianity and humanitarian movements of the Nineteenth Century and emerging in the Social Gospel at around the turn of the century. White and Hopkins state that the period 1830 to 1930 in America can best be understood in terms of this huge surge of religious hope and excitement.⁶

Two important situations arose in the Nineteenth Century which affected this development. The first was the Civil War, centred in Virginia and the surrounding states. The war's devastation seems to have had little effect on the progress of Christianisation in the long term, however. Less violent, but more substantial and wide-ranging in its impact was the effect of urbanisation and industrialisation in the second half of the Nineteenth Century. It was the new industrial society which gave the Christian movement its greatest challenge.

The new cities presented a host of new problems to American society. Protestantism had thrived in the old society of farms and small towns. The big cities presented a far more difficult environment to work in, with their poverty, misery, vice and crime.⁷ Josiah Strong listed the city as the most serious of seven evils threatening American civilisation.⁸ The human problems of industrial strife, unequal wealth distribution and slum dwellings demanded a Christian response, and there began a massive programme of moral crusades and evangelism to deal with it. This was strengthened by the new interest in social Christianity and the task of Christianising society as a whole; an interest reflected world-wide and particularly in England,

---

⁵ Niebuhr, H. Richard, *The Kingdom of God in America*, (Hamden, Conn.: Shoe String Press, 1956), pp. 56-61.

⁶ White, Ronald, and C. Howard Hopkins, *The Social Gospel: Religion and Reform in Changing America*, (Philadelphia: Temple University Press, 1976), p. xiv.

⁷ Handy, Robert T., The Social Gospel in America, 1870-1920: Gladden, Ely and Rauschenbusch, (New York: OUP, 1966), p. 4.

⁸ Handy, *The Social Gospel*, p. 9.

which was to later provide a model of Christian political activism for Niebuhr and the American Left in the form of the British Labour Party.[9]

The crusade to Christianise America, activated by the Great Awakenings, engaged with the challenge of the new industrial society and enjoyed an era of apparent success. The Nineteenth Century Christian humanitarian movements tackled slavery, immigrant exploitation, education and hospitals for the poor, and added weight to the impression that society was improving and that the Kingdom of God was approaching.[10] Secular progressivism added momentum to the Christian social movement, and the century finished in America with a massive general hope and enthusiasm for Christianity.[11] This was the peak of social Christianity, or the Social Gospel as it was now being known under the guidance of Walter Rauschenbusch, its new prophet.

The Social Gospel was the completion of the movement for social Christianity. Religious rather than humanist or rationalist, it was concerned with the task of Christianising society in order to make Christian conversion more possible for the victims of the new industrial order.[12] It combined liberalism[13] with Christianity and the contemporary belief in Progress to create a movement which was activist, optimistic and essentially Christian in so far as it based its core beliefs on the teachings of Jesus. The idea of the Kingdom of God formed the focus for its vision: a new society of justice and peace founded on the law of love; and the Social Gospel movement was at its maximum strength as the new century arrived.[14]

The Effects of History upon Niebuhr's Theology

At the beginning of the twentieth century the Social Gospel was at the height of its power. There was a strong sense of hope, and the expectation that the twentieth century would usher in the era of the Kingdom of God in America. More religious but less apocalyptic than the European optimism, which was more affected by the Marxist expectation of violent revolution, American society as a whole, with its faith in Christian progress looked forward to a new era of peace and prosperity.

The reality could hardly have been more different. Beginning with the First World War, but going forward through Depression and industrial strife, Fascism in Europe and the Second World War, historical reality

---

[9] Meyer, D.B., *The Protestant Search for Political Realism, 1919 - 1941*, (Los Angeles: University of California Press, 1960), pp. 102, 224; Fox, R. W., *Reinhold Niebuhr: A Biography*, (New York: Pantheon, 1985), pp. 77-83, 149-50.

[10] Niebuhr, *The Kingdom of God in America*, pp. 121-2.

[11] Handy, *The Social Gospel*, p. 6; Meyer, pp. 8-15.

[12] Meyer, pp. 27-8.

[13] See the first section of Chapter Two for a definition of liberalism.

[14] Handy, *The Social Gospel*, p. 3.

directly contradicted the optimism of the preceding era. Clearly there was a deep-seated, powerful principle at work in human history which the (broadly liberal) religious optimism of the Nineteenth Century had failed to grasp. It was this force which Niebuhr in time identified as the 'will-to-power', the entrenched sinful egoism of a corrupted humanity. The reality of the will-to-power, as it emerged in the first four decades of the twentieth century, was the source of serious problems for liberal thought, and since it was a factor in human nature it was not prepared to recognise, liberalism had no satisfactory answer to give to deal with it.

1. THE FIRST WORLD WAR: THE FIRST CHALLENGE TO NIEBUHR'S EARLY THEOLOGY

The First World War began the work of Reinhold Niebuhr's theological development, shattering the liberal idealism he had grown up with by exposing some deep-seated shortcomings. In particular, the war demonstrated to him the potency of propaganda, and the ability of the State to mask or override the facts of a situation in order to manipulate the populace and achieve its own ends.[15] This issue of propaganda later formed a key part of his epistemology, particularly when he saw the same instruments effectively employed by the Ford Motor Company in Detroit. The war also demonstrated some unsettling aspects of Government which clashed with the idealistic liberal concepts of humanity and statesmanship he had grown up with. The Versailles settlement in particular revealed an unpleasant cynicism and selfishness in the world of politics. His visit to the Ruhr under French occupation developed his intuition that liberalism was suspect,[16] had even perhaps failed to account for a deep-seated, dangerous side to human nature. The activities of the occupying forces lay too far outside the liberal concept of humanity for it to be able to give an account of such behaviour, and so clearly there must have been a deficiency somewhere in its perspective.

Niebuhr, then, was still a young man, and though he had not really begun writing theology, the war without doubt shook his liberal preconceptions.[17] However, it was his experience as a pastor at Bethel Evangelical Church in Detroit which was more influential in the development of his theology, as he engaged in the struggle for social justice in the industrial arena.

2. THE IMPACT OF THE INDUSTRIAL SITUATION ON NIEBUHR'S THEOLOGY

The world of big business was radically different from the more paternal rural society of America in the period up to the 1870's. This new era was practically an internal war, with thousands of strikes, murders and assassinations each year, beginning in earnest with the railroad strike of

---

[15] Meyer, pp. 219-20.
[16] Related in *Leaves*, pp. 46-7; Fox, pp. 78-9.
[17] Fox, pp. 57-60; Meyer, p. 227.

1877.[18] The powerful capitalists refused to conform to what were regarded as acceptable Christian concepts of morality in their pursuit of wealth.[19] This abuse of power, likened by Henry Adams to an unstoppable dynamo of unrestrained energy,[20] made the lives of their employees most unpleasant, since the industrialists demanded higher productivity while reducing wages. Resistance to the industrial overlords usually took the form of strikes, which could be extremely violent as the private police forces of the industrialists used force, and sometimes machine guns, to break them.

The conflict and brutality of industrial life, highlighted by the Depression, continued the process of exposing the limits of the liberal perception of humanity. Doubts not only about liberalism but also the effectiveness of the Social Gospel were compounded by the failure of the Church to exert any significant influence on either capitalists or labour.[21] For Niebuhr, the disillusionment came through first-hand experience. Despite the relatively comfortable middle class nature of his own Church, he was actively involved in the struggle of the shop-floor workers of Henry Ford's factory.[22] The harsh existence and exploitation he witnessed brought home to him the reality of human sin which contradicted liberal perceptions of human nature. In particular, it was Ford's effective propaganda which revealed to Niebuhr the possibilities of pretence,[23] of disguising egoism behind a facade of reasonableness.[24] Ford presented himself as a caring and enlightened employer while he drove his men to the extremes of exhaustion and then laid them off for months without pay during retooling. This was to be a useful experience for Niebuhr later on as he developed his epistemology and critique of reason.

Meanwhile, the brutality of Ford's private police force, the Ford Service Organisation, and its violent strike-breaking activities, presented Niebuhr with a dilemma. After the First World War he had joined many others in taking a pacifist position against conflict.[25] The plight of the workers in

---

[18] Diggins, John P., *The Rise and Fall of the American Left*, (London: Norton, 1992), pp. 78-81; Handy, *The Social Gospel*, p. 9.

[19] David Bell, 'The Background and Development of Marxian Socialism in the United States', in *Socialism and American Life*, ed. by Donald Drew Egbert and Stow Persons, 2 vols (Princeton: PUP, 1952), vol 1, pp. 213-405 (p. 268).

[20] Diggins, John P., *The Promise of Pragmatism: Modernism and the Crisis of Knowledge and Authority*, (Chicago: University of Chicago Press, 1994), pp. 28-30.

[21] Handy, 'The American Scene', pp. 206-8.

[22] In *Leaves*, p. 78, for example, Niebuhr relates a visit to the factory, a place which he describes as 'hellish'.

[23] Niebuhr uses the US spelling of 'pretense'. Since this book was written in the UK, the British spelling, 'pretence', will be used in the main text, with the US spelling employed when quoting from Niebuhr and other writers using this form of spelling.

[24] Fox, pp. 94-8.

[25] Fox, pp. 78-9; Bingham, J. *The Courage to Change: An Introduction to the Life and Thought of Reinhold Niebuhr*, (Lanham, Maryland: University Press of America,

Detroit in their quest for social justice, though, forced him to reconsider. He recognised that a belief in human reasonableness and the power of love was hopelessly naïve when faced with Ford's thugs. Finally he rejected pacifism in an article in *Atlantic* magazine in May 1927, where he dismissed it as basically a means of keeping the oppressed at heel. Instead, he embraced the use of coercion as a necessary tool to achieve justice, a position he set out in print in *MMIS* a few years later. Historical reality, in the form of the situation in Detroit, had challenged his position and forced him to rethink his theology – a recurring pattern in the development of his theology.

3. THE IMPACT OF RUSSIA ON NIEBUHR'S THEOLOGY

The First World War and the urban reality of Detroit were the first two major situations to challenge the ideas Niebuhr held. The third was the failure of communism in Russia and its collapse into a totalitarian state.

The Russian Revolution in 1917 was met with delight by the American Left, and the emerging communist state was a source of light and hope for many in America, who were struggling to bring social justice to its capitalist society.[26] The apparent success of communism in Russia was seen in direct contrast to the misery of an America blighted first by industrialisation and, following the Wall Street Crash of 1929, the Depression. The early 1930's were marked by a general sense that capitalism had failed and that the Marxist solution of radical change through revolution might be correct. In 20 years matters in America had come a long way from the pre-war euphoria of 1914 which looked forward to the dawning of the new era in the United States. The first New Deal of 1933 was seen as an ineffective palliative by the Left when major surgery was needed.[27] Russia seemed to show that a better alternative than capitalism was possible, and that the Marxist analysis of capitalism as intrinsically flawed was fundamentally accurate.

As early as the late 1920's, though, there was disillusionment in America concerning Marxism. The U.S. Communist Party, pathetically dependent on Moscow for direction and riven by internal strife, began to introduce alienating policies which cost it large numbers of members.[28] More serious, though, was the emerging reality of Stalin's rule. The Moscow trials, beginning in 1936, exposed a more unpleasant state of affairs than the worker's paradise Russia claimed to be. Even so, support remained for communism amongst the Left as a whole through the 1930's, not least due

---

1993), p. 109; Cantor, Milton, *The Divided Left: American Radicalism, 1900 - 1975*, (New York: Hill and Wang, 1978), pp. 137-8.

[26] Diggins, *Rise and Fall*, p. 106; Cantor, pp. 64-73.

[27] Diggins, *Rise and Fall*, p. 189; Shannon, David A., *Between the Wars: America, 1919 - 1941*, 2nd edn (Boston: Houghton Mifflin, 1979), p. 199.

[28] Cantor, p. 86.

to the state of the U.S. economy, which remained in depression. It was not until the Hitler-Stalin Pact of 1939 that the Left in general became disillusioned with Marxism, and that a new perception emerged that the piecemeal reforms in the manner of the New Deal might after all be preferred to radical change.[29] Furthermore, the rise of Fascism in Europe made any kind of democracy, however poor, seem attractive when compared with what was emerging in Germany, Italy and Spain.

Again, Niebuhr's thought was influenced by these events. He had generally supported Marxist socialism, and had employed a Marxist perspective on capitalism and ideology to make a critique of his own liberal tradition.[30] Stalinist Russia, however, disillusioned him. The Hitler-Stalin Pact he found particularly bitter,[31] and he turned against Marxism to become one of its most vehement U.S. critics. He identified the source of Russia's failing with Marxism's essentially optimistic anthropology: like the liberalists, Marxists were essentially 'children of light', too naïve concerning the reality of human nature and the will-to-power and open to manipulation and abuse by the likes of Stalin.[32] Here again, historical reality formed the context in which Niebuhr's thought changed and developed.

4. THE IMPACT OF FASCISM ON NIEBUHR'S THEOLOGY

By the time the Second World War began in Europe, Niebuhr had radically altered his position, and now rejected all forms of humanism, which he now regarded as naïve and optimistic in regard to human nature. Thus he was in a position to analyse the progress of Fascism in terms of a new, deeper anthropology centred on the idea of sin and the will-to-power. Hence even as early as *MMIS* (1932) he was able to recognise and point out the violent nature of the Nazis.[33] In 1940 he actively advocated American involvement in the war and fought vigorously against pacifism, which he perceived to be naïve and based on the discredited liberalism.

The rise of Fascism therefore confirmed and developed Niebuhr's position rather than radically altered it. The reality of the will-to-power and its destructive effect could hardly be more clear. The U.S. Left was generally less well-prepared, though, and the harsh realities of the new era finally soured the original optimism of the turn of the century. The loss of naïveté created a disenchanted generation, more interested in irony,

---

[29] Cantor, pp. 87-95; Sidney Hook, 'The Philosophical Basis of Marxian Socialism in the United States', in *Socialism and American Life*, ed. by Donald Drew Egbert and Stow Persons, 2 vols (Princeton: PUP, 1952), I, pp. 427-51 (p. 451).

[30] See the section below concerning the influence of Marxism upon Niebuhr, especially the Introduction.

[31] Fox, p. 190; John C. Bennett, 'Reinhold Niebuhr's Social Ethics', in *KB*, pp. 45-78 (pp. 72-3).

[32] *CLCD*, p. 76; also pp. 28-9, 45.

[33] *MMIS*, pp. 210, 215-16.

paradox, ambiguity and complexity than grand projects.[34] In particular it was the Spanish Civil War which created the new atmosphere of realism, even cynicism, in that generation.[35] If a moral cause as clear-cut as the resistance to Franco's totalitarianism could fail, what hope was there elsewhere?

In fact, Fascism and Stalinism in Europe changed some important battle lines in America. First, the intellectual agenda changed from attacking capitalism in order to implement socialism, to defending democracy itself against its opponents. For Niebuhr this happened in 1935-6 as he saw the danger of Fascism in Europe.[36]

Second, the perennial issue of pacifism and the use of force to control evil resurfaced. Pacifism, in Niebuhr's view, was no match for the Nazis. Only a philosophy which was prepared to sanction force could provide a realistic opposition to Fascism. Marxism, though realistic in the necessity of using coercion by its advocation of violence for the revolution, was clearly inadequate in other areas. An alternative was needed to deal with the human evil which historical events had clearly exposed. This was the challenge to which Niebuhr rose with his theology.

Conclusion

The impact of the first decades of the twentieth century on optimistic thinkers of all kinds was obviously tremendous. In particular the American Social Gospel movement found itself in disarray.[37] The times called for a more profound theology, one which plumbed the depths of humanity, as Kierkegaard had for example, and so be better able to deal with intrinsic human nature than Marxism.[38] Without completely abandoning the heritage of the Social Gospel, Niebuhr sought a theology able to deal effectively with human evil. We now turn to the intellectual resources which were at his disposal.

---

[34] Bell, Daniel, *The End of Ideology: On the Exhaustion of Political Ideas in the Fifties*, revised edition (New York: The Free Press, 1962), p. 300.
[35] Diggins, *Rise and Fall*, pp. 175-8; Cantor, p. 112.
[36] Fox, pp. 168-9.
[37] Handy, 'The American Scene', pp. 206-8.
[38] Diggins, *Rise and Fall*, p. 192.

CHAPTER 2
Philosophical and Theological Schools of Thought Significant for the Development of Niebuhr's Theology

Niebuhr's Concept of Liberal Protestantism

Introduction

There has already been a substantial amount of discussion by Niebuhr's commentators concerning his relationship with liberal Protestantism.[1] However, despite the thoroughness of their considerations, a clear definition of the term 'liberal Protestantism', also called liberalism, seems to be lacking. As a preliminary stage of this chapter it will be worth taking the trouble to define this term clearly. The task of this section of the chapter, therefore, will be to set out briefly the main characteristics of the liberal Protestantism with which Niebuhr was familiar.

Regarding the use of the term 'liberal', it should first be noted that we are concerned primarily with the liberal Protestantism to be found in the school which took up the theology of Albrecht Ritschl. With this in mind we may exclude the political aspect of the term 'Liberal' found for example in the philosophy of John Stuart Mill. Furthermore, it is the liberal Protestantism found in America with which Niebuhr would have been familiar that particularly interests us. While followers of Ritschl in Europe, such as Adolf Von Harnack and Ernst Troeltsch, may have had some influence upon Niebuhr, it was with the liberal Protestantism of the Social Gospel movement in America, headed by Walter Rauschenbusch, that he had by far the greater contact and which proved to be a key influence upon him.[2]

---

[1] See particularly Daniel D. Williams' analysis in 'Niebuhr and Liberalism', *KB*, pp. 194-213, and Durkin, Kenneth, *Reinhold Niebuhr*, (London: Geoffrey Chapman, 1989), Chapter 1; also Grenz, Stanley and Roger Olson, *20th Century Theology: God and the World in a Transitional Age*, (Carlisle: Paternoster, 1992), pp. 105-7, Rasmussen, L., ed., *Reinhold Niebuhr: Theologian of Public Life*, (London: Collins, 1988), pp. 26-9.

[2] Arthur Schlesinger, Jnr., 'Reinhold Niebuhr's Role in American Political Life and Thought', in *KB*, pp. 125-50 (pp. 127-31).

A Definition of Liberal Protestantism

What should we understand by the term 'liberal', then?[3] First, liberalism can be identified by its attempt to make Christianity relevant and accessible to the modern mind, working hard to make a religion which could be regarded as ancient and outdated, up-to-date and relevant.[4] This is one of liberalism's greatest contributions to modern theology, and in fact a task Niebuhr himself undertook, despite his general hostility towards the school. The liberal agenda to modernise the gospel reflected a deep-seated regard for Christianity: a matter often overlooked amongst those often classified as 'Neo-orthodox', Niebuhr included. Many liberals took a positive view of modern developments in philosophy, sociology and psychology and attempted to incorporate valid insights into their theology; [5] and Niebuhr likewise followed this approach. They were also prepared to discard dogmas they considered to be irrecoverably outdated in order to keep Christianity relevant and acceptable to the modern world.

Second, liberal Protestantism assimilated Enlightenment thinking into its theology. Of particular importance was its desire to show the essential reasonableness of Christianity. There was also a commitment to the concept of 'natural religion', of there being a single, rational, complete religion which lay behind the various incomplete historical religions, and would furthermore be compatible with the natural sciences. From this arose the search for an 'essential Christianity', which they believed would emerge if they stripped away aspects of theology and the New Testament they considered irrational or unscientific: the 'husk and kernel' idea. Some theologians, however, considered that this had occurred to excess, and that some key elements of Christianity had been lost. H. Richard Niebuhr's famous comment summarised this perception: 'A God without wrath brought men without sin into a kingdom without judgment through the ministrations of a Christ without a cross'.[6]

Third, liberal Protestantism tended to accept the findings of the Tubingen school and the quest of the historical Jesus too uncritically. Liberal Christologies therefore tended to present Jesus as the ideal man, a profound religious teacher or poet uniquely inspired to proclaim the Kingdom of God before dying a tragic death. It stopped short of recognising the divinity of Christ. Furthermore, those areas of Christ's teachings which seemed to affirm the essential goodness and worth of human nature were highlighted somewhat at the expense of those dealing with human sinfulness. Also,

---

[3] This definition is constructed by drawing on descriptions found in the following works: Grenz and Olson, pp. 51-2; Handy, *The Social Gospel*, pp. 10-11; Schlesinger in *KB*, pp. 128-9, and Williams in *KB*, pp. 197-206.

[4] Reardon, *Liberal Protestantism*, p. 64; Fox, p. 183.

[5] Mackintosh, Hugh Ross, *Types of Modern Theology: Schleiermacher to Barth*, (London: Nisbet, 1937), pp. 181-4; Welch, vol II, p. 223.

[6] Niebuhr, *The Kingdom of God in America*, p. 193.

those aspects of theology they considered to be irrational or supernatural were regarded as the result of ancient ignorance, or of the long-gone battles with encroaching heresies. So the miracles recorded during Jesus' ministry and his Resurrection were stripped of their factual status and interpreted as 'myths' or just simple misunderstandings.[7]

Fourth, the concept of the Kingdom of God, of a society operating according to the law of love, took pride of place in American liberalism, as one might expect, considering the country's Christian foundations. The Kingdom was presented as the central point of Christ's existence and teachings, particularly in the Social Gospel movement headed by Walter Rauschenbusch. Jesus' job was seen to be to proclaim the coming of the Kingdom of God as an imminent possibility for humanity, achieved by applying his principles of love as set out most clearly in the Sermon on the Mount. The law of love itself was seen as effective and sufficient for the task of establishing social justice. All that would be required would be for good men to work hard at bringing it into effect. Consequently, there was a strong belief that progress towards a more Christian, perhaps even a perfect society was underway, and would soon be achieved.

Fifth, liberal Protestant anthropology drew substantially from secular humanism, which had Renaissance and Enlightenment ideas as the basis for its position on human nature.[8] Liberalism presented humanity as essentially good and rejected Christian orthodox concepts of original sin as obscurantist. For liberalism, sin was basically anti-social behaviour as a result of ignorant selfishness – something which could be remedied fairly easily by effective education. The reality of human evil which Niebuhr regarded as essential for accurate theology found no place in their understanding. In fact it was this failure which formed the heart of Niebuhr's critique of liberalism, which he saw as being too optimistic about humanity and so inadequate for the task of dealing with the reality of human evil. Of particular significance in this context was the idea of pacifism: he saw liberal Protestantism as affirming pacifism, expecting human love to be successful in the task of fighting evil. This position was based on a belief in the power of love and the basic goodness and reasonableness of humanity, a faith Niebuhr considered to be ill-founded.[9] This belief in human nature was also reflected in liberal theological doctrine. Human personality was considered naturally divine, on an equal footing with God himself, while personal religious experience was regarded as the primary source of divine revelation. The liberal method of doing theology reflected this position: following Schleiermacher, the correct

---

[7] Reardon, Bernard M. G., *Religious Thought in the Nineteenth Century: Illustrated from Writers of the Period*, (Cambridge: CUP, 1966), p. 18; Mackintosh, pp. 14-6.

[8] Reardon, *Liberal Protestantism*, p. 11.

[9] *KB*, pp. 7-8, 64-71.

starting point of theology was thought to be the believer's inner experience of God.

Conclusion

These five points can be taken as the defining features of liberal Protestant theology. The effect of this theology at the time was to increase the emphasis on divine immanence at the expense of the 'otherness' and separateness of God.[10] God the Father and Christ the Son were made more approachable as concepts of sin and judgment were laid to rest, while progressively, humanity and society were applauded and made the focus of theological thought. Expectations for change in this world, and salvation in the next, were placed in the realm of human qualities and endeavours rather than in the character and power of God; and in America, this emerged in the practical activities of the Social Gospel movement which we saw in the previous section. Most crucially for our study of Niebuhr, though, the darker aspects of human nature which could have accounted for the evils he witnessed around him were removed from the picture. This meant that, as he became increasingly aware of those evils, and his conviction that they required a Christian response grew, he became progressively more critical of the liberal tradition. Niebuhr felt that the liberal understanding of God, the world and humanity lacked the resources he needed to deal effectively with human evil. His response was to seek philosophies which were prepared to be more realistic about human nature and the problems prevalent in society. The first of these was Marxism.

The Influence of Marxism on Reinhold Niebuhr

Introduction

The influence Marx, or perhaps more accurately, Marxism, had on Reinhold Niebuhr, has been much noted,[11] and it is accepted that Marxism had a profound effect upon Niebuhr, especially in the early part of his adult life. One has only to glance at the Contents page of *MMIS* to see how much Marxist thought penetrated his own ideas at this time. However, Niebuhr's

---

[10] Grenz and Olson, p. 52.

[11] See Allen, E.L., *A Guide to the Thought of Reinhold Niebuhr: Christianity and Society*, (London: Hodder and Stoughton, no date), Chapter 2; Bennett, pp. 72-5, and Schlesinger, pp. 138-41 in *KB*; and McCann, Dennis, 'Reinhold Niebuhr and Jacques Maritain on Marxism: A Comparison of Two Traditional Models of Practical Theology', *The Journal of Religion*, 58 (1978), pp. 140-68 (pp. 141-51).

position towards Marxism became progressively more hostile through the rest of his life, and in fact even at its most influential time, Marxism never seduced him entirely. Though adopting a number of its insights, he remained consistently critical of certain aspects throughout his engagement with it. What is thus interesting and important is to understand the nature of this mixed reaction.

Niebuhr's appreciation of Marxism, we contend, grew out of two factors. The first was Niebuhr's progressive disillusionment with his early liberal Protestantism as he was exposed to human suffering during his pastorate in Detroit. Marxism seemed to provide a more realistic understanding of the situation than liberalism, and so could provide better answers to the problems of suffering than the liberalism he was having increasing doubts about. The second was Marxism's strong similarity to Pragmatism in the important areas of epistemology and the role of human agency in overcoming injustice and evil. Both of these will be considered.

Niebuhr's Social Encounter with Marxism

Niebuhr encountered Marxism during his time in Detroit – in its social rather than its philosophical form. The result was that primarily he engaged with Marxism as a movement and ideology, investigating Marx's actual ideas only secondarily. This is significant since his attitude towards Marxism was strongly based on its social effect rather than any intellectual appeal; so when Marxism failed so spectacularly in the USSR, Niebuhr's reaction was particularly vehement. Very much a Pragmatist, for him the true nature of the idea was to be found in the material reality it produced rather than the abstract philosophy behind it.[12] Stalin's purges and the Stalin-Hitler Pact were, for Niebuhr, Marxism's true nature.

At his early stage, though, prior to Stalin's purges, Marxism seemed to be an effective social force, realistic rather than sentimental, and despite its faults more effective than the Social Gospel in making a difference in society.[13] To quote Richard Pells,

> To this point, Niebuhr's disenchantment with liberalism resembled that of other intellectuals in the 1930s. And like them, he found himself irresistibly attracted to Marxism - though for reasons that were not particularly ideological. Instead, Marxism seemed the perfect antidote to

---

[12] In the section on William James below, see 'The Philosophy of Pragmatism', especially the first section, 'Pragmatism as method', for elaboration on this point.

[13] McCann, p. 145; Schlesinger in *KB*, p. 138.

the liberal virus because it offered a more realistic - and a more religious - understanding of man and his society.[14]

Marxism was also sufficiently radical in its appraisal of capitalism to appeal to an idealistic young activist striving to achieve social justice. As the Great Depression began to take its grip in the late 1920s, the notion that capitalism itself as a system was flawed became increasingly attractive. The failure of the government to respond to the Depression, prior to Franklin D. Roosevelt's first New Deal in 1933,[15] indicated that there were serious problems with the economic system, something only a radical reorganisation could cure. Despite his Pragmatic spirit, Niebuhr scorned Roosevelt's New Deal as a palliative offered when major surgery was needed.[16] Later he would rescind his position; but at the time his desire for radicalism was too strong, and Marxism was the more attractive philosophy.

So in the time from about 1920 to 1936, Marxism exerted a serious influence on Niebuhr as his disillusionment with liberal Protestantism developed. Realistic, activist, and power-based, it filled the vacuum left by the receding tide of liberal Protestantism on Niebuhr's horizon. Still more importantly, Marxism had strong similarities to another, particularly important philosophy by which Niebuhr had long been influenced, American Pragmatism. It seems strongly possible that the second reason Niebuhr was attracted to Marxism was because it confirmed many of the ideas he valued in Pragmatist thought. Marxism complements Pragmatism in that it has both a materialist anthropology, with consequences for its epistemology, and a sense of the importance of human activism.[17]

Marxism and Niebuhr's Theological Development

Marx reverses Hegel's position of regarding Pure Thought as the ground of material existence, and asserts instead that material existence is the source of consciousness.[18] The practical problem of physical survival is the primary reality, from which arise the secondary products of thought and knowledge. In existential terms, existence creates essence, not visa versa. It is through existence, and more importantly, action, that history and thought are created.

---

[14] Pells, Richard H, *Radical Visions and American Dreams: Culture and Social Thought in the Depression Years*, (Middletown, Conn.: Wesleyan University Press, 1973), p. 143.

[15] Shannon, pp. 182-5.

[16] John C. Bennett and Arthur Schlesinger in *KB*, pp. 74-6 and 141-7 respectively.

[17] See 'The Philosophy of Pragmatism' in the section on William James below.

[18] McLellan, David, *Marx*, (Glasgow: Fontana/Collins, 1975), pp. 27-8.

> In direct contrast to German philosophy which descends from heaven to earth, here we ascend from earth to heaven...We set out from real, active men, and on the basis of their real life-process we demonstrate the development of the ideological reflexes and echoes of this life-process...Morality, religion, metaphysics, all the rest of ideology and their corresponding forms of consciousness, thus no longer retain the semblance of independence. They have no history, no development; but men, developing their material production and their material intercourse, alter, along with this their real existence, their thinking and the products of their thinking. Life is not determined by consciousness, but consciousness by life.[19]

Since knowledge comes through material creation, knowledge is a consequence of material reality. With material reality being primary, when knowledge emerges, it does so from a material basis; hence material reality is the source of knowledge and knowledge is created through and conditioned by its material basis. This is not to say that only the material is real: rather, standing against (Hegelian) idealism Marx says that, while ideas do exist in some way, they are not independent of their material source.

Knowledge, then, does not exist independently of material reality, and is an expression of the material basis from which it arises. Thus human truth is contingent, inseparable from the contingent (social and material) situation which gives rise to it. No thought or form of knowledge is independent of the situation from which it arises.[20] For Marx, the production of goods is the main work, or substance, of society; thus the knowledge society has arises from that production and so is conditioned by it.[21] Consequently all knowledge is socially created, conditioned by the social situation which is its source; and this means essentially that a social system determines the ideas which are regarded as true in a given society. Since our modern society is set up by the industrial oligarchies, our 'knowledge' is in fact little more than an expression of the ruling classes' ideas; and, Marx argues, since society is run for the benefit of those classes, their interests condition the knowledge which is accepted as true in society.

> The ideas of the ruling class are in every epoch the ruling ideas, i.e. the class which is the ruling material force of society is at the same time its ruling intellectual force. The class which has the means of material production at its disposal, has control at the same time over the means of

---

[19] From 'The German Ideology, The Premisses of the Materialist Method', in *Karl Marx: Selected Writings*, ed. by David McLellan (Oxford: OUP, 1977), p. 164.

[20] McLellan, *Marx*, p. 39.

[21] Marx, Karl, and Friedrich Engels, *The Communist Manifesto*, (London: Penguin, 1967), p. 99.

mental production, so that thereby, generally speaking, the ideas of those who lack the means of mental production are subject to it. The ruling ideas are nothing more than the ideal expression of the dominant material relationships, the dominant material relationships grasped as ideas...[22]

This is basically Marx's radical critique of epistemology. It is power interests which generate and so condition knowledge.

Marx uses the word 'ideology' to describe this type of knowledge which exists to serve the interests of the ruling classes. Ideology does not arise consciously, however: there is a distinction between ideology and propaganda. While propaganda is the conscious attempt to manipulate information, ideology arises naturally and spontaneously throughout a society.[23] It is a corporate, unconscious production arising from the substance of the society, based on class divisions, the institution of private property and methods of production. Ideology, like culture, is a manifestation of deeper, hidden realities of life in a given social situation. As only the 'symptom' of deeper realities, the method of dealing with ideology is to sweep away the class divisions and means of production from which it arises, rather than trying to engage with it rationally. It is through the reorganisation of society, a radical solution, that ideology is overcome and justice is achieved. Attempting to change the ideology will not change society: in his reversal of idealism, Marx places the emphasis on changing material reality, particularly the class structure, rather than philosophically engaging with ideas in order to change the world. These developments will then change the ideology spontaneously.

One aspect of the complementarity of Marxism and Pragmatism thus becomes evident: both have a low view of knowledge as something secondary, a contingent, materially dependent (and alterable) servant of material and social factors. Reason is conditioned and finite, an expression of class interests, not something detached, eternal and purely objective.[24]

Marxism was also forceful about the practical realities of bringing about change in society. In opposing powerful interests, power, in the form of coercion or even violent revolution, would be necessary. Niebuhr's radical endorsement of coercion in *MMIS* reflects the chord Marxist 'Realism' struck with him: as opposed to the belief in the power of love favoured by liberal Protestantism, which he had come to regard as insipid, Marxism presented him with a philosophy which he reckoned could deal adequately with the abuse of power he saw in Detroit at first hand. Its radicalism and power-based philosophy answered the need for realism which liberalism had clearly failed to do.

---

[22] From 'The German Ideology, Communism and History', in McLellan, *Karl Marx: Selected Writings*, p. 176.

[23] Turner, Denys, *Marxism and Christianity*, (Oxford: Blackwell, 1983), pp. 64-5.

[24] See the section on William James below entitled 'Anthropology and Epistemology'.

Furthermore, the Marxist critique of epistemology was extremely interesting to him. From the justifications Ford gave for exploiting his workforce, Niebuhr could see that reason could be used to serve self-interest.[25] Niebuhr's disillusionment with the supposed power and purity of reason and its ability to overcome entrenched interest found its answer in the Marxist critique of reason, which showed how knowledge and rationality could be made to serve material interests. Further, the concept that ideology was spontaneous and unconscious went well with the development of his own ideas concerning original sin and self-deception: here was a philosophy which acknowledged that self-justification, though selfish, could be successfully disguised to the perpetrator himself.

But while subscribing to Marxism's radical social solution for a time, Niebuhr was soon drawn more towards the more Christian, existential[26] solution of self-knowledge as the means of overcoming evil. Hence, while he gave weight to the Marxist solution of using coercion in the corporate realm, he complemented it with an essentially individualistic concept concerning the ultimate source of evil and the means of dealing with it. In time the individualist focus of his thought took over, perhaps due in part to the colossal failure of the USSR and what it revealed about Marxism.

Secondly, Marxism and Pragmatism came together as influential forces in Niebuhr's development in the role both gave to human agency as important for shaping history. For James especially this was essential, since he had an almost pathological fear of determinism and was highly committed to a belief in the power of human freedom as its antidote. But Niebuhr, while being committed to the potency of human vitality, also had a sense of the inexorable power of God driving towards the fulfilment of history's ideal perfection, the Kingdom of God. This teleological perspective, in tension with the necessity of human action actually to bring it about, is paralleled in Marx, so that both of them have an unresolved, or even logically inconsistent tension between human action and determinism.[27] So both Niebuhr and Marx subscribe to a belief in the unstoppable power of history to achieve a determinate goal. For Marx, this consists of historical determinism operating dialectically to produce an inevitable revolution followed by communism.[28] For Niebuhr, this is expressed in terms of the power of God working towards the fulfilment of the 'myth' of the Kingdom of God.[29] But balanced against this determinism is the necessity of human action which is required to bring these ends about.

---

[25] Fox, pp. 95-100, 109-10.
[26] Existential in terms of self-awareness creating authenticity, self-definition or salvation. See the section on Kierkegaard below, entitled 'Kierkegaard and Niebuhr'.
[27] Hook, 'The Philosophical Basis of Marxian Socialism in the United States', in *Socialism and American Life,* pp. 439-42.
[28] Marx, *The Communist Manifesto,* p. 94.
[29] *NDM II,* Chapter X.

It is only through *human* action that communism or the Kingdom of God is realised in history, despite its 'inevitability'. This leads Marx to exhort the world-wide proletariat to shake off their chains, and Niebuhr to adopt an energy-generating epistemology based on myth.[30] So while both Niebuhr and Marx subscribe to some form of determinism, they also have a strong commitment to human activity as the means of achieving historical goals. Hence it is unsurprising that Niebuhr found in Marxism a philosophy with which he could identify.

A third area of common ground between Niebuhr's agenda, Pragmatism and Marxism is the attempt to deal with the 'problem of power'.[31] Inherent in capitalism is the problem of unrestrained egoism, as self-interest becomes socially acceptable or sometimes even encouraged in the name of 'wealth creation'. Both Pragmatism and Marxism can be seen as arising in the first half of the Nineteenth Century in response to the problem of power created by an essentially capitalist civilisation. Hence the general Pragmatic agenda, which was taken up by Niebuhr, found an ally in the realism of Marxism for the task of reconstructing an ethical society out of the basic amorality of a modern industrial civilisation.

One final possible area of similarity between Marx and Niebuhr concerns their understanding of the development of history. Marx follows Hegel in seeing history in terms of a dynamic, dialectically unfolding system revolving round two opposing classes, the bourgeoisie and the proletariat. Niebuhr's position follows a similar line, in that he consistently presents two polarised fields which establish a dynamic relation between themselves: Creator and Creation; human and divine; rational and empirical; social and individual; form and vitality. However, while the setting up of opposites in this way indicates a dialectical approach, in fact it is not strictly the case. In Niebuhr's thought, the two poles are more often left in an unresolved tension which becomes a source of vitality and dynamism. This is seen particularly in his concept of myth, where an ideal, such as the Kingdom of God, is kept in tension with the reality of society. Rather than reconciling the opposites, Niebuhr prefers to leave them in tension. Thus, while his method at first sight might appear dialectic, in fact his thought is really dualist, although one has to be equally careful of imposing that label upon him.

For someone with Niebuhr's Pragmatic commitment, Marxism would have seemed to be a philosophy talking the language of life. The Pragmatist commitment to human action for the task of creating a better world was echoed in Marxism. Marx was not a pure philosopher concerned with flawlessly constructed, abstract systems of logic, but rather, a

---

[30] See the section below on Niebuhr's Epistemology Part 2, particularly 'Making use of the will-to-power' and 'Setting up the tension of an impossible ideal'.

[31] See the section below on William James, 'Modernism and the Problem of Power' for elaboration.

practical, activist thinker who used his intelligence to engage with real-life situations.[32] His position is summed up in his famous 11th Thesis on Feuerbach, 'The philosophers have only <u>interpreted</u> the world in various ways; the point, however, is to <u>change</u> it'.[33] This is reflected in the unresolved tension of historical determinism and the necessity of human action, found also in Pragmatism and Niebuhr's own approach. Finally, like Niebuhr, Marx's thought developed through his engagement with contemporary issues, and it was largely through Marx's dealings with the unfolding historical situations that his ideas emerged.

Niebuhr's Disillusionment with Marxism
If Marxism was so attractive a philosophy for Niebuhr in his early years, what lay behind his later vehement rejection of it? Two major factors account for this change. The first was historical reality. Niebuhr's appreciation of Marxism was closely linked to its actual effectiveness in confronting human evil effectively and creating a better society. This task was also intrinsic to much of Niebuhr's agenda. Niebuhr was attracted to Marxism because its insights and activism offered something which he perceived theology lacked at that time, namely a realistic appraisal of human problems emerging in an effective social philosophy. He thought that the employment of Marxist ideas would produce a more just society. This was why Stalin's purges (1936-1938), and then the Hitler-Stalin Pact, seriously disillusioned him.[34] If this was the reality of Marxism, it was seriously flawed.

In addition to the situation in the USSR, the rise of Fascism in Europe altered the ideological battle lines generally, not just for Niebuhr but for the whole of the Left in America.[35] Suddenly the war was not between socialism and capitalism, but between democracy (of whatever kind) and totalitarian Fascism, the brutal regimes of Mussolini, Hitler and Franco.[36] The victory of Franco in the Spanish Civil War was a severe blow to hopes concerning the ability of good to conquer evil, and made the necessity of protecting democracy all the more urgent.[37] At the same time, events in the United States during the mid-late 1930's were influencing thought about radicalism and Marxism generally. Improvements in American society following the (partial) success of the New Deal, made piecemeal and

---

[32] Jeffrey Reiman, 'Moral Philosophy: The critique of capitalism and the problem of ideology', in *The Cambridge Companion to Marx*, ed. by Terrell Carver (Cambridge: CUP, 1991), pp. 143-67 (pp. 148-9).

[33] The 11th thesis on Feuerbach, in Marx, Karl, and Friedrich Engels, *Collected Works*, 47 vols (London: Lawrence and Wishart, 1975-1998), V, (1976), p. 8.

[34] McCann, p. 147.

[35] Cantor, p. 142.

[36] Pells, pp. 296-99; Cantor, p. 131.

[37] Diggins, *Rise and Fall*, p. 178.

gradual reforms more attractive than revolutions, especially when the U.S. was compared to the dire situations found in Russia and Germany. At the same time, those changes undermined the Marxist prophecy that capitalism is unable to save itself from self-destruction.[38] The relative well-being of the US when compared with the terror of the USSR made the Left wing in America more sceptical towards Marxism, and more willing to support democracy.

The second major factor to change Niebuhr's mind was his own, growing, appreciation of 'prophetic' Christianity. Increasingly aware of its depth of insight, he became more critical of alternative philosophies, and more dissatisfied with its detractors, whether they were liberalist attempts to water down Christian doctrine or the more overt attacks of hostile opponents like Marx. In time, Niebuhr's comparison of Marxism with Christianity led him to dismiss Marxism on two counts. The first was its failure to deal with the reality of human nature, both its possibilities and limits. This was his general test for philosophies: whether they could do justice to both the good and the evil in humanity. On the one hand, Niebuhr noted that Marxism failed to notice or account for the human capacity for selflessness, and in particular self-sacrificial love. Despite his keen awareness of the shortcomings of human goodness, it seemed to Niebuhr that it was necessary to recognise the capacity to love where it did occur if an unwarranted cynicism was to be avoided. At the same time, though, the Marxist analysis which placed the source of evil in social institutions actually reflected an optimistic anthropology which in Niebuhr's view totally failed to deal with the issue of how evil arises in the first place and how it should be dealt with. In Marxism, it is the social system, in particular the class structure and the institution of private property, which is the source of evil. But the social system, and the classes themselves, consist of nothing which is not human; therefore it is the human beings who make up society which are the ultimate source of the evil which society then perpetrates. Marxism failed to probe beneath the surface and look for the real source of the problem, which Niebuhr identified as actually being in human nature itself. It was this failure to recognise the depth of the problem which had left Russia vulnerable to the manipulations of men like Stalin. So Niebuhr finally dismissed the Marxists as foolish and naive, 'children of light'.[39]

Thus Marxism's first weakness when compared to Christianity was its inadequate anthropology, which lacked the depth of insight of the Christian analysis, and failed to do justice to the limits and possibilities of human nature. The second was its failure to apply to itself its own radical critique of epistemology. Niebuhr considered the Marxist concept of ideology as being insightful, and adapted it for his own use. His concept of original sin,

---

[38] Diggins, *Rise and Fall*, p. 189; Pells, p. 297.
[39] *CLCD*, pp. 28-9, 76-8.

for example, draws strongly on the idea that some forms of knowledge can become vehicles for egoistic action. The real test, however, is whether this insight is applied to the self. If not, then the very critique of ideology becomes a form of ideology. Supposedly objective knowledge concerning the nature of knowledge is used by a group to criticise others, advance its own world view and, through that, its own interests. The test of Marxist integrity, therefore, was whether or not the concept of ideology was applied by the Marxists to themselves; and this manifestly failed to happen. The Marxists were as absolute and dogmatic about their own ideas as the classes they criticised, most crucially for Niebuhr in their belief in the absolute worth and purity of the proletariat.[40] Niebuhr regarded this as a highly significant failure. The Marxists, so good at criticising other philosophies as ideologies, idolised Marxism and the proletariat, failing to see that they were using the Marxist philosophy as a vehicle for their own interests. Even in the early stages of his thought Niebuhr was critical of this failure.[41] As time passed and the reality of the USSR emerged, Niebuhr saw that it was an intrinsic flaw which Marxism was incapable of overcoming. The unprecedented vindictiveness of the Russian Communist Party towards even those who had been heroes in the revolution proved that Marxists had failed to recognise the ideological nature of their own beliefs and so could not be trusted.

Aspects of Marxism Retained by Niebuhr

So what aspects of Marxist thought did Niebuhr retain? Several key points remained useful to him. The first was the radical critique of epistemology as ideology, that ideals can be used at vehicles for a hidden agenda of self-interest. Throughout his work the thought emerged that egoism could, and often did, use apparently high-minded interests to hide the true, selfish motivations for action from both itself and those around it, who might seek to stop it if the true cause for action were known. The second was the Marxist political realism, especially the necessity of using coercion to establish a just society. This, though most obviously a theme of *MMIS*, remained a consistent subject through his writings. Third, and connected with this, was the realistic analysis of political and economic structures. The structures of society could be used as the powerful instruments of group interests. This meant social institutions can be manipulated and become dangerous; and this in turn has two consequences: the first, that no society is perfect, and that even a well-intentioned institution – a Government, the Church or democracy itself, can be manipulated and made to serve self-interested parties. Therefore checks and safeguards, preferably in the form of active self-criticism, are required. The second implication is

---

[40] See for example *BT*, pp. 36-8, *ICE*, pp. 27-9.
[41] *MMIS*, pp. 157, 167.

that since no social system is sacred, criticisms and improvements should be made. All forms of society are temporal and provisional and should not be idolised. Fourth, and finally, that capitalism has a tragic internal contradiction which results in self-destruction if not refined and moderated. *REE* expresses this most clearly, but it remained a recurring theme in his work.

Conclusion

It may be said in conclusion that Niebuhr's loyalty to Marxism owed much to circumstances. His disillusionment with liberal Protestantism came at a time when Marxism was still being taken seriously enough for him to be attracted to its realism, and when his more 'prophetic' Christianity had yet to emerge. Despite that, however, Niebuhr made good use of several of Marx's best insights, and Marxism without doubt helped him develop the Christian 'Realism' for which he became famous.

The Influence of Søren Kierkegaard upon Reinhold Niebuhr

Introduction

We are considering the intellectual influences which developed Niebuhr's thought, helped him understand human nature and so provide an answer to the problems he observed in society. Of key importance in this was the Christian Existentialist, Søren Kierkegaard.

The Theology of Kierkegaard

The main significance of Kierkegaard for Niebuhr is that he confirmed Niebuhr's belief that the key to the problem of sin and evil ultimately lies in the nature of the individual as a self-conscious being. Niebuhr follows Kierkegaard in embracing the doctrine of original sin, rejecting contemporary beliefs in the basic goodness and potency of humanity, and in the power and purity of reason. For both of them, this progresses into an insistence upon the essential sinfulness of humanity and the universal corruption of human nature. A common foundation is found in their closely allied anthropology.

Kierkegaard presents the human individual as consisting of two forms of existence, the physical and the psyche, which are united by the synthesising power of a third element of existence, the human spirit.

Man is a synthesis of the psychical and the physical; however, a synthesis is unthinkable if the two are not united in a third. This third is spirit.[42]

Sharing physical existence with the other creatures, the human person inhabits the natural world. At the same time, though, there is a unique quality resident: self-conscious freedom, consisting of 'possibility'. This quality sets humanity apart from other creatures. By a third, uniting force, 'the spirit', these two aspects of existence are held together to form the human person.

From the psyche comes the possibility of choice. The personality as self-consciousness detaches itself from the objective, defined limits of concrete existence so that it can create an unlimited range of options for the future.[43] Its freedom as subject over object gives it the possibility of an infinite number of contingencies. This means that the consciousness, as the means of these infinite possibilities, has an aspect of infinity to it. Consequently the psyche consists of something utterly different from physical existence, an infinite quality within finite creatureliness. The final result is that human, self-conscious existence consists of the infinite within the finite; and this self-consciousness, which is freedom, is the source of the possibilities from which the infinity within the self is derived.

The personality of the individual is the same as the self-consciousness. As such, the personality is the possibility of the infinite in the finite. Since the objective is the defined, and therefore the limited, the subjective is the opposite, in fact the antithesis, of the objectivity which constitutes physical reality. The personality, therefore, is the subjective: personal, indefinable, without limits or wholly perceptible qualities, consisting of pure freedom and possibility. As such it is also the means of communicating with the infinite Absolute. But God is also personal, the ultimate Subject, the final Thou. Of course the individual is not God; but through the infinity of the personality, the self has the means of communicating with God. (Kierkegaard is careful to maintain the difference between a person's infinite striving towards God, and the God who is The Infinite.) The personality of the self makes communication possible between the person and God in a thou: Thou exchange.

For Kierkegaard, the personality, as the means of including the infinite in the finite, is also the possibility of the eternal in the temporal. 'Man, then, is a synthesis of psyche and body, but he is also a *synthesis of the temporal and the eternal.*'[44] Through the personality, which as freedom and subjectivity is non-objective and transcendent, the eternal enters the

---

[42] *The Concept of Anxiety: A Simple Psychologically Orienting Deliberation on the Dogmatic Issue of Hereditary Sin*, ed. and trans. by R. Thomte and A. Anderson (Princeton: Princeton University Press, 1980), p. 43.

[43] *Concept of Anxiety*, p. 91.

[44] *Concept of Anxiety*, p. 85 (italics in the original).

temporal through the creativity of the choice of the consciousness. This event of choice, particularly ethical choice, lies at the centre of Kierkegaard's thought. For Kierkegaard, the event of choice is the means by which the essence of the individual is actualised and history is created.

> The synthesis of the temporal and the eternal is not another synthesis but is the expression for the first synthesis, according to which man is a synthesis of psyche and body that is sustained by spirit. As soon as the spirit is posited, the moment is present...Only with the moment does history begin.[45]

> [T]he eternal is for representation the infinitely contentful present...The present is the eternal, or rather, the eternal is the present, and the present is full.[46]

The present thus has an infinite aspect to it. As such it is the eternal in the temporal. As a temporal event with an infinite quality it exists as something eternal. The infinity of the present distinguishes it from the finitude of the past, and its actuality distinguishes it from the possibility of the future; hence from the present, the past and the future are distinguished and come into existence. Creatures which lack self-consciousness have no (eternal) present and therefore no past or future: they simply exist.

This view of course necessitates the existence of human freedom. Hence Kierkegaard has a certain view of causality, namely that while effect is derived from cause, *which* effect is subject to infinite possibilities. [47] This idea also emerges in Niebuhr's thought, as we shall see. While maintaining the validity of causality, both Kierkegaard and Niebuhr assert that the cause-effect sequence is not fixed, and that an infinite number of possibilities can arise from a given cause. Hence they dispose of determinism and concentrate instead on the source of human possibilities, especially the possibility of sin, through the psychological method and the analysis of human consciousness as freedom.

The concept of humanity as a unity of finitude and infinity, a temporal being with a transcendent eternal element, is one key element of Kierkegaard's philosophy to emerge in Niebuhr's thought. Yet the most important contribution of Kierkegaard's thought to Niebuhr's theology is his attempt to produce a psychological explanation for the existence of sin. Kierkegaard believes the source of humanity's sinfulness to lie in the

---

[45] *Concept of Anxiety*, pp. 88-9.
[46] *Concept of Anxiety*, p. 86.
[47] Kierkegaard, S., *Philosophical Fragments*, ed. and trans., with an introduction and notes, by Howard V. Hong and Edna H. Hong (Princeton: Princeton University Press, 1985), p. 93.

psychological perception of the human situation. This means that the origins of sin can be discovered through an analysis of the human situation and the way it gives rise to anxiety in the human psyche. Hence for both Kierkegaard and Niebuhr, the ultimate source of sin is to be found in the anxious human consciousness.

Kierkegaard turns away from traditional, ontological approaches for providing an explanation for the origins of sin, since they implied that created, finite being itself was intrinsically sinful. Instead, he concerns himself with the question of *how* it is possible to sin. What are the psychological conditions necessary to bring sin about?[48] At the centre of his explanation lies his concept of anxiety and the leap into knowledge.

Anxiety is the spirit's awareness of its own possibilities.[49] Its possibilities are endless, unrestricted; yet, as something unactualised, they are essentially mysterious and unknown. Its possibilities exist as 'nothingness', things that, although non-existent, have a form of being of which the spirit is aware *as* its possibilities. They exist, but not in the full sense of the word, since they do not exist *yet*, and may never do so. As existing in possibility they threaten the self; but as unactualised, they are nothing definite or specific on which the spirit can focus on and deal with. Hence the spirit's concern is unfocused, and cannot be described as fear since there is precisely *nothing* to fear.

> In this state there is peace and repose, but there is simultaneously something else that is not contention and strife, for there is indeed nothing against which to strive. What, then, is it? Nothing. But what effect does nothing have? It begets anxiety.[50]

> [Anxiety] is altogether different from fear and similar concepts that refer to something definite, whereas anxiety is freedom's actuality as the possibility of possibility.[51]

Thus anxiety is the spirit's awareness of its own possibilities. The 'nothing' about which it is anxious is essentially unknown to it *as* nothing. If the anxiety is to be overcome, the spirit must have something specific to become aware of, thus translating its anxiety into fear (of the specific) which can be overcome. When something definite exists, it can be faced and overcome, but only when it is known is this possible, since an unknown factor cannot be mastered.

---

[48] *Concept of Anxiety*, pp. 21-2.
[49] *Concept of Anxiety*, Chapter I, section 5, esp. pp. 42-3. See also Malantschuk, pp. 260-72.
[50] *Concept of Anxiety*, p. 41.
[51] *Concept of Anxiety*, p. 42.

According to Kierkegaard, then, anxiety is the result of ignorance, an ignorance born of the fact that there is nothing to be known.[52] The lack of knowledge concerning the self's possibilities generates an unfocused worry about things which are not-yet, not-existing, nothing. But the state of ignorance is, by virtue of its lack of knowledge, also a state of innocence, especially if no leap into actuality and knowledge has ever occurred. Prior to the leap ever occurring, therefore, a state of innocence exists. Kierkegaard identifies this as the pre-Fall state of Adam: a state of dreaming innocence, when the person is in immediate unity with his natural surroundings and when the activity of the spirit in its powerful actualisation lies dormant in its dreamlike state.[53]

The reality of spirit does exist, however, and in its dreaming state it is still aware of the possibilities of its freedom. Adam in his pre-Fall state was no less (and no more) human than ourselves, and had the complete human reality of the physical, the psyche and the spirit. The spirit is thus aware of the 'nothingness' which is the not-yet-existing, even in its dreaming state. Despite Adam's blissful unity with his world, then, the self-consciousness-produced nothing exerts its effect upon him. Precisely *because* of his innocence, he has no knowledge of his possibilities, yet is aware of them. The state of innocence is thus one of anxiety, unrelieved by any degree of self-actualised certainty.

Temptation is awakened by the prospect of actualisation.[54] When God prohibits taking fruit from the tree, and supports his command with a threat, the first possibility of actualisation arrives. The man is presented with the possibility of 'being able', with a specific possibility of actuality in mind. This increases his anxiety as the first not-yet-known possibility of taking the fruit arises. As of yet, he does not know what choice is, nor the reality of sin and the accompanying guilt, nor even the meaning of good and evil.[55] He is only aware of their possibility, and his ignorance in the face of them. His ignorance makes him increasingly, acutely anxious, to the point when a leap into the unknown becomes enormously desirable. The mystery of the unknown thus attracts him. At the same time, he has been warned not to eat/act/leap. Hence the danger of the act is clear, and the prospect is repellent to him. The possibility of the action thus both attracts and repels him at the same time, just as someone suffering from vertigo is both repelled and attracted by the possibility of jumping over the precipice.

---

[52] *Concept of Anxiety*, pp. 37, 41.

[53] *Concept of Anxiety*, pp. 41-3.

[54] *Concept of Anxiety*, p. 44; Lee Barrett, 'Kierkegaard's "Anxiety" and the Augustinian Doctrine of Original Sin', in *The Concept of Anxiety: Vol. 8 of The International Kierkegaard Commentary*, ed. by Robert Perkins (Macon: Mercer University Press, 1985), VIII, pp. 35-61 (pp. 55-6).

[55] *Concept of Anxiety*, p. 44.

Philosophical and Theological Influences

Anxiety may be compared with dizziness. He whose eye happens to look down into the yawning abyss becomes dizzy. But what is the reason for this? It is just as much in his own eye as in the abyss, for suppose he had not looked down. Hence anxiety is the dizziness of freedom, which emerges when the spirit wants to posit the synthesis and freedom looks down into its own possibility, laying hold of finiteness to support itself. Freedom succumbs in this dizziness.[56]

The vertigo of anxiety overwhelms him through his contemplation of it: he leaps into actuality, making his first conscious choice, and thus leaps into knowledge. By the same token, he leaps into sin and guilt. He has disobeyed God and broken his commandments. In doing so, he has acquired forbidden knowledge. Hence the leap into knowledge and into sin are the same. The Fall event consists of exactly this occurrence, of leaping from anxiety into certainty and knowledge by forbidden action.

The narrative in Genesis also gives the correct explanation of innocence. Innocence is ignorance...innocence is always lost only by the qualitative leap of the individual.[57]

With this event, though, self-actualisation, and therefore the individual history, begins. The leap into knowledge becomes an ongoing event of decision and action. In time, this activity builds up a personal history. This history, though, is also the history of sin; hence human history and the history of sin are the same.[58] As generations pass, the build-up of personal histories as a quantitative accumulation of qualitative leaps begins to form a corporate identity; and since this history is also the history of sin, the accumulation of history is the accumulation of sin. Just as the corporate history and social identity build up into something definable, and they begin to affect individuals, so the history of sin does the same; and this is precisely Kierkegaard's concept of original sin.[59] The acts of the individual are unique, and add to the corporate history/sin, thus developing and changing it; but the history/sin of the race affects the individual and predisposes him to sin. In terms of state versus act, the state of original sin consists of the accumulation of the acts of the individuals. The state in turn creates a powerful effect on the individuals who conversely actualise the state in their own events of synthesis, and so on. In this way sin presupposes itself through its interactive relationship between state and act in the individual.

---

[56] *Concept of Anxiety*, p. 61.
[57] *Concept of Anxiety*, p. 37.
[58] *Concept of Anxiety*, pp. 28-9, 33-4, 52-6, 89-91.
[59] Barrett, pp. 45-7.

Sin came into the world by a sin. Were this not so, sin would have come into the world as something accidental, which one would do well not to explain. The difficulty for the understanding is precisely the triumph of the explanation and its profound consequences, namely, that sin presupposes itself, that sin comes into the world in such a way that by the fact that it is, it is presupposed.[60]

Kierkegaard's concept of sin bears substantial resemblance to the traditional Augustine - Lutheran model.[61] In essence, it is negative, existing to be negated.[62] All through the description of the psychology of sin, the motif of negativity appears. Its effect on the individual is derived from nothingness through anxiety: anxiety, derived from nothingness, is enhanced by sin, and the actualisation of the self by the leap is essentially sinful since it is prohibited by God and consists of a leap into forbidden knowledge. Sin thus has the magnetic-repulsive quality of vertigo which results in its ongoing actualisation through the self's fall into knowledge. Also like Augustine, sinning is a universally human trait which corrupts the very essence of the person. For Kierkegaard, the actual process of self-actualisation is sinful, and the history of the person is the unfolding story of his sin. Furthermore, the issue of guilt is strongly represented by Kierkegaard, especially in the ethical/Judaic stage of the individual's development towards Christianity[63] but also generally, as the consequence of the Fall and ongoing sin. The fact that it is through the person's own event of choice that sin is actualised justifies the allegation of responsibility, while the effect of the historical accumulation of the guilt of the race makes the inevitability of guilt equally powerful. Finally, Kierkegaard emphasizes the paradoxical nature of original sin as he insists that, ultimately, original sin is a mystery to be experienced through a specific mood, and not a rational doctrine to be analysed and dissected.[64]

Kierkegaard and Niebuhr

Niebuhr follows Kierkegaard in placing the ultimate source of sin and evil not in any such accidental feature such as a lack of education or in social structures, but in human nature itself. For Niebuhr, it is the actual human constitution of existing as a finite creature aware of infinite possibilities that gives rise to the possibility of sin through anxiety and the attempt to become secure. As Richard Kroner asserts, Niebuhr shares with

---

[60] *Concept of Anxiety*, p. 32.
[61] Barrett, pp. 42, 51.
[62] *Concept of Anxiety*, p. 15.
[63] Copleston, F., *A History of Philosophy*, 9 vols (London: Burns and Oates, 1946-75), VII (1963), pp. 341-3; Malantschuk, pp. 268-70.
[64] *Concept of Anxiety*, pp. 15, 32-4, 146-51.

Kierkegaard an individualist, psychological approach to uncovering the real source of sin and the problem of evil.[65] It is in the anxious human psyche, the individual aware of the fragility of his existence, that sin arises. It is to be expected, therefore, that Niebuhr's views of the human personality and the nature of sin, particularly the paradoxical nature of original sin, bear substantial similarities to Kierkegaard's. Using the same terminology of the infinite in the finite, the eternal and the temporal, Niebuhr presents humanity as having an existence which participates in, but also transcends, the natural, physical, temporal realm.

> The eternity which is part of the environment of man is neither the infinity of time nor yet a realm of undifferentiated unity of being. It is the changeless source of man's changing being. As a creature who is involved in flux but who is also conscious of the fact that he is so involved, he cannot be totally involved. As spirit who can set time, nature, the world and being per se into juxtaposition to himself and inquire after the meaning of these things proves that in some sense he stands outside and beyond them.[66]

The self-consciousness which facilitates this transcendence is by nature subject and not object, and forms the interface between the individual and God while remaining human and not absolute or divine.[67] This ability is also the means by which humanity transcends history and thus is able to shape it: like Kierkegaard, Niebuhr places the source of human history in the self-consciousness.[68] From this, the two aspects of existence for humanity form the means of interpretation by which Niebuhr explains the unfolding of history.[69] Furthermore, the importance of the individual and the personality is upheld by Niebuhr as something intrinsically human and essential to maintain.[70] Like Kierkegaard, he views the loss of the individual as a symptom of the demonic, or the sinful, be it through Fascist politics or sensualism.

Despite these similarities, Niebuhr's anthropology differs from Kierkegaard's. Niebuhr prefers to keep the thesis-antithesis tension unresolved and instead of uniting opposite qualities through a moment of synthesis, derives meaning from the uncompleted dialectic. Niebuhr then

---

[65] Richard Kroner, 'The Historical Roots of Niebuhr's Thought', in *KB*, pp. 177-192 (p. 183).

[66] *NDM I*, p. 133. See also *BT*, Preface; *NDM I*, pp. 155, 193, 286.

[67] *NDM I*, pp. 169, 275.

[68] *NDM I*, p. 27; *NDM II*, pp. 1-2.

[69] *NDM II*, Chapter I, sections 1 and 2.

[70] *NDM I*, Chapter III.

commits himself to the notion of paradox to describe the human situation of finitude and infinity together.[71]

Niebuhr's use of anxiety likewise shows similarities to and differences from Kierkegaard's. While using the same term, Niebuhr's concept of anxiety differs significantly from Kierkegaard's. For Niebuhr, it is a less technical concept, and more aligned with the common idea of anxiety. Fundamentally, it is anxiety about personal well-being rather than a self-consciousness' concern in the face of its possibilities. But like Kierkegaard, Niebuhr's anxiety is derived from self-consciousness.[72] It is this which gives the person the ability to be conscious of the self as a self, as a finite being in a world of infinite dangers. The result of this awareness of the true state of the self brings on insecurity, which is the source of the anxiety.

> Thus man is, like the animals, involved in the necessities and contingencies of nature; but unlike the animals he sees this situation and anticipates its perils...In short, man, being both free and bound, both limited and limitless, is anxious. Anxiety is the inevitable concomitant of the paradox of freedom and finiteness in which man is involved.[73]

The person is anxious about the perils he faces. Technically it could be argued that this is therefore fear rather than anxiety since it has an object: the threats to the person's well-being. However, the source of the concern is the existence of unknown possibilities which threaten the self in the future; hence anxiety is the correct term, despite its slightly different focus.

It is because of this position that Niebuhr may be described in this specific respect as an existentialist.[74] The situatedness of the human person as a finite being with an infinite aspect to its existence is what gives rise to anxiety. Anxiety emerges from the actual constitution of human being.

Niebuhr follows Kierkegaard in stating that it is anxiety which leads to sin as the result of the individual's self-consciousness. Rather than being a leap into knowledge, though, for Niebuhr, anxiety develops into sin as a grasping at power in order to become secure. The insecurity of the self emerges in anxiety: a state which can be overcome by gaining power for the self, which in turn can be used to deal with the forces which threaten its existence.

Niebuhr therefore follows Kierkegaard in employing a psychological method for the analysis of human sinfulness. Both are concerned with the

---

[71] *NDM I*, pp. 24, 187-8.

[72] *NDM I*, p. 180.

[73] *NDM I*, p. 194.

[74] Though the understanding of the term varies, this is the description of Niebuhr given by various commentators, particularly Paul Ramsey, 'Love and Law' in *KB*, pp. 79-124 (p. 82), Richard Kroner in *KB*, p. 183, and Grenz and Olson, pp. 101-4.

question of how it is possible for a person to sin. Niebuhr shares Kierkegaard's belief that to understand the human race you must first understand the individual; and so his discussion of human nature (*NDM I*) precedes his analysis of human history (*NDM II*). It is also the case that Niebuhr follows Kierkegaard in his Augustine/Lutheran view that sin is universal, corrupting the whole of humanity, but also that it entails guilt in the individual despite its inevitability. Kierkegaard goes into much greater depth in his discussion of the possibility of sin and our responsibility for it through the race – individual relation, though. Niebuhr avoids this depth of analysis, and instead resorts to declaring the origins of sin to be mysterious or paradoxical with relatively little discussion.[75]

Kierkegaard's influence can also be seen in Niebuhr's attitude towards knowledge and rationality. Both thinkers are hostile to the rationalist belief in human reason as the means of salvation, and so both sought to dismiss the rationalist concept that knowledge carried with it saving power. The 'ought implies can' of Kant and the dynamic rationalism of Hegel implied that knowledge of sin brought with it the means by which sin may be overcome. This also implied that the power of reason was sufficient to achieve salvation. Kierkegaard, writing in a world dominated by Hegelian thought, resisted this influence strenuously by restating the subjective aspect of salvation and the need for the personal appropriation of knowledge.[76]

Niebuhr concurred on this matter. He made it clear that, with original sin in particular, knowing about sin did not equate with overcoming it. Understanding sin only makes apparent the individual's enslavement to it and the consequent dependence upon grace for salvation. Furthermore, Niebuhr specifically regarded both reason and ideology as vehicles for egoistic activity. While he was careful to maintain the value of reason, he was equally careful to point out its limitations for achieving good ends, and its susceptibility to manipulation by the self. His view of sin as 'pretence', whereby the self uses apparently reasonable arguments and selfless ideals to mask its egoist agenda,
made it clear that he regarded the rationalists, especially Hegel, as having a dangerously optimistic view of the power and purity of reason.[77] Also like Kierkegaard, Niebuhr emphasized the importance of paradoxes –not as leading to the leap of faith, but rather because of their capacity to be expressions of the limits of reason and as indicators of the transcendent, non-rational nature of some Christian truths.[78] For him, paradoxes were the expression of the eternal in the temporal, the infinite in the finite. Realities which consist of essentially irreconcilable qualities thus appear as

---

[75] See *NDM I*, pp. 268-80 for his main consideration of the matter.

[76] *Concept of Anxiety*, p. 16; Malantschuk pp. 284-90.

[77] *NDM I*, pp. 124-31.

[78] *BT*, pp. 4-21; *NDM I*, pp. 158-9.

paradoxes in historical existence, and should be understood as expressing revealed truths about God, humanity, and the nature of reason.

Conclusion

It is now clear that Kierkegaard's great contribution to Niebuhr's development was a clear understanding that the ultimate source of the problem of evil lies in the human psyche itself. This engendered a psychological approach to the question of how sin arises. Furthermore, his theology was influenced by Kierkegaard in the four important areas of anthropology, anxiety, the nature of sin, and epistemology. Like the other thinkers who influenced his thought, however, Niebuhr's relationship with Kierkegaard was one of making use of the aspects of Kierkegaard's thought he considered insightful without actually becoming a disciple. Hence while it would be inaccurate to label him as an existentialist, there are without doubt existentialist aspects to his thought.

The Influence of Romanticism on Reinhold Niebuhr

Introduction

In Chapter One, we saw how harsh experiences in Detroit revealed to Niebuhr that a powerful and destructive force was at work in human affairs, a force that his earlier liberalism had failed to provide a satisfactory explanation for. This force was deep seated, a part of human nature itself emerging consistently throughout society and human activity. As such, it was the source of the suffering he had observed. To form an effective theological response to it, it would be necessary for Niebuhr to understand this power thoroughly, for which he required a clear understanding of its characteristics, how it arose, and how it should be dealt with. Romanticism, as he understood it, had a significant role to play in this development. In this section we will seek to define the term 'Romantic' and examine the role Romanticism played in the development of Niebuhr's theology.

Niebuhr's Concept of Romanticism

When considering Niebuhr's discussions regarding 'Romanticism', it is clear that he has a certain school in mind, a school in which vitality and power, coloured by tragedy, take a central role, and in which reason is the slave to the will, id or will-to-power of the individual. From examining a definition of

Philosophical and Theological Influences 35

Romanticism, for example Copleston's in his *History of Philosophy*,[79] it emerges that Niebuhr's understanding of the term is idiosyncratic. Copleston's definition acknowledges the importance of human creativity and originality, and the rejection of rationalist value systems in favour of individually-created values established by Romanticists to facilitate the full enjoyment of life. However, he also includes the love of Nature, bordering on worship, as an important feature, and a strong spiritual element, a yearning for the Infinite, which tends to lie behind much of Romantic thinking. In Niebuhr's discussion of Romanticism,[80] though, vitality and creative energy are the elements which come to the fore, with Schopenhauer and Nietzsche (also bringing in Bergson, Rousseau, and Freud) as the main examples. Furthermore, Copleston makes no mention of tragedy,[81] while for Niebuhr this seems to be an important aspect of Romantic thinking. This indicates that Niebuhr is concerned with a specific kind of Romanticism, where human vitality with an undertone of tragedy is the central element. When it is recalled that Niebuhr consistently mentions Romanticism in relation to Nazi ideology,[82] it is clear that for him the typical Romantic thinker was in fact Nietzsche. Therefore, whether this characterisation is misleading or not,[83] it is Nietzsche the Romantic which we must consider in order to map Niebuhr's background in 'Romanticism'.

The Will to Power in the Philosophy of Nietzsche

Born in 1844, Nietzsche came to intellectual maturity not under the influence of Hegel, but of Schopenhauer, attracted by his atheism and pessimism.[84] Nietzsche takes up Schopenhauer's basic idea that Will defines reality, and that the world is essentially chaotic, terrifying, beyond understanding or hope. For Nietzsche, the whole of history, truth and humanity is in a state of Becoming, in constant change.[85] This constant flux makes a nonsense of fixed ideas of truth, of rational unchanging objective ideas or values, since no part of existence is stable enough to support them. On the contrary, he states, all

---

[79] Copleston, *A History of Philosophy*, VII, pp. 14-20.
[80] See particularly *NDM I*, pp. 34-45.
[81] Likewise Geoffrey Brereton in the definitions of Romanticism he gives in *Principles of Tragedy: A Rational Examination of the Tragic Concept in Life and Literature*, (Miami: University of Miami Press, 1968), p. 114, footnote 7, and pp. 183-4.
[82] See for example *BT*, p. 238; *CPP*, pp. 84, 103.
[83] Walter Kaufmann certainly regards the title to be misleading. See *Nietzsche: Philosopher, Psychologist, AntiChrist*, 4th edn (Princeton: Princeton University Press, 1974), pp. 15, 124.
[84] Copleston, F., *Friedrich Nietzsche: Philosopher of Culture*, (London: Search, 1975), pp. 143, 158.
[85] Copleston, *Nietzsche*, p. 158; Young, Julian, *Nietzsche's Philosophy of Art*, (Cambridge: CUP, 1992), p. 41; Blackham, H.J., *Six Existentialist Thinkers*, (London: Routledge and Kegan Paul, 1961), p. 24.

values are purely arbitrary, the fossilisation of contingent and temporary ideas belonging to some social group.[86] Asserting the universal personal interpretation of all ideas, Nietzsche replaces truth with fiction and objectivity with arbitrariness, particularly where moral values are concerned.[87] The result is a total loss of meaning and value in the world.

> Nihilism represents an intermediary pathological condition (the vast generalisation, the conclusion that there is no purpose in anything, is pathological): whether is be that the productive forces are not yet strong enough - or that decadence still hesitates and has not yet discovered its expedient.

> The conditions of this hypothesis:- That there is no truth; that there is no absolute state of affairs - no "thing-in-itself." This alone is Nihilism, and of the most extreme kind. It finds that the value of things consists precisely in the fact that these values are not real and never have been real, but that they are only a symptom of strength on the part of the valuer, a simplification serving the purposes of existence.[88]

> What is belief? How is a belief born? All belief assumes that something is true.

> The extremest form of Nihilism would mean that all belief - all assumption of truth - is false: because no real world is at hand. It were therefore: only an appearance seen in perspective, whose origin must be found in us (seeing that we are constantly in need of a narrower, a shortened, and simplified world).[89]

But some kind of value system is necessary, he asserts, some source of meaning for existence based on some sort of absolute.[90] The will is the only constant, the only continually present aspect of human existence, itself in a state of becoming but in a *constant* state of becoming, always evaluating and changing but ever-present,[91] and also the absolute upon which the existence of

---

[86] Nietzsche, F., *The Will to Power: an Attempted Transvaluation of All Values*, trans. by A.M. Ludovici (London: Foulis, 1914), aphorism 12. (All references to Nietzsche's works will be given by aphorism rather than page number, with the exception of *The Birth of Tragedy*.

[87] Copleston, *History of Philosophy*, VII, pp. 410-11.

[88] *The Will-to-Power*, aphorism 13.

[89] *The Will-to-Power*, aphorism 15.

[90] *The Will-to-Power*, aphorisms 18-20.

[91] Blackham, pp. 25, 33.

the rest of (contingent) existence must be based. Hence, following Schopenhauer, and in a Romantic twist of the Cartesian quest for the indubitable, Nietzsche makes the will define reality, the only firm ground upon which knowledge can be built.

Nietzsche's concept of the will has specific qualities. It is something more than the unobtrusive will-to-live found in Darwin's evolutionary theory.[92] The will Nietzsche has in mind is the 'will-to-power', an aggressive and self-centred drive for power, a will which forges its own destiny and overwhelms its opponents. In his early writings, the will-to-power is a feature of the weak members of society who feel inadequate and crave power for themselves.[93] This emerges in a contempt for others and the attempt to manipulate and control those who pose a threat to them, most importantly their stronger neighbours. The main means of control is not through force, though, but by an objective value system.[94] Values, Nietzsche thinks, originally emerged within a group context to justify the group's own way of living.[95] For the aristocracy, courage and power were applauded since these qualities gave the group ascendancy. The slaves, however, encouraged servility, humility and compassion to give themselves a sense of moral superiority in their slavery. In time, this value system was used to deprive the nobility of their sense of superiority, and so eventually to enslave them to the weaker parties who could then manipulate the stronger members of society for their own ends. In this Nietzsche makes clear his position that reason, beliefs and values are no more than the servants of self-interest, particularly the 'will-to-power'.

Nietzsche regards Christianity as the classic case of the slave mentality gaining ascendancy. His view is that the priestly types created 'the Holy Lie', supposedly objective moral values based on divine revelation, to exert their control over society according to their own designs.[96] The foundation of this was the notion of God, to whom the priests claimed exclusive access and who was supposed to have issued the commandments the priests used to exercise mastery in society. The disposal of the idea of an omniscient, omnipotent and judgmental God as the source of slavish moral values was therefore the vital step in demolishing manipulative priestly religion, releasing the strong from

---

[92] Nietzsche, F., *Twilight of the Idols and The AntiChrist*, trans. by R.J. Hollingdale (London: Penguin, 1990): *Twilight of the Idols*, 'Expeditions of an Untimely Man', aphorism 14.

[93] Walter Kaufmann, 'The Discovery of the Will to Power' in *Nietzsche: A Collection of Critical Essays*, ed. by Robert C. Solomon (New York: Anchor, 1973), pp. 226-42 (pp. 226-8).

[94] Copleston, *History of Philosophy*, VII, pp. 410-11.

[95] Nietzsche, F., *Beyond Good and Evil*, trans. by Helen Zimmern, vol XII of *The Complete Works of Friedrich Nietzsche*, ed. by Oscar Levy (London: Allen and Unwin:1923), aphorism 260.

[96] *The Will to Power*, aphorisms 135, 141 and 142; *The AntiChrist*, aphorism 49.

the thrall of objective values enforced by a vengeful God, and allowing them to regain their rightful place of ascendancy.

In *The Dawn of Day*, Nietzsche's thought undergoes a radical change as he realises that in fact the will-to-power is present in all humanity and society, even the Greek culture he thought so impressive.[97] Indeed, he believes that the will-to-power was the driving force behind Greek culture itself. From this point on his agenda is to facilitate the release of the will-to-power from the bondage imposed upon it by the objective value systems so that the strong can create a new culture of courage and nobility. In *Thus Spake Zarathustra* this attempt emerges in full force,[98] beginning with the 'death of God' in the second part of Zarathustra's Introductory Speech: a theme vividly expressed in the proclamation of the madman in *The Gay Science*:

> The madman. - Have you not heard of that madman who lit a lantern in the bright morning hours, ran to the market place, and cried incessantly: "I seek God! I seek God!" - As many of those who did not believe in God were standing around just then, he provoked much laughter. Has he got lost? asked one. Did he lose his way like a child? asked another. Or is he hiding? Is he afraid of us? Has he gone on a voyage? emigrated? - Thus they yelled and laughed.
>
> The madman jumped into their midst and pierced them with his eyes. "Whither is God?" he cried; I will tell you. We have killed him - you and I. All of us are his murderers...God is dead. God remains dead. And we have killed him.[99]

It is the will-to-power that becomes the basis for epistemology and also anthropology for Nietzsche following the 'death of God'. All humanity has the will-to-power, and through it knowledge is established. For the weak, the will-to-power emerges as an objective value system intended to control the powerful members of society in the struggle for power. For the powerful, though, the quest for power is unnecessary since the strong man already has an abundance of it. The powerful figure, an individual of culture, hard and strong, free of self-doubt or pity, is Nietzsche's idea of the overman.[100] He is a creature of vitality, powerful, serene, magnanimous and generous, while being fully aware of the arbitrariness and absurdity of existence. Rather than being bound by convention or impersonal ideas of morality, he creates his own

---

[97] Nietzsche, F., *The Dawn of Day*, trans. by J.M. Kennedy, vol. IX of *The Complete Works of Friedrich Nietzsche*, ed. by Oscar Levy (London: Allen and Unwin, 1924), aphorism 360; Kaufmann, 'Discovery of the Will to Power', pp. 227, 234.

[98] See also Kaufmann, *Nietzsche*, p. 193.

[99] Nietzsche, F., *The Gay Science*, trans. and with commentary by Walter Kaufmann, (New York: Random House, 1974), Book 3, aphorism 125.

[100] Copleston, *Nietzsche*, pp. 83-94.

values according to his personality and ideas. It is through these values that he is able to give his will-to-power free reign and so live his life to the full. Hence ultimately it is through his own willing and the values he creates that he fulfils his own existence and destiny.

The will-to-power therefore is a matter of overcoming. For the weak, it is the overcoming of those they fear and feel inferior to. For the strong, however, domination of others is transcended to become the overcoming of oneself: an altogether more impressive achievement by which they overcome their neighbours by the sheer immensity of their power.[101] Thus the ascetic is Nietzsche's ultimate overman. The ascetic's great mastery emerges in self-torture, an activity which so appals those around him that his power unintentionally tortures and subdues his neighbours.

Nietzsche's view of power, then, is essentially positive. It is power which makes the weak strong, and transforms them from ignoble manipulators into noble aristocrats. All human power is, at its root, the will-to-power, but by quantitative distinction it is transformed from the lesser to the higher, from power-grasping to greatness.[102]

Niebuhr and the Will-to-Power

Nietzsche's idea of the will-to-power gave Niebuhr the concept he needed to describe the destructive force at work in human affairs. The will-to-power captured the sense of a forceful nucleus of energy, dominating and controlling the world around it according to its own self-centred agenda. It gave the right sense of aggression, of ruthless acquisition and of the indifference to the well-being of others he had observed in the destructive activities of industrialists and powerful nations. Most visible of all, the aggressive rise of Nazism in Germany in the 1930's with its open adherence to Nietzschean ideas was a clear indicator that this was the term he sought. The term 'will-to-power' emerges forcibly and for the first time in Niebuhr's major work *MMIS*. It is notable that Niebuhr wrote *MMIS* a year or so after the arrival at Union of Dietrich Bonhoeffer, a theologian heavily influenced by Nietzsche,[103] so that the latter would seem to be the likely source of Niebuhr's acquaintance with these ideas of Nietzsche's. From this point onwards, the concept of the will-to-power forms an important part of Niebuhr's anthropology as the description of the virile element of human nature from which the problem of human evil arises.

To the question whether Niebuhr's use of the phrase is synonymous with Nietzsche's, the answer is that it is. However, while Niebuhr's concept of the will-to-power correlates with Nietzsche's, his attitude towards it is

---

[101] Kaufmann, *Nietzsche*, pp. 195-7.
[102] Kaufmann, *Nietzsche*, pp. 193-6.
[103] Fox, pp. 124-26; Woelfel, James W., *Bonhoeffer's Theology: Classical and Revolutionary*, (New York: Abingdon, 1970), pp. 68-71.

diametrically opposed. While Nietzsche regards it as essential to affirm the will-to-power and give it free reign, at least for the overman, Niebuhr's position is that the will-to-power is practically the definition of human evil, and that since power corrupts, the pursuit of power by the will-to-power is not only to be deplored, but actively resisted.

Niebuhr's understanding of the will-to-power, then, approximates to Nietzsche's. First, for Niebuhr it is the will which forms the identity of the individual by fusing together the mind and the natural impulses.

> The ideal of love is thus first of all a commandment which appeals to the will. What is the human will? It is neither the total personality nor yet the rational element in personality. It is the total organized personality moving against the recalcitrant elements in the self.[104]

So the will is the main player in the human person rather than the rational faculty, and is the aspect of humanity which is to be addressed primarily. This has important consequences for Niebuhr's epistemology, since effective communication must therefore be addressed not to the mind through rational methods, but to the will through non-rational forms of communication such as myth, symbol or paradox.[105] It is the will which dominates the person and which must be dealt with to bring about change.

But the concept of the will which Niebuhr has in mind is not something generally docile or restrained, accepting the limits of its existence, simply a will to live. For Niebuhr, the will is the aggressive driving force of the will-to-power, striving to become secure in a world of infinite threats through the ceaseless acquisition of power. Through the anxious self-consciousness, the natural will-to-live is transformed from its relatively harmless struggle for survival into the will-to-power as it competes ruthlessly with its rivals in the struggle for power.

> [T]he will-to-live is also spiritually transmuted into the will-to-power or into the desire for "power and glory". Man, being more than a natural creature, is not interested merely in physical survival but in prestige and social approval. Having the intelligence to anticipate the perils in which he stands in nature and history, he invariably seeks to gain security against these perils by enhancing his power, individually and collectively.[106]

> How curiously nature and sin are involved in this process; for human imagination transmutes nature's harmless will-to-live into a sinful will-to-

---

[104] *ICE*, p. 220.

[105] See the sections on Epistemology in Chapter Three for the main discussion on this matter.

[106] *CLCD*, p. 21.

power. But the will-to-power always hides behind the natural will-to-live.[107]

Once the effort to gain significance beyond himself has succeeded, man fights for his social eminence and increased significance with the same fervor and with the same sense of justification, with which he fights for his life. The economy of nature has provided that means of defense may be quickly transmuted into means of aggression. There is therefore no possibility of drawing a sharp line between the will-to-live and the will-to-power.[108]

Thus in the human situation, it is the most aggressive and strongest will-to-power which gains ascendancy, to the detriment of those around it. So with the will-to-power as the basis of human life, humanity is in a constant state of conflict, a struggle for power in which the strong members of society thrive at the expense of the weaker members. With his increasing awareness of the evils of humanity, Niebuhr could see in Nietzsche's concept the description of human egoism he wanted, and adopted both the expression and the concept more or less uncritically.

The function of the concept in Niebuhr's thought is very different from Nietzsche's, though. Nietzsche wanted the force of the will-to-power released from its bondage to create a noble culture suitable for nurturing the overman. Niebuhr's position is that the will-to-power is the quintessence of sin, the source of evil in the world.[109] The failure of liberalism consisted in its inability to recognise the depth and strength of the will-to-power. This left it unaware of the truth regarding human evil, and unable to provide an adequate answer to its presence.[110] For Niebuhr it was the will-to-power at work in human society which required a vigorous Christian response if the evil in society was to be overcome. Niebuhr's actual agenda, we contend, was to provide a theological resource which would facilitate an effective battle against the evil present in the world. It is in this sense that Niebuhr's theology is a form of theodicy, a theological response to the problem of evil.

Following Nietzsche, Niebuhr makes extensive use of two key aspects of the will-to-power in his discussion of human behaviour. As a full discussion of his anthropology will be presented in a later section of the book, at present these two points need only be mentioned briefly. First, Niebuhr identifies the

---

[107] *BT*, p. 103.
[108] *MMIS*, p. 42.
[109] *NDM I*, p. 26.
[110] 'Ten Years That Shook My World.' Fourteenth Article in the Series "How My Mind Has Changed in This Decade", *The Christian Century*, 56 (26 April 1939), pp. 542-6 (p. 544).

essential aspect of sinful behaviour as egoistic striving of the will to gain power for the self. With strong overtones of Promethean tragedy,[111] he asserts that this striving is intrinsically sinful since it consists of defying the limits of existence set by a holy God. Like Prometheus, this defiance results in tragedy as the transgression is punished severely. Second, there is his view that the will-to-power uses reason or objective ideals as means of gaining power for itself, which has a prime place in his discussions regarding power, sin and epistemology. The concept of pretence, of the will-to-power using noble-sounding ideals to mask its egoism, forms an essential part of his theology and has clear Nietzschean overtones. 'The will-to-power uses reason, as kings use courtiers and chaplains to add grace to their enterprise'.[112]

Two final points should be made regarding Niebuhr's relationship with Nietzsche. The first is that while Niebuhr recognised the insight of Nietzsche's thought, he could not accept the consequences of Nietzsche's analysis and so never became a disciple. In particular, Niebuhr regarded Nazism as the direct result of Nietzsche's teachings, and while this may be unfair, for Niebuhr the Pragmatist the reality of Nietzschean thought lay in its practical consequences, which in this case meant Fascism. The second point, briefly mentioned earlier in this section, is that Niebuhr's view of power is very different from Nietzsche's. Nietzsche's mature view of power was essentially positive, as something bringing nobility. By contrast, Niebuhr's consistent perception was that power corrupts, and that it exacerbates the worst aspects of human nature and gives rise to the problem of evil. The lack of a positive doctrine of power is a serious weakness in Niebuhr's theology, as Hinze points out.[113] However, Niebuhr's undertaking, to deal with the problem of human evil in contrast to the optimism of his time would inevitably have made him more concerned with the problems humanity creates for itself through effects of power than with its beneficent aspects.

Tragedy in Romanticism

We have seen how the work of Nietzsche influenced the development of Niebuhr's thought by giving him the concept of the will-to-power. In as much as Nietzsche can be described as a Romantic thinker, this is the first major contribution Romanticism made to Niebuhr's theology. The second is the motif of tragedy, which for Niebuhr describes both the effects of the will-to-power in the human situation, and the actual human state of sinfulness. It should be noted that in Romanticism as a whole, tragedy only plays a minor

---

[111] *BT*, pp. 161-5.
[112] *MMIS*, p. 44.
[113] See the 'Considerations' discussion in the Christian Realism section of Chapter Three.

role.[114] In the thought of Schopenhauer and Nietzsche, however, the picture is significantly different, with both thinkers having a strong feeling for the tragic and incorporating it into their philosophies. For Schopenhauer this consists of the tragic state of the Primal Being, with its endless frustrating striving and misery. Thus he sees reality itself as essentially tragic. In Nietzsche the position is slightly different. Spurning Schopenhauer's pessimism and negation of life, Nietzsche seeks to affirm vitality and power, most importantly the will-to-power of the overman. Nietzsche's role for tragedy in his philosophy comes in terms of his desire for a 'tragic' culture akin to that of the ancient Greeks.[115] In his early work *The Birth of Tragedy* he gives the perspective that the power of tragedy lies in the interrelation between Dionysian vitality and Apolline art.[116] It is a similar balance, between primal urge and self-control, that is to be found in the overman. Hence, when a culture strives towards such a balance to achieve a tragic nature, the conditions obtain which foster the emergence of the overman.[117] For Nietzsche, then, the emergence of the overman, a figure he modelled on the tragic hero,[118] is achieved by establishing a culture where the elements of tragedy as force balanced by control, are present. It is under these terms that tragedy plays an important role in Nietzsche's philosophy.

In the Romanticism of Schopenhauer and Nietzsche, then, the motif of tragedy plays a prominent role. If, as seems likely, Niebuhr's commitment to tragedy comes from a Romantic influence, then we may be confident that it arises from the same source which provided him with the other main Romantic idea, the will-to-power. This theory is further supported by the type of tragedy Niebuhr has in mind: a matter which will be discussed presently. Sufficient to note that the term 'Dionysian', an important term for Nietzsche, is incorporated in Niebuhr's definition of pure tragedy;[119] also, that Niebuhr specifically refers to *The Birth of Tragedy* in *NDM I* (pp. 9, 35), indicating his familiarity with Nietzsche's work. It should be noted, however, that other important influences upon him such as Pascal and Kierkegaard also had a strong sense of the tragic,[120] and so the source should not be restricted to Nietzsche.

To gain a clearer understanding of what is meant by 'tragedy' and the 'the tragic' let us begin with Aristotle's *Poetics*. In Chapter Six, Aristotle gives us this definition.

---

[114] Brereton, pp. 183-4.
[115] Silk, M.S., and Stern, J.P., *Nietzsche on Tragedy*, (Cambridge: CUP, 1981), pp. 235, 328.
[116] *The Birth of Tragedy*, trans. by S. Whiteside (London: Penguin, 1993), pp. 43-5.
[117] White, Richard, 'Art and the Individual in Nietzsche's Birth of Tragedy', *British Journal of Aesthetics*, 28 (1988), pp. 59-67 (pp. 63-4).
[118] Silk and Stern, p. 296.
[119] *BT*, pp. 156-60.
[120] *KB*, pp. 182-7; Brereton, pp. 148-54.

> Tragedy is an imitation of an action that is admirable, complete and possesses magnitude; in language made pleasurable, each of its species separated in different parts; performed by actors, not through narration; effecting through pity and fear the purification of such emotions.[121]

As distinct from this dramatic context, Niebuhr is concerned with the tragedy of historical action such as the plays represent. However, Aristotle's definition includes two important aspects which should be noted. First of these is the sense of greatness which surrounds tragic events, captured in the terms 'admirable' and 'possess[ing] magnitude'. One key aspect of tragedy, as opposed to the merely pitiful, is the sheer impressiveness of the action.[122] The tragic figure is outstanding, commanding respect and admiration bordering on reverence. The appearance of royalty in tragedy, for example in *Oedipus Rex* or *Hamlet*, reflects this, as does the sense of awesome power in *Prometheus Bound*. It is this impression of greatness which raises the tragic above the pitiful. The second aspect of Aristotle's definition we should consider is the idea of 'catharsis', the potent emotions of pity and fear, the hallmark of experiencing tragedy. There has been much debate as to what this is, exactly. Essentially, it seems to be a combination of reactions; first, of pity for the person at the centre of the drama, the hero, who suffers terribly for his actions; second, of awe, or a sense that the action of the hero is beyond the capabilities of mere mortals; third, of fear, or even terror, often triggered by the destruction of the hero by gigantic forces such as Fate or the gods.[123] It is this last element which provides a sense of identity between the hero and those who observe. Pity and awe separate the hero from the rest of humanity; but his destruction by the same forces faced by all humanity reminds us of our own vulnerability to them. For if the great hero is destroyed, what chance have we?

It is this mixture of pity and fear based on awe and identity which makes tragedy so powerful. Brereton provides a further definition of tragedy which, being broader and more applicable to real life rather than its theoretical representation, is a useful development of Aristotle's when considering Niebuhr's use of the concept of tragedy.

> A tragedy is a final and impressive disaster due to an unforeseen or unrealised failure involving people who command respect and sympathy. It often entails an ironical change of fortune and usually conveys a strong

---

[121] *Poetics*, trans. with an introduction and notes by Malcolm Heath (London: Penguin, 1996), p. 10.

[122] See also Brereton, pp. 6-8.

[123] For a useful discussion of catharsis, see Brereton, pp. 28-32.

impression of waste. It is always accompanied by misery and emotional distress.[124]

This captures the impressiveness of tragedy, its sense of greatness, disaster and terrible waste. Yet even to this definition there are two aspects of tragedy which should be added. One is that tragedy tends to involve a deliberate act of some kind, often in the form of defiance against great powers. Brereton mentions this (p. 9) but does not include it in his definition. The second is the notion of a character flaw, of some intrinsic quality which is both the source of greatness and of the destruction of the character. The reckless self-assertion of, for example, Ixion or Peleus, reflects this and is mentioned by Aristotle in the *Poetics*.[125] Both these elements are important for Niebuhr's understanding and use of the tragic.

Niebuhr's Concept of Tragedy

We see very clearly in *BT* (pp. 156-60) that Niebuhr's idea of pure tragedy follows the pattern of Prometheus, where titanic defiance against huge forces results in the destruction of the central character. Significantly, in the case of Prometheus, it is a divine command in relation to the acquisition of knowledge by humanity which is involved. This parallels the Fall narrative, where the violation of God's command not to eat from the Tree of Knowledge results in calamity. Thus for Niebuhr, the concept of pure tragedy includes an action in defiance of divine limitations, which results in self-destruction.

A second motif of tragedy Niebuhr discusses is that of Dionysian vitality.[126] Here, unbridled passions emerge in a reckless disregard for prudence or virtue. It is the sheer exuberance of Dionysus which produces tragedy, as the necessary laws for life to be sustained are swept aside by its power. Thus, the vitality of life, when unrestrained, becomes self-contradictory and self-destructive as life itself destroys the means by which it may continue.

These first two kinds of tragedy, the Promethean and the Dionysian, are closely allied in Niebuhr's view in that they correspond to the force of the will-to-power breaking through barriers of limitation or natural prudence in its activity of self-assertion. It is this representation that results in Niebuhr placing the motif of tragedy at the heart of his concept of sin, and thereby his model of salvation. Since his concept of sin, or human evil, revolves around the concept of the will-to-power, it is to be expected that the destructiveness of the will-to-power should be expressed in terms which capture the force and vitality of that concept, namely, the motifs of Promethean and Dionysian tragedy. Furthermore, Dionysian religion is integral to Nietzsche's philosophy and concept of tragedy, beginning with its central role in *The Birth of Tragedy*,

---

[124] Brereton, p. 20 (his italics).
[125] as 'Tragedy of character' in Chapter 18 (p. 29 of the Penguin edition.)
[126] *BT*, pp. 159-60.

a work Niebuhr was familiar with, but continuing through the whole of Nietzsche's thought;[127] so once more we can detect here the influence of Nietzsche on Niebuhr.

In this way, the tragic motif can be seen as describing accurately the manifestation of the will-to-power as Niebuhr perceives it. But this indicates that, in fact, the concept of tragedy Niebuhr has in mind is reflective of a single element, the will-to-power. Both the Promethean and Dionysian motifs express the nature of this one thing: it may be stated, then, that in fact the two main types of tragedy Niebuhr refers to have one final identity, the unrestrained disregard for limitation or prudence resulting in self-destruction which is the will-to-power. Hence in Niebuhr's thought, Promethean and Dionysian tragedy may be collated and regarded as one.

This is reflected in the way Niebuhr makes clear what types of tragedy he is not concerned with. He dismisses the figures of Thomas Hardy's novels as not tragic but pitiful, since their lives consist of impotent struggle against and destruction by the forces of Fate.[128] Whether 'pitiful' rather than 'tragic' is the true definition of Hardy's characters is open to debate: its significance here is that Niebuhr considered them not to be tragic since they lacked the wilful self-assertion of the will-to-power. For Niebuhr, the will-to-power and the true definition of tragedy are to be seen as inextricably linked.

For Niebuhr, then, the key aspect of Promethean tragedy is the great act of defiance of divine powers or limits, resulting in the destruction of the character. This must be borne in mind in Niebuhr's discussion of sin, which for him consists of humanity's rebellion against the God-given limits of human existence. Unlike Greek tragedy, this form of defiance may be considered intrinsically immoral, since it consists of rebellion against a holy, good, and loving God rather than the arrogant, capricious, and self-seeking gods of Greek mythology.[129] The Greek hero defying the gods for some noble purpose may be considered virtuous, but an aggressive egoist attempting to grasp power for himself in opposition to God's righteous instructions must be regarded as debased.

While the Promethean notion of tragedy is clearly dominant for Niebuhr, a second form of tragedy also plays an important role in his theology. This is the tragic idea of greatness destroying itself through some intrinsic flaw. For Niebuhr, this takes the form of the self-destruction of humanity through its unique quality of self-consciousness which is the source of man's creativity and evil together.

> The tragedy of human history consists precisely in the fact that human life cannot be creative without being destructive, that biological urges are

---

[127] Kaufmann, *Nietzsche*, pp. 32-3.

[128] *BT*, pp. 156-8.

[129] Brereton, p. 273.

enhanced and sublimated by daemonic spirit and that this spirit cannot express itself without committing the sin of pride.[130]

This was Niebuhr's antidote to the optimism of the late nineteenth century; for humanity's great creativity brings progress to greater good, but with it, greater evil.[131] It is this tragic flaw, by which the uniqueness of humanity gives rise to good and also to evil, that creates the hopeless state of sin which requires God's salvation. In contrast to liberal or Marxist concepts of human nature which practically guaranteed human progress to Utopia, Niebuhr asserts the inevitable growth of evil alongside the good. This tragic element is further demonstrated by his discussion of the will-to-power's drive for security. The will-to-power seeks power for itself by aggressive self-assertion in order to become secure. But the force of dominion results in injustice, a reaction by the oppressed, and finally rebellion and the destruction of the aggressive will-to-power by its enemies. Thus, in a cycle of tragic self-destruction, in trying to avoid insecurity, final destruction comes about. The intrinsic flaw of the will-to-power guarantees that, through its striving, it destroys itself.

Niebuhr's position, then, is that the state of sinful humanity is essentially tragic. The human state consists of a hopeless striving, in defiance of God and the God-given limits of existence, to overcome the vast power of God at work in nature and humanity. This sinful activity, arising from the very nature of humanity as self-conscious finitude, is the source of human evil, and ultimately incurs the wrath of a holy God, who destroys humanity through the forces of nature and history. Thus, for Niebuhr, tragedy lies at the heart of the human situation and is essential for understanding the true nature of life.

Conclusion

In conclusion, we may briefly summarise the influence of Romanticism as we have defined it upon Niebuhr: it contributes two key concepts (derived from Nietzsche) to his theology. The first is the concept of the will-to-power, which he makes use of to represent the element of evil in humanity which he has identified. Thus the idea of the will-to-power forms the central motif of his anthropology and also his ideas regarding sin, power, and Christian ethics. The second is the concept of tragedy, which has a pivotal role in his thought. For Niebuhr, tragedy expresses the true state of humanity, both its sinful defiance of God and the result of sin being self-destruction. Hence, while Niebuhr cannot be described as a Romantic philosopher (his limited appreciation of humanity, and the absence of the glorification of Nature putting him outside that school), Romanticism clearly contributed some very important ideas to his theology – and we shall see evidence later of how pervasive the influence was.

---

[130] *NDM* 1, p. 11.
[131] *CLCD*, p. 46.

The Influence of William James on Reinhold Niebuhr

Introduction

In the recent *Cambridge Companion to William James*, Ross Posnock[132] analyses James' contribution to American culture and presents his influence on theologians such as Niebuhr in terms of the impact of his analysis of religious experience. James' impact on Niebuhr can seen as considerably broader than this, however. Richard Fox describes Niebuhr as 'a thoroughgoing Jamesian pragmatist' (p. 84), a title confirmed by Niebuhr himself[133] and a number of his commentators.[134] We must ask, then, in what sense was Niebuhr a Pragmatist in the Jamesian tradition? Our particular concern here is to see how that tradition contributed to Niebuhr's theological response to the existence of human evil. After a brief consideration of the circumstances in which Pragmatism arose, we will consider James' Pragmatic method, certain aspects of his epistemology, and his strong interest in two issues, the problem of determinism and (for him) the closely related problem of evil.

Modernism and the Problem of Power

By the middle of the Nineteenth Century, American society had outgrown its Puritan beginnings, its Republican social ethic and its Enlightenment assurances concerning the power of reason to promote morality.[135] The raw existence of the Frontiersman, the 'tough-minded' to use James' expression, consisting of practical self-interest and hard irreligiousness, was emerging as a dominant philosophy, especially in the political arena, while democracy had come to be regarded as nothing more than 'the systematic organisation of hatreds'.[136] This change in society, combined with the cold accuracy of empiricism, revealed the true nature of harsh reality unsoftened by ideals or religion.

---

[132] Ross Posnock, 'The influence of William James on American Culture', in *The Cambridge Companion to William James*, ed. by Ruth Anna Putman (Cambridge: CUP, 1997), pp. 322-42 (p. 322).

[133] Bingham, p. 224.

[134] Arthur Schlesinger in *KB*, pp. 131-32; West, Cornel, *The American Evasion of Philosophy: A Genealogy of Pragmatism*, (Basingstoke: Macmillan, 1989), p. 152. Robin Lovin draws out the role the Pragmatic coherence theory of truth plays in Niebuhr's theology in *Reinhold Niebuhr and Christian Realism*, pp. 46-54.

[135] Diggins, *Promise of Pragmatism*, pp. 23, 59.

[136] Henry Adams, quoted by Diggins, *Promise of Pragmatism*, p. 62.

This, says John P Diggins, presented the 'problem of modernism', the issue of power without authority, or autonomous, self-justifying power.[137] The changes in philosophy and society made manifest the true nature of existence as being defined ultimately by power alone. The power to survive could be seen to be a wholly sufficient reason for existence, without any higher ideal or justification. No matter how constructive or destructive something's nature, its sole requirement for existence would be the power to sustain itself, the power to exist. In other words, it is power itself which defines reality.

The problem of the autonomy of power had far-reaching implications. The random, amoral and capricious aspects of reality emerged as the actual events which constitute history became the primary source of knowledge. This challenged the longstanding theistic view, implicit in philosophy from Plato onwards and of course in theology, that the universe has an intrinsically moral basis which rewards and implements justice and selflessness. It also changed the nature of perceived truth. As events became the primary source of knowledge, the rationalist view that truth consists of eternal, unchanging abstracts, was replaced. In its stead came the more scientific idea that truth emerges from studying events, which gives rise to provisional hypotheses which are developed and modified as time passes and further events or experiments are observed.[138] This scientific approach detaches events from imposed rationalist patterns and allows their real natures to emerge. It also means that that truth appears in situations and is the consequence of them, i.e. it is something created rather than discovered, and is something situational, contingent and dynamic.[139] This change in epistemology lies at the heart of Pragmatism, as we shall see presently.

This emergence of the problem of modernism gave a new understanding of authority. Henry Adams described the power of existence as a dynamo, irresistible and self-serving, and operating to laws which made it possible to plot its future course.

> [Adams] now became a philosopher of history, and as such he reconceived history not as politics and diplomacy but as a fateful process of force, energy, and power, a process that could be plotted according to the new laws of physics. Convinced that knowledge of the universe must now be found in objective forces independent of men, Adams developed a "dynamic theory of history" to present to the society of American historians.[140]

Since existence is governed by the dynamic power of history, anything which exists and has the power to challenge ' the dynamo' is by definition

---

[137] See particularly Diggins, *Promise of Pragmatism*, pp. 14-5, 39-40 and 97-8.
[138] Diggins, *Promise of Pragmatism*, pp. 126-33.
[139] William James, *Pragmatism*, (New York: Dover, 1995), Lecture VI.
[140] Diggins, *Promise of Pragmatism*, p. 83.

itself a part of that same force. Hence all supposed challenges to power are actually part of the process of history. This applies even to the power of reason, to the extent that philosophy has been seen to be used as a tool of power by rationalising self-interested action.

If history is governed by power rather than morality or rationality, then the ultimate questions of philosophy must be concerned with the nature of power, and with devising a means of dealing with the newly perceived, true nature of reality. Pragmatism arose from this challenge, endeavouring to replace the old, passive and sterile metaphysics with an action-focused, practical philosophy. It would be forward-looking and seeking to establish a new role for human creative energy in the battle to regain a sense of meaning for human history. It may be because James, as Posnock says, invited American intellectuals to turn toward facts, action and power that his influence on Niebuhr was far-reaching.

James and Niebuhr: Matters of Style

An obvious reason for calling Niebuhr a Jamesian Pragmatist is their similar style of writing. James was not a particularly thorough or systematic thinker but rather an essayist, writing on matters he found interesting.[141] Nor are his works particularly aimed at fellow academics; they appeal to non-professionals, who find them accessible and readable. Likewise, many of Niebuhr's writings appeared in newspapers and lay journals, and even his theological works, despite their profundity, are not so difficult that those who are not professional scholars would find them intractable.

Second, both Niebuhr and James take what Cornel West calls a 'dialectic' approach to other traditions and thinkers (p. 57). By this he means that they select the elements from a tradition they find interesting, usually at the extremes, and ignore or reject the rest. This might also be called a rhetorical style, employed more to make a point than to do justice to the ideas held by the opponent. Niebuhr certainly used this approach, for example in *NDM I* to expose the supposed shortcomings of the schools of thought against which he wanted to argue.[142] Whether Niebuhr's method is in fact 'dialectic', or instead aggressively rhetorical, is a matter for debate. Thus John C. Bennett makes the point that the result of Niebuhr's approach is that his own way of thinking

---

[141] Marcell, David W., *Progress and Pragmatism: James, Dewey, Beard and the American Idea of Progress*, (London: Greenwood, 1974), pp. 172-73; West, American Evasion, p. 54.

[142] See pp. 1-12 particularly, but the first four chapters of *NDM I* might accurately be described as 'rhetorical' in this sense, as Niebuhr caricatures various philosophical alternatives to Christianity as a preparation for presenting his own ideas.

Philosophical and Theological Influences 51

is exposed (including its shortcomings) more than the true position of his opponent.[143]

Third, James, like Kierkegaard, takes a psychological approach to matters of human existence, and has an essentially individualistic philosophy.[144] Niebuhr's philosophy too is individualistic and psychologically orientated. Whether or not Niebuhr developed his approach directly as a result of these thinkers' influence, he clearly was indebted to them and so a closer examination of James will be useful.

The Philosophy of Pragmatism

1. PRAGMATISM AS METHOD

'Pragmatism' was a term taken from an essay written by Charles Peirce in 1878,[145] and in James' use primarily defines a method.

> The pragmatic method is primarily a method of settling metaphysical disputes that otherwise might be interminable. Is the world one or many? - fated or free? - material or spiritual? - here are notions either of which may or may not hold good of the world; and disputes over such notions are unending. The pragmatic method in such cases is to try to interpret each notion by tracing its respective practical consequences. What difference would it practically make to anyone if this notion rather than that notion were true? If no practical difference whatever can be traced, then the alternatives mean practically the same thing, and all dispute is idle...To attain perfect clearness in our thoughts of an object, then, we need only consider what conceivable effects of a practical kind the object may involve – what sensations we are to expect from it, and what reactions we must prepare. Our conception of these effects, whether immediate or remote, is then for us the whole of our conception of the object, so far as that conception has positive significance at all. This is the principle of Peirce, the principle of pragmatism.[146]

James sees the first task of Pragmatism to be to define the limits of authentic philosophical inquiry and so eliminate intractable 'pseudo-problems' which he perceived had brought traditional metaphysics to a halt.[147] He employs the

---

[143] John C. Bennett, 'Reinhold Niebuhr's Contribution to Christian Social Ethics' in Landon, Harold R., *Reinhold Niebuhr: A Prophetic Voice in Our Time*, (Greenwich, Conn.: Seabury Press, 1962), pp. 55-96 (p. 60).

[144] Berstein, Richard J., *Praxis and Action*, (London: Duckworth, 1972), pp. 166-7.

[145] James, *Pragmatism*, p. 18.

[146] James, *Pragmatism*, p. 18.

[147] Moore, Edward C., *American Pragmatism: Peirce, James and Dewey*, (New York: Columbia University Press, 1961), p. 116; Diggins, *Promise of Pragmatism*, p. 12.

method of verification used by scientific inquiry to state that truth is to be defined in terms of what can be tested, observed, measured and corroborated. Consequently, true ideas can be verified by experimentation and empirical research; false ideas cannot.[148] By defining truth in these terms, by what can be measured, he sidelines many of the traditional problems of metaphysics which had resulted in insoluble antinomies. True ideas will make a difference. Identifying knowledge with material reality, if the results of using an idea cannot be seen in material, measurable ways, the idea is simply irrelevant, a piece of sophistry, to be discounted. The issue must therefore lie outside the boundaries of authentic, valuable philosophy.

> Pragmatism, on the other hand, asks its usual question. "Grant an idea or belief to be true," it says, "what concrete difference will its being true make in anyone's actual life? How will the truth be realised? What experiences will be different from those which would obtain if the belief were false? What, in short, is the truth's cash-value in experiential terms?"

> The moment pragmatism asks this question, it sees the answer: *True ideas are those that we can assimilate, validate, corroborate and verify. False ideas are those that we cannot.* That is the practical difference it makes to us to have true ideas; that, therefore, is the meaning of truth, for it is all that truth is known-as.[149]

Thus the first stage of the Pragmatic method establishes the correct objects of philosophical inquiry, while the second concerns the way it solves those (authentic) philosophical problems which remain. James' point is that questions which had proved insoluble by rational means can be solved empirically, by trying out the various ideas on offer as solutions and seeing what practical, measurable difference each one makes. In this respect, Pragmatism can be understood as the application of the scientific method to philosophy. It is an approach based on measurable consequences and concerned with active experimentation in concrete situations to produce factual results. Forward-looking, the Pragmatist is interested in the near-future as different ideas are put to use and the results emerge. For James, therefore, the process of accumulating knowledge is an active, living process whereby currently held beliefs are constantly tried out and modified, and so the truth about an idea or theory is discovered by it being put to the test in a situation rather than dealt with through abstract reason. This step alone is a dramatic move for epistemology; but James goes further still. He states that truth is created in a situation, according to the

---

[148] James, *Pragmatism*, p. 77.

[149] James, *Pragmatism*, p. 77.

usefulness of the idea. For him, an idea is neither true nor false till it is tried out; and its truth-value is determined by its usefulness in concrete situations. Hence truth is generated by its use in real life.

> The truth of an idea is not a stagnant property inherent in it. Truth *happens* to an idea. It *becomes* true, is *made* true by events. Its verity *is* in fact an event, a process: the process namely of verifying itself, its veri-*fication*. Its validity is the process of its valid-*ation*.[150]

Prior to being tested, an idea has no truth-value; it simply exists. To become true, the idea must be tried out and verified, and through its usefulness its value can be ascertained. This process of creating truth consists in the living of 'live hypotheses',[151] ideas which connect with an existing set of beliefs sufficiently to make them relevant and interesting. Testing out a live hypothesis consists in trying it out in real-life situations. The new idea will be employed by the person, and as the consequences emerge in the near future its truth will be revealed in terms of its actual effects. The intention of the consciousness is personal well-being;[152] so the ability of the idea to fulfil its purpose for the consciousness in this overall plan is the measure of its truth.[153] Ideas are therefore teleologically measured: their truth-value consists of their final result, the consequences of the idea as it is employed in existence. If the true nature of the idea is revealed by the sum of its effects,[154] then the effects of an idea reveal the reality of its true nature, its 'cash value' or truth content. This is James' development of Peirce's principle of 'meaning-*effect*',[155] a Pragmatic technique of weighing up ideas according to their real-life consequences.

In introducing this discussion of the influence of James on Niebuhr we mentioned the strong similarity of philosophical style, in terms of approach and expression. Clearly, the similarity of method goes deeper than just the style employed. Niebuhr consistently uses the criteria of noting the actual effects of a principle or ideology when weighing up the various philosophies he encounters. Thus because the reality of the idea was the sum of its consequences,[156] then the truth of Marxism was, for him, the Stalinist Russia of betrayal and pogrom. It was by judging the concrete situations arising from an ideology that he was able to critique, in turn,

---

[150] James, *Pragmatism*, pp. 77-8.
[151] William James, *The Will to Believe and Other Essays in Popular Philosophy*, (New York: Longmans Green and Co., 1904), pp. 2-3, 58-60.
[152] Marcell, pp. 159-62.
[153] James, *Pragmatism*, pp. 23, 79; *The Will to Believe*, pp. 10-11; Moore, pp. 141-4.
[154] James, *The Will to Believe*, p. 117.
[155] Thiselton, A.C., *New Horizons in Hermeneutics*, (London: HarperCollins, 1992), p. 84.
[156] Cf. Harvey J. Cormier, 'Pragmatism, politics, and the corridor', in *The Cambridge Companion to William James*, pp. 343-62 (pp. 343-44).

liberalism, Marxism and Neo-orthodoxy to expose their shortcomings. Most important amongst the criteria employed was the ability to recognise and deal with human evil in the form of the will-to-power. It was the failure to produce a satisfactory response to the factor which caused him to reject liberalism and turn to Marxism in the late 1920s. Marxism in turn proved inadequate and Niebuhr progressed into his own form of Christian ethics which has been called Christian Realism. It is therefore likely that he discovered in Pragmatic philosophy the principle he needed for assessing the validity of any ideology or theology. Furthermore, he could be said to have sought a theological development of Pragmatic thinking that would deal adequately with human evil which would be consistent with this approach. His mature affirmation of prophetic Christianity was an argument about the *effect* of Christian truth in a world of the will-to-power, the effect of bringing about the social justice that overcomes human evil.

2. Ontology and Epistemology

It is by the Pragmatic method of empirical results that James sidelines some of the most difficult and fruitless problems of traditional metaphysics. Rather than presenting logical arguments regarding the nature of being or of knowledge, James simply asserts the existence of being, the accuracy of the mind's perception of its surroundings and the existence of God and of freewill.[157] Bypassing the intractable arguments concerning substance and phenomenology, James assumes that the world exists as it appears to be and that interaction with the world consists in truthful engagement with it through use. James' means of justifying this realist ontology[158] and his 'correspondence'[159] theory of truth is an immediate consequence of his Pragmatism. He never argues the case for Realism or accurate perception, presumably regarding them as examples of the dry metaphysical discussions his Pragmatism was intended to eliminate. His defence of this position, if there is one, is simply that the consequences which flow from it

---

[157] Richard M. Gale notes that James' passionate defence of freewill was due to his dependence on it to sustain him through his emotional crises, rather than its logical coherence. 'John Dewey's naturalisation of William James', in *The Cambridge Companion to William James*, pp. 49-68 (p. 56).

[158] James, *Pragmatism*, p. 94; West, *American Evasion*, p. 67.

[159] Or more accurately, 'commerce' theory of truth, as new perceptions and ideas challenge, interact with and modify the existing set of beliefs. See *Pragmatism*, p. 27. In his discussion of Gramsci's and West's criticisms of James in *The Cambridge Companion to William James*, though, Harvey J. Cormier mentions that James was hostile to the 'whole realism-versus-idealism debate' and was seeking to establish a new way of looking at truth which moved beyond ideas of truth as internal ideas corresponding to external entities (pp. 344-7). Strictly speaking, this makes normal epistemological terms such as 'correspondence theory' redundant, and the term 'commerce theory of truth' should be understood as only a description of what James had in mind.

are the most advantageous; also it is the 'common sense' view which has proved most useful down the centuries.[160] Effectively, he justifies his position on the basis that it is these ideas which make the most sense and have the most beneficial consequences.[161]

James' epistemology and ontology are closely connected. This is clear in his Pragmatic theory of knowledge just considered, in which usefulness defines truth. If the truth of a concept lies in its ability to make use of the world, to mine the world of its resources, as it were, for the battle for survival, there must be an external world in which the concepts can be used.

Those truths held by consciousness engage with the world around it through personal experience. Reality is 'what truths have to take account of'.[162] As the person carries on through life making use of the body of beliefs for personal well-being, he encounters the world through sensations and perceptions, and the resistance hard reality gives to its flow of ideas and activities. It is the difference the material world makes to the person's activities which indicates the reality of that world. So, just as the truth content of an idea is formed as its effects emerge in the world, so the reality of the world is revealed by the difference it makes to the consciousness.

Niebuhr takes exactly the same approach concerning matters of metaphysics. From his days at Yale Divinity School onwards, he avoided metaphysics, finding them tedious and unproductive.[163] Niebuhr, like James, simply assumes the existence of being and a coherence theory of truth in which perception is expected to correspond to reality and the coherence of reality be reflected by a generally coherent body of beliefs held by the person.[164] This assumed ontology and epistemology was something of a source of frustration for his colleague Paul Tillich, who on one occasion attempted without much success to establish Niebuhr's ontology,[165] and devoted his chapter in the Kegley and Bretall volume on Niebuhr to Niebuhr's lack of a specific epistemology. For Niebuhr, such discussions were a distraction from the more important task of dealing with the ethical challenges of the social and political world he, and most of his audience, were engaged in. This also bears striking resemblance to James, who was hugely influential not least because of the practical flavour of his thought,

---

[160] James, *Pragmatism*, pp. 69-71.

[161] Hilary Putman makes the point that James does not give any accurate definition of truth; James' discussion of the matter proceeds through a series of examples. 'James' theory of truth', in *The Cambridge Companion to William James*, pp. 166-85 (p. 172).

[162] James, *Pragmatism*, p. 94.

[163] Fox, p. 34.

[164] Lovin, pp. 46-54.

[165] Paul Tillich, 'Sin and Grace in the Theology of Reinhold Niebuhr', in Landon, pp. 27-54.

underpinned by his exceptional moral fervour.¹⁶⁶ Also like James, Niebuhr, when considering ways in which evil can be overcome, simply assumes the possibility of freewill and positive moral action without attempting to provide any kind of justification for his position.

So far we have indicated the more general ways in which James can be seen to have influenced Niebuhr. Here was a philosopher who wrote and spoke to the general public, arguing with a passion rather than logic-chopping – an intellectual after Niebuhr's own heart. His approach to the business of philosophy was similarly concrete and the Pragmatic method with its voluntaristic epistemology and ontology would also have strengthened Niebuhr's mode of thinking. We turn now to more specific features of his ontology, his anthropology and his concept of reason.

3. ANTHROPOLOGY AND EPISTEMOLOGY

Several factors unite to form James' anthropology. By profession, he was an early pioneer of psychology in America. First, then, and as might be expected, his approach to questions of existence begins with the workings of the mind (as it also did for Kierkegaard). Furthermore, James's version of Pragmatism is focused primarily on the individual as the means by which truth is formed and also moral action occurs in the world. In fact, James holds a near-anarchic position and regards individual freedom and creativity as the highest of human goods, and his philosophy is partly an attempt to defend these qualities against the deadening influences of monolithic bureaucracies and deterministic philosophies.¹⁶⁷ Second, his anthropology, like his epistemology, is firmly grounded in the materialist tradition, such that he understands the human person primarily in terms of a natural, physical being out of which arise the qualities of self-consciousness, reason and so on. Third, he draws on Darwin's concept of the survival of the fittest, so that survival in a dangerous world is of paramount importance for the individual. James' concept of the person therefore is of a material-biological unity in which the mind is a function of a material object (the brain).¹⁶⁸ The mind and body form a unity which physiologically interact to maximise personal well-being.¹⁶⁹ Darwinist that

---

[166] Posnock in *The Cambridge Companion to William James*, p. 327. Kierkegaard likewise, incidentally, though to a lesser extent: as a pastor his thought has a practical basis and important implications for active Christian faith.

[167] Diggins, *Promise of Pragmatism*, pp. 122-3.

[168] Diggins, *Promise of Pragmatism*, p. 127; Moore, p. 155.

[169] James, *The Will to Believe*, p. 117; Moore, pp. 141-2; Gay Wilson Allen, 'William James', in *Makers of American Thought: An Introduction to Seven American Writers*, ed. by Ralph Ross (Minneapolis: University of Minnesota Press, 1974), pp. 49-84 (p. 62).

he was, James viewed the mind as an evolved aspect of human existence, extremely useful in the general struggle for survival.[170]

Rather than being a passive, unchanging receptacle, James sees the mind as a powerful and active organiser, constantly modifying its stock of ideas and employing them as new situations arise.[171] It is creative and complex, affected by other parts of the person's body and situation. As an interactive force it is constantly changing, flowing through its existential position and channelling resources according to its goal of personal welfare. James describes it as a 'stream of consciousness', a complex flow of thoughts, ideas, objects and memories, all directed according to the person's intentions.[172] Although reason forms part of the flow, its role is limited and conditioned, forming only part of the constant decision-making process. Overall it is the will of the person which formulates decisions and creates the person's identity, which James describes as the 'passional nature', and consists of the entire complex of the self directed by the consciousness.[173]

Since the focus of the self is personal well-being, the stream of consciousness is organised and directed by the self towards this end. Reason, rather than being the cause of action, is employed by the self for its own ends as it acts according to its personal goals. Hence the consciousness only acts reasonably as far as it finds it useful to do so, and no further. Rather than being governed by reason, human beings act according to self-will and use reason to achieve their goals, and to justify their actions should the need arise.

> Our reason is quite satisfied, in nine hundred and ninety nine cases out of every thousand of us, if it can find a few arguments that will do to recite in case our credulity is criticised by some one else...We want to have a truth; we want to believe that our experiments and studies and discussions must put us in a continually better and better position towards it; and on this line we agree to fight out our thinking lives. But if a pyrrhonistic sceptic asks us *how we know* all this, can our logic find a reply? No! certainly it cannot. It is just one volition against another, – we willingly go in for life upon a trust or assumption which he, for his part, does not care to make.[174]

---

[170] James, *The Will to Believe*, pp. 226-7; Marcell, pp. 159-60; C. Wright Mills, *Sociology and Pragmatism: The Higher Learning in America*, (New York: OUP, 1966), pp. 227-8. As Owen Flanagan points out, though, James should not be regarded as a straightforward naturalist, cf. 'Consciousness as a pragmatist views it', in *The Cambridge Companion to William James*, pp. 25-48 (pp. 26-7).

[171] James, *The Will to Believe*, pp. 129-30, 141.

[172] James, *The Will to Believe*, pp. 63-4, 75; Marcell, pp. 161-5; Allen in Ross, *Makers of American Thought*, p. 62; Diggins, *Promise of Pragmatism*, p. 127.

[173] James, *The Will to Believe*, p. 11; Allen in Ross, *Makers of American Thought*, p. 65.

[174] James, *The Will to Believe*, pp. 9-10.

So, like Nietzsche, James sees self-will as the defining factor where truth is concerned, and reason serves the will rather than vice versa; and as a result of his Darwinism and materialist anthropology, James sees reason as a tool used by the person in the struggle for survival, rather than a dominant ordering or controlling principle.

We see the same line of thought in Niebuhr. For him, the whole person, including the rational faculty, is created by God as a material entity.[175] While the self-consciousness has a transcendent capacity, the faculty of reason is not separate from the material body in any way or capable of disinterested detachment.[176] On the contrary, he consistently states that it is the will which governs and manipulates rationality for its own ends. In the section on Romanticism we saw how Niebuhr accepted Nietzsche's concept of the will-to-power as an accurate description of the human will. In James' materialism he saw the actual anthropology which underlies this perspective, since it is by the fused unity of a single composite (material) existence that the will is able to exert such control over other parts of the self, including the rational element. In the rationalist dualism of Plato and Descartes the distinctiveness and separateness of reason ensures its freedom from the passions of the body and therefore its objectivity. For Niebuhr, no such dualism exists: the material unity of the person makes pure detachment impossible, and instead he asserts the government of the will. Thus it is the will that is the locus of the person, the powerful controlling factor creating personal coherence and identity, and not the cognitive faculty.[177] This perspective, that the will is the key player in human nature, determines Niebuhr's epistemology since it is the (non-cognitive) will which must be reached if personal behaviour is to be influenced.

James' Darwinism is also crucial for Niebuhr. It is the practical issue of survival through the acquisition of power which forms the centrepiece of Niebuhr's understanding of human existence, since it is from the insecurity of a threatened state that the quest for power of the will-to-power arises, which in turn is the source of human evil.[178] Hence the source of anxiety in humanity which is at the heart of his understanding of human nature is derived from the very practical matter of survival. Unlike Kierkegaard, who sees angst as a consequence of self-conscious freedom, Niebuhr sees it in the more common-sense terms of anxiety regarding one's own physical well-being. The agenda of the will, as the will-to-power, is domination in order to become secure against the threats to material existence; and since this is a practical matter, Niebuhr's whole theology has a uniquely down-to-

---

[175] *NDM I*, pp. 12-3.

[176] *BT*, pp. 293-4.

[177] *ICE*, p. 220.

[178] See the section in Chapter 3 on Anthropology and Sin, 'Anxiety: the source of sin and the will-to-power' and 'Security and the will-to-power' for a full account of this matter.

earth character. Consequently, his influence in the practical world, not least in the realm of politics, was huge. Deriving his theology from the concrete issues facing humanity, he has immediate and practical ideas for such matters. Ultimately, this crucial aspect of his thought comes from the problem of personal survival and material well-being we also see in James.

4. GOD, FREEDOM AND EVIL

The final aspect of James' Pragmatism we will consider directly concerns the problem of evil. At the start of this section we considered how the problem of autonomous power formed the crucible out of which Pragmatism arose. The problem of power can be seen as a particular form of the problem of evil in which it is human depravity which creates the suffering. Diggins and West both argue that James' philosophy is a response to the problem of power arising in a modern industrial society. Marcell even says that James was almost obsessive about this matter, and that this was reflected in his lifelong fight with determinism (p. 150). For James, determinism gives rise to the problem of evil since, if God is both in total control and omnipotent, then He must be directly responsible for the evil in the world. So James' philosophy can be seen as an attempt to give an effective antidote to determinism and at the same time to provide a response to the problem of evil. Three aspects of his thought deal with this task: a pluralist universe open to human influence, an emphasis on human striving and a finite God.

James extends his dynamic and forward-looking philosophy beyond the realm of the individual to the world as a whole. He regards human history itself as malleable and open to different possibilities,[179] describing the universe as a moral background where the future is uncertain and the triumph of good over evil is dependent upon the effects of human creative energy.[180] Meliorism is neither wholly optimistic nor pessimistic. Unlike the optimistic universalist, the future is not guaranteed to be good, consisting of certain salvation for all; but neither is it certain to be evil consisting of unavoidable damnation. James' own type of meliorism is more optimistic than pessimistic. His pluralism breaks up the structure of history into blocks of human-sized dimensions, where human effort can make a measurable difference within a confined sphere of influence. This means that the future can be influenced by human action and so James establishes human activity as ultimately significant. Human activity is the means by which change can occur and good can triumph over evil; hence James' philosophy overall is geared to generating dynamic human power. He regards traditional metaphysics as a disaster in this respect since they deprive humanity of its most cherished powers.[181] Religion he views more

---

[179] James, *Pragmatism*, Lecture VIII, especially pp. 108-14; Marcell, pp. 188-90.

[180] James, *Pragmatism*, pp. 110-12; Diggins, *Promise of Pragmatism*, p. 127.

[181] James, *The Will to Believe*, p. 126.

positively, seeing it as more radical and provocative and therefore an active promoter of passions; philosophy he sees as too weak and diffident to be useful.[182] The uncertainty of history's outcome is integral to making the struggle real, a genuine adventure. The possibility of salvation exists, but it is only a possibility, and needs actualisation. This can be achieved by human activity, which can realise the potential for good in the world. James' main belief is in human will and struggle,[183] and salvation, rather than being the work of God, is a human affair. In fact, James presents a God similar to J. S. Mill's: a being of finite power, attempting to master evil but dependent upon humanity for a successful outcome. For James, the role of religion is to provide galvanising beliefs and demands to activate humanity to battle for good against evil. The existence of freewill, a melioristic universe, and a finitely powerful God makes evil a matter of human responsibility.

Niebuhr's universe bears visible similarities to this picture. As we argue here, his theology as a whole is an attempt to deal with the existence of evil. Unlike James, Niebuhr shows no sign of grappling with determinism. Perhaps his own boundless energy, even after his stroke in 1952, was proof enough for him that humanity can change the world. Like James, though, a significant role in the work of overcoming evil is placed in the hands of humanity. It is partly through the moral striving of human agents that evil is defeated and justice established in the social realm.[184] A notable point of his early theology is how little God is actually mentioned, to the point that it might be thought that God's personal activity in history is not significant for him. His position at that time seemed to be that God established certain moral structures in the Creation to facilitate and reward moral activity, and left humanity to determine the content of history to a large extent. The role for God is broadly set in terms of establishing the general pattern of history as a process of salvation, with final success of goodness over evil guaranteed. Consequently, a viewpoint notably similar to James' meliorist universe is apparent at this stage, whereby the future is open, dependent upon human activity for the degree to which goodness and justice prevail, at least in the short and medium terms. In his later works Niebuhr modifies his position somewhat, developing the role of God more fully, particularly in terms of God's power being at work in the individual through faith. This concentrates on the work of God in terms of individual salvation, though, while the role of corporate activity of the Church as the body of Christ through the power of the Holy Spirit remains practically absent. In his early theology Niebuhr is more interested in the role of religion as a social force, presenting it in terms of being useful for underpinning morality and

---

[182] James, *The Will to Believe*, pp. 213-4.

[183] West, *American Evasion*, p. 66.

[184] West, *American Evasion*, pp. 227-8.

releasing powerful human energies.[185] This speaks powerfully of a Jamesian mindset, complementing a Social Gospel foundation perhaps, and a similar commitment to human vitality rather than divine activity as the means by which evil is overcome.

Conclusion

We have seen how certain Jamesian notions emerge in Niebuhr's theology. Primary amongst them is the unity of truth and reality whereby the truthfulness of an idea is to be understood in terms of its material results, or 'cash value' as James puts it. It was by this method that Niebuhr evaluated the various schools and ideas he encountered. Most important in this context was the ability to provide an effective response to the force of human egoism, expressed by him in terms of the will-to-power. Also of great importance was James' material anthropology, with its emphasis on personal survival, which formed the foundation for Niebuhr's version of the anxious self and his model of reason as the tool of the will-to-power in its struggle for survival and security. There are also the unstated assumptions of ontology, epistemology, freewill and the nature of history which, though hidden, formed the structure which shaped Niebuhr's approach to life. Finally, bearing in mind his view of religion as a social resource and the related role of God in history, we can understand why Niebuhr the theologian thought as a Jamesian Pragmatist.

We should consider, however, the locus of Niebuhr's Pragmatism. Unlike some of the areas of thought discussed in this chapter, Niebuhr does not seem to have reacted aggressively against it; on the contrary, his later writings seem, if anything, more Pragmatic than his earlier ones. As we have already noted, the flexibility of Pragmatism as primarily a method enabled him to relate his theology to a rapidly changing world with consistently useful results.[186] The exception to this longstanding appreciation concerned John Dewey; and perhaps this gives a clue as to its durable appeal for Niebuhr. For Pragmatism, at heart, was a method, a way of going about things, and not an ideology. It did not attempt to provide a world view which Niebuhr would have to compare with Christianity at some point and find wanting. On the contrary, he was able to combine Pragmatism with Christianity: using the one to enhance the other, he presents Christianity's insights in a way which was relevant and useful, and which at the same time proved its truthfulness. It was only when Dewey attempted to present a humanist doctrine, dismissing human evil as merely a matter of poor education, that Niebuhr reacted against a fellow Pragmatist.[187] So Pragmatism was influential for Niebuhr mainly because it

---

[185] *CRSW*, p. 44; *MMIS*, Chapter III.
[186] *KB*, p. 148.
[187] *NDM I*, pp. 117-9.

gave him a method for doing theology. Here was a philosophy without an ideology to contradict or detract from his Christian perspective. It was a means of approaching issues of thought in a practical and dynamic way and which would also, by its very nature, contribute answers which were useful for engaging with the issues of life. This, with James' influence as a moral figure passionately concerned with the practical issues of the day, makes it clear why Niebuhr felt himself to be in the Jamesian Pragmatic tradition.

Reinhold Niebuhr and Neo-orthodoxy: A Debate with Karl Barth

Introduction

In the final section of this chapter we will consider the 'Neo-orthodox' title often given to Reinhold Niebuhr[188] which despite its popularity is problematic and which Niebuhr himself disputed.[189] Neo-orthodoxy was a school which arose in Europe and North America in the first half of the twentieth century and includes within its ranks the hugely influential Continental theologians Karl Barth, Emil Brunner and Rudolf Bultmann, and in America, Reinhold Niebuhr and his brother H. Richard. To a certain extent, Niebuhr's inclusion in this prestigious list is fully justified, and in the first part of this section his basic common heritage will be sketched briefly. What is of particular interest in the context our study, however, is the way in which Niebuhr distanced himself from this group, or more accurately, from its greatest and most prolific advocate, Karl Barth. It will be argued here that the reason for Niebuhr's disquiet with Barth's theology is directly the result of Niebuhr's primary focus on the problem of evil for his theology. First and foremost it was because Niebuhr regarded Barth as a threat to the key matter of overcoming consequences of the will-to-power that he became so hostile to a theologian with whom, on the surface, he had a great deal in common.

---

[188] See, for example, Daniel Bell, *The End of Ideology*, p. 311; Grenz and Olson, pp. 99-100; McGrath, A. E., *Christian Theology: An Introduction*, (Oxford: Blackwells, 1994), p. 99.

[189] See Fox, pp. 117, 164-6, 265-6.

Niebuhr as a Neo-orthodox Theologian

While Niebuhr made clear his hostility to Barth,[190] at first sight this might be somewhat surprising, since Niebuhr and Barth had much in common and shared a broadly similar agenda. Barth, like Niebuhr, was educated in the liberal tradition but turned against liberalism when too many of its presuppositions, particularly those regarding human goodness and the Progress of humanity, were exposed as so much wishful thinking by the First World War and its aftermath.[191] Also as with Niebuhr, in answer to the crisis of liberalism Barth turned towards the classical Christian doctrines of human sinfulness and divine grace, where he discovered the 'strange new world' of God's revelation from which he eventually built his *Church Dogmatics*.[192] Again like Niebuhr, the influence of Kierkegaard came into play at this time and became extremely important; in fact Kierkegaard has been described as the foundation upon which Neo-orthodoxy was built.[193] His influence emerges in Barth's theology primarily in terms of his dialectical theology of 'No' and 'Yes'. Here, Barth decisively separates humanity from God through the 'infinite qualitative difference', which precludes any attempt by sinful humanity to bridge the gap. This in turn makes special divine revelation a necessary prerequisite for knowledge of God, precluding (for Barth) the possibility of natural revelation through the analogy of being, and re-establishing the judgment of God upon a sinful humanity, overcome only through divine grace.

In these terms, particularly the otherness of God, the sinfulness of humanity and necessity of grace for salvation, Niebuhr and Barth can be seen to share the same foundation, and from that developed their shared task of demolishing liberalism in its various forms to make way for these biblical and Reformation principles. Yet despite this common ground, Niebuhr and Barth held very different ideas regarding theology, to the point of mutual hostility. At root, this reflects, not a superficial misunderstanding, but a radically different perspective on the nature of theology itself and the essential doctrines of the nature of sin and of salvation by grace.

Niebuhr in Opposition to Barth

Niebuhr reached his so-called 'Neo-orthodoxy' through a process of disillusionment brought on by the problem of evil. The liberalism of his younger days was simply inadequate to deal with the destructive force of

---

[190] See, for example, *MMIS*, pp. 68-71; *REE*, pp. 134-5, 217-24, 286-9; *CPP*, p. 58; *NDM I*, p. 234.

[191] Grenz and Olson, pp. 66-7; Livingston, James. C., *Modern Christian Thought: From the Enlightenment to Vatican II*, (New York: Macmillan, 1971), p. 310.

[192] Livingston, p. 310; Grenz and Olson, pp. 63, 100.

[193] Grenz and Olson, p. 64.

the will-to-power. He first turned to Marxism for a more realistic understanding of human relations, before encountering the depth of understanding he required in the classical Christian doctrine of original sin.[194] Consequently, Niebuhr's Neo-orthodox orientation may be understood as incidental: rather than setting out to prove the traditional doctrines' worth, he searched for a set of concepts which would marry well with what he had seen of the will-to-power in Detroit, Nazi Germany and so on. Presumably, if another school of theology (or philosophy) had provided the insights he required, he would have identified with that instead of the Marxism that originally attracted him. Niebuhr's theology is derived from the situations and problems he encountered during the turbulent era of the first half of the twentieth century. Developed from this basis, his theology is by nature practical, intended to deal with concrete situations around him, and concerned with matters of ethics. It might be said that, for him, Neo-orthodox theology was the best tool he found for the work of dealing with the theological problem of the will-to-power.

Barth's idea of theology is somewhat different. For him, theology is defined in terms of its object: it is the study of the nature of God in order to reach a clear and undistorted picture of who God really is. His social or practical considerations arise out of this, and in that sense are incidental. Barth's theology does not start with the problems currently facing humanity, but with the revelation of God through his Word, embodied in the person of Jesus Christ. For him, the task of theology is to ensure the accurate representation of God's Word by referring the proclamation of the gospel to its origin in God himself as represented solely by Christ. Hence Barth has an unswerving commitment to the unique revelation of God through Christ, reflected in the thoroughgoing Christocentrism which defines not only the content of his theology but the method also.[195] This Christological method indicates his determination to establish the singular nature of Christian theology, insisting that it is to be carried out according to its own standards and methods in a way which will reflect the unique revelation of God through Christ. So emphatic is Barth on this matter of revelation that he refuses to consider any form of natural revelation occurring apart from Christ: a point of dispute with his colleague Brunner so strong that Barth's pamphlet *No!*, objecting to Brunner's minimal affirmation of natural theology as supporting special revelation, ruined their friendship.[196]

For Barth, therefore, the classical Christian doctrines are not incidental or 'useful', but intrinsic to the method and content of his theology. It is

---

[194] Emil Brunner relates Niebuhr's excitement at his encounter with the idea of sin during a discussion with himself and Van Dusen in 1928. Cf. *KB*, p. 28.

[195] Heron, Alasdair, I. C., *A Century of Protestant Theology*, (Cambridge: Lutterworth, 1980), p. 88; McGrath, p. 108; Grenz and Olson, pp. 70-72.

[196] Heron, pp. 78-9, 84-7; Grenz and Olson, pp. 68, 84; Livingston, p. 333.

impossible to imagine him giving priority, or even a place of significance, to anything which might query the uniqueness of Christ, regardless of its usefulness or practical consequences. Similarly, a doctrine considered by Barth to be important in terms of God's revelation would be fully affirmed and extrapolated, regardless of any apparently undesirable practical consequences. This obviously contrasts significantly with the attitude towards doctrine and ideas in general Niebuhr reveals, taking as he did his criteria of truth from the Pragmatic idea of 'meaning-effect'. For Niebuhr, the material results of employing a concept are decisive for demonstrating its validity and truth-content. With his main interest being to deal theologically with human depravity, the criteria for assessing a doctrine are heavily influenced by its ability to overcome evil and establish social justice. It begins to become clear why Niebuhr became so hostile to Barth: if Barth's theology should threaten Niebuhr's social agenda, Niebuhr would begin to wonder if that theology was an ally or an enemy.

This reflects an underlying difference in their understanding of what theology should actually do. For Niebuhr, theology is a means of providing the framework within which humanity can understand its position in relation to God and recognise both the limits and possibilities of what could be achieved. In turn this would give a full understanding of what could be expected from God, with particular reference to the task of overcoming the problem of evil. For Barth, however, theology should be concerned with unpacking God's revelation in Christ so that the work of God could be acknowledged and accepted. For both of them only the judgment of God reveals the true position of humanity in its complete dependence in God. But while for Niebuhr this means that humanity makes its contribution to the task of salvation within its God-given limits, for Barth the whole point is that humanity has *no* contribution to make, and must be *utterly* dependent upon God. So while Niebuhr regards theology as a means to the end of activating humanity within a framework of its dependence upon God, Barth regards theology as an end in itself: a radically different perspective and one which, unsurprisingly, caused considerable conflict between them.

It has been suggested that the issue of salvation lies at the heart of the difference between Barth and Niebuhr. We will now consider this matter further.

Key Issues: Evil, Sin and Salvation

Niebuhr came to his Neo-orthodox position because he needed to come to terms with the reality of the will-to-power in society. Only in the classical Christian doctrines of human sinfulness and the salvation of God could he find not only an explanation of the power at work in the desperate situations he met, but also an adequate means of overcoming that force of evil. The focus of his theology, therefore, was the will-to-power and the way it affected the world around him. It was in relation to this factor that his theology emerged and developed and took on the strongly practical relevancy which made him such an influential thinker, not only in theological circles but in the world of politics also. It also meant that, with his theology being shaped by contemporary events rather than doctrinal matters or systematic exposition, it tended to focus on those aspects of Christian thought which were practical and relevant to contemporary situations. This was his greatest strength – but also his greatest weakness, since it meant that some areas of his thought remained under-developed or in the background where a more dogmatic thinker would have been more systematic. His priority was to give the perspective 'from below' of what God does and the contribution humanity makes. This emerges in an account of what sin and salvation means *for us* primarily, rather than from God's perspective. Of course this has its advantages, not least its relevance; but the unpacking of the divine perspective, in terms of what sin and salvation means in terms of God's nature and being, is lacking.

Barth's theological agenda, on the other hand, is set by his view that theology is to be the study of God revealed by his Word. The focus of his theology therefore is the nature of God and his saving activity – matters very much concerned with the transcendent realm of God, of looking at what God does, with very little reference to the immanent realm. His concepts of evil and sinfulness reflect this primary focus and so, unlike Niebuhr, Barth presents these doctrines almost exclusively in terms of the being of God. This means that the human aspects and consequences of the matter are practically excluded. So, while for Niebuhr evil is consistently considered in terms of social deprivation and human suffering, for Barth, evil is an ontological category, a 'nothingness', dark and chaotic, created by God but passed over or rejected by God, 'that to which God, in his wisdom, has said "no" from all eternity'.[197] Evil exists at the edges of Creation, having no form of its own but gaining its definition and power by virtue of God's hostility towards it.[198] 'Nothingness' it is not simply nothing, though, but a dangerous and destructive force, threatening the order of Creation.

> Nothingness is that from which God separates Himself and in face of which He asserts Himself and exerts His positive will...Nothingness has no existence and cannot be known except as the object of God's activity as always a holy activity...That which God renounces and abandons in virtue of His decision is not merely nothing. It is nothingness, and has as such its own being, albeit malignant and perverse. A real dimension is disclosed, and existence and form are given to a reality *sui generis*, in the

---

[197] Balthasar, Hans Urs von, *The Theology of Karl Barth*, trans. by John Drury (New York, Chicago, San Francisco: Holt, Rinehart and Winston, 1971), p. 189.

[198] Berkouwer, G. C., *The Triumph of Grace in the Theology of Karl Barth*, (London: Paternoster, 1956), pp. 62-3, 244.

fact that God is wholly and utterly not the Creator in this respect. Nothingness is that which God does not will. It lives only by the fact that it is that which God does not will...Nothingness "is," therefore, in its connexion with the activity of God. It "is" because and as and so long as God is against it...It is evil.[199]

Human sinfulness consists of turning away from the grace of God's positive affirmation towards this nothingness in an attitude of insistent self-autonomy.[200] As such, it is primarily a rejection of God and a breach of a covenant relationship.[201] Sin is therefore first and foremost an offence against God, something which can only be fully known and understood in relation to God's being. In this way it corresponds to the nothingness of evil to which it turns, as something which only gains its substance and definition in terms of the rejection of God; and like the nothingness of evil, it has no positive nature of its own, but exists only as being *not* the positive Yes of God. This means that sin has no real substance, no nature of its own, no real existence in fact. It is an 'ontological impossibility'. Furthermore, this means that there is nothing in its favour which would merit choosing it over and against the grace of God. Consequently the event of sin, of rejecting God in favour of something which has nothing of its own to offer, is incomprehensible, absurd, a mystery, something that should be impossible. 'Sin is that which is absurd, man's absurd choice and decision for that which is not...Sin exists only in this absurd event.'[202] In this way, both Niebuhr and Barth draw on Kierkegaard's understanding of the ultimate mystery of sin, presenting it in moral and ontological terms; but what is obvious in Barth is the ontological rather than the practically moral.

It is manifest, then, that Barth's understanding of sin is substantially different from Niebuhr's. Where Niebuhr's focus is on the virulence of the will-to-power, Barth is concerned with the ontological impossibility of evil and sin, and its nature as nothingness, negativity, absence. This is not to say that for Barth sin does not have destructive consequences; but Niebuhr's concept of sin is much more positive in terms of its empirical reality. For Niebuhr, sin or evil has its own identity, whereas for Barth sin is purely negative, actually impossible, absurd. It has no being of its own, deriving its identity only from the holy activity of God which is opposed to it.[203]

---

[199] Barth, Karl, *Church Dogmatics, III/3: The Doctrine of Creation, Part 3*, trans. by G.W. Bromiley and R. J. Ehrlich (Edinburgh: T & T Clark, 1960), pp. 351-3.
[200] Berkouwer, pp. 62-3; Balthasar, pp. 189-90.
[201] Barth, Karl, *Church Dogmatics, IV/1: The Doctrine of Reconciliation, Part 1*, trans. by G.W. Bromiley (Edinburgh: T & T Clark, 1956), p. 140.
[202] *Church Dogmatics, IV/1*, p. 410.
[203] *Church Dogmatics, III/3*, pp. 351-53; Berkouwer, pp. 216, 225-8.

This fundamentally different approach to sin and evil is reflected in their very different models of salvation. Niebuhr's concept of salvation focuses heavily on the task of overcoming the will-to-power, as we will argue in more detail later. For Niebuhr, it is the corrupted nature of human power in which goodness and power become mutually contradictory in the human situation that makes salvation impossible for humanity. It then requires the power of God to break into the historical realm to overcome the force of the will-to-power and achieve salvation. Hence salvation for Niebuhr is primarily something practical, a matter of God dealing with the consequences of sin in the social sphere as much as the spiritual. Furthermore, within the scheme of salvation, Niebuhr gives a prominent place to the role humanity plays in God's work of overcoming evil. Having had some very positive experiences concerning those outside the Christian camp fighting for justice, Niebuhr is affirmative of the efforts of all humanity, Christian or not, in the effort to overcome evil. Consequently he has a positive role for humanity, within its sinful limits, and of natural theology as a source of inspiration, in his overall scheme of salvation by the grace of God.

In this area particularly, Barth's theology could hardly be more different; and here lies the root of the problem between Niebuhr and Barth. For Barth, even as sinfulness and evil are to be understood in terms of God's being, so salvation is to be understood entirely in terms of God's activity. Salvation concerns the return of humanity from the nothingness of that which God has rejected, and reinstatement in the positive order of the realm of being which God affirms. But more than this: since evil consists of nothingness or lack of being, and sinfulness corresponds to this state, salvation consists of the completion of being by the grace of God and his power.[204] It is by encounter with God, making manifest the absence of completion in the sinful state, that the true nature of that state as impossible and absurd comes to the fore and so is overcome. It is as the true ontological impossibility of sin is made apparent that the state of sinfulness is made impossible and the sin of humanity is dealt with once and for all by Christ. Salvation therefore consists of sinful humanity being made complete in Christ. 'Salvation is more than being. Salvation is fulfilment, the supreme, sufficient, definitive and indestructible fulfilment of being.'[205]

The crucial point of Barth's scheme is that this act of restoration, of completion, of overcoming the ontological impossibility of sin, is entirely the work of God, brought about by Christ's work on the Cross in which the effects of sin were overcome and all humanity was redeemed in one event of salvation. Thus it is through the grace and power of God, and that alone, that evil is overcome for all. Through divine grace, all evil in its full historical significance is dealt with. 'Thus it follows that the controversy

---

[204] Balthasar, p. 295.
[205] *Church Dogmatics*, *IV/1*, p. 8.

Philosophical and Theological Influences

with nothingness, its conquest, removal and abolition, is primarily and properly the cause of God Himself.'[206] With evil and sinfulness overcome in this way, it only remains for God to make the completion of being, the work of salvation, effective for humanity; and this occurs in Barth's scheme by the universal election of the human race into its fulfilment, which is Christ.[207]

This doctrine, of course, has serious consequences for the traditional scheme of salvation, most importantly the concept that the decision of the individual has some kind of bearing on his eternal destiny. Barth negates all aspects of human involvement in the work of salvation,[208] a stance at odds with most forms of Christian thought, and wholly in contradiction to Niebuhr's position that the human contribution to salvation is important, if not essential. According to Barth, humanity simply has no positive contribution to make in this area, simply accepting and acknowledging the irresistible work of grace. At most, the only active role taken by the person is the rejection of God and a maintained preference for the nothingness of evil.[209] But even this is only provisional and illusory: the acceptance or rejection of the work of God in no way affects its objective reality. Thus all humanity is included in Christ, and so is redeemed and made complete, regardless of the individual's appropriation of the work. Disbelief is ultimately impossible and inconsequential in the face of God's omnipotence.

> For Barth, unbelief is, in view of the omnipotence of the divine decision, an *impossible* matter...In Jesus Christ – the object of faith – the possibility of unbelief is "rejected, done away with, emptied." Therefore the inevitability of faith exists "objectively, really, ontologically for all men." Jesus Christ is *not* presented to us as an alternative, he is not an *offer*, for every other alternative has been wiped away. In God's decision "the root of man's unbelief, the man of sin, has been destroyed," so that unbelief has become "an objective, real, ontological impossibility; faith, however, has became (*sic*) an objective, real, ontological inevitability for *all*, for *every* man."[210]

---

[206] *Church Dogmatics*, III/3, p. 357.
[207] Barth, Karl, *Church Dogmatics, II/2, The Doctrine of God, Part 2*, trans. by G.W. Bromiley et al (Edinburgh: T & T Clark, 1957), pp. 122-7; also Berkouwer, pp. 102-12, 290; Grenz and Olson, p. 74.
[208] Livingston, pp. 336-7.
[209] Berkouwer, p. 112.
[210] Berkouwer, p. 266.

Barth's wholehearted rejection of any human contribution to God's work extends to all aspects of human life.[211] The problem of evil, so important for Niebuhr, is only incidental to sin in the first place, but for Barth even at most it consists of no more than the inconsequential remnant of evil remaining after God has dealt with its substance in Christ.[212] Hence ultimately even the most important and demanding aspects of historical existence are insignificant in Barth's scheme of things, overcome as they are by God's grace. Activity in this world is deprived of all substantial meaning when seen in the light of God's saving work; and Barth is so absolute in his view of God's activity that there is no significant place for human self-sacrifice, wisdom or achievement.

Conclusion

Barth's theology is so fundamentally different from Niebuhr's in conception, method, focus and conclusion that it inevitably evoked Niebuhr's hostility. Most importantly, Niebuhr's views concerning the nature of sin, the meaning of grace and the work of salvation were simply emptied of their meaning by Barth, who reduced the struggle against the will-to-power to a pointless activity. Barth's absolutism renders all aspects of the human realm insignificant, destroying important, if contingent, temporal distinctions between the relatively good and the relatively evil. It is these distinctions which Niebuhr regarded as essential for making human self-sacrifice meaningful: something vitally important if the fight against the will-to-power was to be successful. Barth's theology refuses to allow this entire battle any eternal significance, and so negates what Niebuhr's theology is trying to achieve. As far as Niebuhr is concerned, Barth is simply too absolute in his judgment; and it is these absolutes which threaten to overwhelm the historical realm and render it meaningless.

> The difference between a little more and a little less justice in a social system, and between a little more and a little less selfishness in the individual, may represent differences between sickness and health, between misery and happiness in particular situations. Theologies, such as that of Barth, which threaten to destroy all relative moral judgments by their exclusive emphasis upon the ultimate religious fact of the sinfulness of all men, are rightly suspected of imperilling relative moral achievements of history.[213]

Affirming the classical Christian doctrines of the transcendent otherness of God, original sin and salvation by grace through faith, both Niebuhr and

---

[211] Heron, pp. 95-6.
[212] Berkouwer, p. 253.
[213] *NDM I*, p. 234.

Philosophical and Theological Influences 71

Barth can correctly be described as 'Neo-orthodox'. Yet the contents of these doctrines, reflecting their respective understandings of the nature and function of theology, are radically different. Hence, despite such common ground, including the same agenda in terms of their hostility to liberal ideas of God and humanity, it is now clear why in time they came to view each other with suspicion, if not downright hostility. The foundation for this opposition is derived from Niebuhr's fundamental task, which was to provide a substantial theological answer to the problem of evil arising from the reality of the will-to-power. So while we have made clear the mood, attitude and themes that Niebuhr shares with Neo-orthodox theology, his opposition to its 'heavenly rather than earthly' character has been more obvious. Consequently, while the use of the label to describe Niebuhr's theology is understandable, it is extremely doubtful whether, strictly peaking, that description is appropriate.

CHAPTER 3
The Various Doctrinal Motifs in Niebuhr's Theology

Cosmology

Introduction

Having discussed Niebuhr's relationship with certain streams of thought, and the way they influenced his work, we will now consider aspects of his actual theology. Here we will be seeking to interpret his thought systematically, in order to establish the hypothesis that Niebuhr's intent is to provide a theological response to the existence of human evil. The first doctrinal issue to be considered will be his cosmology.

Niebuhr's cosmology sets the scene for much of his theology. In this section, we will set out his position on the nature of reality, using three sets of dualisms which can be identified in his thought. These are, first, an ontological distinction between God the Creator and his Creation; second, a differentiation between transcendence and immanence; and third, a distinction of different kinds of power, in particular contrasting the divine power of God with human power. In turn, these three schemata will provide the background for his anthropology, his doctrines of sin, salvation and Christology, his epistemology and Christian Realism.

Two realms of Being: Creator and Creation[1]

The foundation of Niebuhr's theology is the nature of God.[2] It is the revelation of God as Creator which goes forward into a two-fold emphasis on the nature of reality, with the transcendent being of God above and apart from the Creation on the one hand, and Creation itself on the other. Bridging these two realms of being is God's personal revelation and

---

[1] See No. 1 on the cosmological diagram, included in Appendix 1.
[2] As Lovin notes, pp. 63-5.

activity in Creation, giving rise to an intimate involvement in the cosmos.[3] Yet, in keeping with his determination to move beyond the liberalism of his early years, Niebuhr asserts an absolute gulf of being between God and his Creation.[4] Following Kierkegaard,[5] Niebuhr decisively separates the divine, eternal and infinite nature of God from the created, finite, temporal realm of Creation; and this ontological status of 'created' applies, not least, to humanity itself and includes its self-conscious freedom.

By beginning with this assertion of the otherness of God, Niebuhr presents his credentials as an opponent to the liberal elevation of the best in humanity to a state of continuity of God. As Cornelison states,

> In his usual dialectical style, Niebuhr contended that Christian revelation equally emphasizes the transcendence of God over creation, and also God's intimate relationship to it…in Niebuhr's thought, because most of his thought in his Christian Realism period was directed toward the danger of liberalism and idealism, the preponderance of his writing emphasized the distinction between God and world. Against Liberal Theology and the idealist temptation to find God in the world, Niebuhr placed the 'vertical' transcendence of God.[6]

Niebuhr, then, is determined to make clear this understanding of the ultimate nature of Creation, particularly in terms of its separateness from God – a gulf which is unbridgeable, at least from humanity's side. The ontological qualities of Creation will now be considered.

CREATION AS THE WORK OF GOD

For Niebuhr, the Creation is the cosmos in its entirety.[7] Importantly, this includes not only material reality but certain kinds of transcendence, human self-consciousness being taken as a form of self-transcendence. As the cosmological diagram illustrates (Appendix 1), key qualities of the cosmos include its ontological status as created by God, together with its intrinsic finitude, temporality and causal sequence. As God's Creation, the cosmos is the result of an act of God's will; furthermore, Creation is maintained and sustained by the ongoing work of God. Therefore, all reality that we know of is the result of God's creative will and power, and so these are the source and ground of all being. Ultimately it is God who defines reality.

---

[3] *NDM I*, p. 136.
[4] *NDM I*, pp. 143, 181.
[5] Kroner in *KB*, p. 184.
[6] Cornelison, Robert T., *The Christian Realism of Reinhold Niebuhr and the Political Realism of Jurgen Moltmann in Dialogue: The Realism of Hope*, (San Francisco: Mellen Research University Press, 1992), p. 40.
[7] Note the Creation line of the cosmological chart in comparison with the Transcendence/Immanence line.

Niebuhr identifies this creative will, which is the ground of cosmic being and the pattern of Creation, with the Logos. It is the Logos which is the means by which God created and continues to sustain reality, and the means by which nature comes to reveal the being of God. In *NDM I* he states,

> The God of the Christian faith is the creator of the world. His wisdom is the principle of form, the *logos*. But creation is not merely the subjection of a primitive chaos to the order of *logos*. God is the source of vitality as well as of order. Order and vitality are a unity in him. Even the *logos*, identified with the second person of the Trinity in Christian faith, is more than *logos*. The Christ is the redeemer who reveals God in His redemptive vitality, above and beyond the revelation of the created order. "The world was made by Him" indeed. He is the pattern, the *logos* of creation. But He is also the revelation of the redemptive will which restores a fallen world to the pattern of its creation. (p. 29)[8]

> The Biblical doctrine of creation derives both the formless stuff and the forming principle from a more ultimate divine source, which it defines as both *logos* and as creative will, as both the principle of form and the principle of vitality. The supra-rational character of this doctrine is proved by the fact that, when pressed logically, it leads to the assertion that God creates *ex nihilio*, the idea at which all logical concepts of derivation must end – and begin. (pp. 144-45)

In the Creation then we have an analogy of being. Although the Creation is not God, through Creation and its definition in terms of the Logos we have our first glimpse of the being of God. Niebuhr therefore holds some form of natural theology, asserting against Barth but with Brunner that some revelation and understanding of God is possible by fallen humanity in an unredeemed state.[9] This has an important bearing on his recognition of the possibility of valid secular insights and therefore his openness to non-theological ideas.

---

[8] This bears strong similarity to Bonhoeffer's idea of the 'ontological Logos' whereby it is God who defines reality, and the pattern of his Creation is revealed by Christ: 'In Jesus Christ the reality of God entered into the reality of this world. The place where the answer is given, both to the question concerning the reality of God and to the question concerning the reality of the world, is designated solely and alone by the name Jesus Christ. God and the world are comprised in this name. In Him all things consist.' Bonhoeffer, D., *Ethics*, ed. by E. Bethge (London: SCM, 1955), p.167; also pp. 51-2, 161-8.

[9] Kroner in *KB*, pp. 184-5.

CONSIDERATIONS

Niebuhr's understanding of the Creator and his Creation is particularly significant in relation to the focus of our study on his theology as an attempt to deal with the problem of evil.

First, his ultimate ontology concerning the separateness of God from his Creation has important consequences for his model of divine revelation and the question of God's relationship and involvement with the world. Whilst determined to maintain the separation of being, Niebuhr is equally determined to assert God's 'intimate relation to the world'.[10] To make this possible, Niebuhr presents God's revelation and activity in the world in terms of power relations. Employing an epistemology strongly reminiscent of Berdyaev,[11] he presents effective revelation in terms of non-rational conduits of power whereby, through divine encounter, myth or symbol, Creation (and humanity) are exposed to the presence of God. God also relates to his Creation directly through divine power, whereby his providence guides, controls and changes historical existence to conform to his purposes. Finally, as already mentioned, it is by the power of God that the being of the cosmos is actually sustained. Consequently, for Niebuhr, Creation remains entirely dependent on God, and God is intimately involved with the cosmos, but confusion of being is avoided. By these means Niebuhr attempts to steer between the deism of an overly detached God and the pantheism of an overly intimate one. Furthermore, by affirming the ongoing dependence of Creation upon God for existence, his doctrine of Creation sets the scene for his version of eschatology, whereby Creation remains dependent upon God for sustenance, and also for completion and redemption.[12] However, the role of completion is presented not so much in terms of the end of time; the main role Niebuhr allows eschatology, particularly the Kingdom of God, is moment to moment within history.[13]

Second, the incorporation of the concept of Logos into his actual definition of reality results in his perception of reality as an intrinsically moral, even holy, structure. With the Logos as the power and presence of God through all Creation, the whole of that Creation, though separate from God, has the holiness of God himself as part of its fabric. This means that Creation itself shares and actively participates in the moral agenda of God, even to the level of his holiness. As a result, just as God in his holiness is implacably hostile to human sin, so is the cosmos. This means that our environment, the natural world, being intrinsically hostile to sin, is hostile

---

[10] *NDM I*, pp. 136, 143.

[11] Berdyaev, N., *Freedom and the Spirit*, trans. from the Russian by O. F. Clarke (London: Bles, 1935), particularly Chapter 2.

[12] *NDM II*, Chapter X.

[13] This is discussed further in Epistemology Part 2, 'Three roles for epistemology', and 'Myth, symbol and paradox', below.

towards us sinful creatures.[14] This has important implications for the problem of evil; for this explains why living in this world is so harsh and conflict-ridden for humanity. It is Creation itself, infused with the holiness and power of God, which reacts aggressively, one might even say wrathfully, to our unholy presence in its midst.

The second major point in relation to the intrinsically moral nature of reality concerns the source of evil itself. If Creation is intrinsically good, indeed holy, then the source of evil cannot be placed in material reality and must lie elsewhere. Thus Niebuhr is explicit in stating that the Creation itself is not evil, but on the contrary is intrinsically good.[15]

> It is important to recognise how basic the Christian doctrine of the goodness of creation is for a conception of man in which human finiteness is emphasized but not deprecated. In the Biblical view the contrast between the created world and the Creator, between its dependent and insufficient existence and His freedom and self-sufficiency, is absolute. But this contrast never means that the created world is evil by reason of the particularization and individualization of its various types of existence. It is never a corruption of an original divine unity and eternity, as in neo-Platonism; nor is it evil because of the desire and pain which characterize all insufficient and dependent life, as in Buddhism.[16]

Niebuhr's point is that, contra Gnostic ideas regarding the corruptness of matter, historical existence is not evil by reason of its material finitude, contingency, historicity and dependence upon God.[17] Rather, the source of evil is to be found elsewhere, in a sinful human race. It is human sin which has damaged and corrupted an essentially good cosmos, not vice versa; and this means that the Christian attitude towards Creation is essentially positive. The material world is to be respected and cared for, not shunned nor viewed with disgust, nor ruthlessly exploited. Furthermore, this means that the means of overcoming evil is not a matter of escaping, overcoming or even destroying the material world. The destiny of Creation is to be seen in terms of renewal and its ultimate fulfilment by the power of God, not its annihilation.[18] This in turn has consequences for pinpointing the true source of evil, identified by Niebuhr as lying in human nature, and the means by which it arose. Human evil does not arise from its created state of finitude and temporality. On the contrary, humanity was created as something good, along with the rest of the cosmos; it is sinfulness arising from the anxious self-consciousness which is the source of the problem of evil. Sin

---

[14] *NDM I*, pp. 151-3.
[15] *NDM I*, pp. 143-4, 179-81; *BT*, p. 188.
[16] *NDM I*, p. 181.
[17] *NDM I*, p. 158.
[18] *BT*, p. 302.

is not an inevitable aspect of createdness: there is no 'Fall into particularity' to be blamed on the Creator-God. Instead, the source of evil lies in human self-consciousness and arises by choice, and therefore is humanity's responsibility.

Third, and finally, Niebuhr's ontology of Creation has important consequences for his approach to truth and praxis. Since the whole Creation shares the same basic ontological status of being-created, ultimately it forms a single coherent unity. The whole of the historical realm, including some kinds of transcendence, and also human ideas and self-consciousness, has no final separateness from the material world, and so there is no real division between ideas and the world in which we live. True to his Pragmatic inheritance, therefore, Niebuhr holds a coherentist-correspondence theory of epistemology, expecting reality, truth and understanding to integrate naturally. Following from this, it is reasonable for him to expect the physical world to correspond to (true) knowledge, and for genuine concepts to cohere well together. This means that there can be no final conflict between science and religion, truth and fact, nature and scripture. Where truth occurs, there also is harmony of knowledge and being. Of course there is in fact conflict between ideas; but more accurately these should be called ideologies, reflecting the conditioned and sinful nature of all human knowledge. So, for Niebuhr, it is not some supposed impossibility of human consciousness to grasp reality which causes conflict between ideas; he simply assumes that the norm is the conformity of human understanding with reality. On that understanding it is the distortion of sin which generates conflict, as simple truth becomes the vehicle for the ego.

Placing the source of the perennial conflict between ideas in human sinfulness in this way makes use of a certain understanding of human knowledge. Niebuhr assumes that all human knowledge, religious and otherwise, is sinful and therefore prone to distortion. Consequently, contra Barth, he is prepared to put secular understanding on a par with religious insight, making no ultimate distinction between theology and the other disciplines. This emerges in his affirmation of natural theology, and his openness to secular sources of knowledge as a source of insight. However, this brought him into conflict with Barth and others because he assumed human beings had some ability to discern truth unaided by divine grace or revelation – one reason why the label of Neo-orthodox is inappropriate for him. Perhaps this is an inconsistency, inasmuch as he asserts the corruption of human knowledge but seems to affirm the validity of the same without much qualification. Yet surely it is the case that all manner of people, including the 'unsaved', can discern truth to a certain extent, while religious knowledge can be misused; and Niebuhr is, after all, only expressing a qualified acceptance of human knowledge. So Niebuhr's position seems to be that human knowledge of all kinds, though corrupted by sin and so somewhat untrustworthy, is useful and provides valid insights. This seems an entirely reasonable position for a Christian theologian to hold.

Two Orders of Reality: Immanence and Transcendence

We come now to the second form of dualism which Niebuhr employs. This consists of two realms, the immanent and the transcendent. To some extent these are also ontological distinctions, in so far as they form two different orders of reality. However, as the cosmological diagram illustrates, substantially both immanence and some forms of transcendence belong to the ontological category of created being. There is some confusion in this matter in respect of certain kinds of transcendence. Is the quality of divine justice, upon which the Kingdom of God is based, and which will one day be realised in history at the Eschaton, an aspect of the created realm, or of the Creator? Generally speaking, though, Niebuhr seems to regard transcendence as organically related to the cosmos.

IMMANENCE AND TRANSCENDENCE

First, it should be noted that immanence, in Niebuhr's scheme, consists of historical reality *as it is*. It emerges day-to-day as the temporarily-realised reality which concretises at the ongoing moment of the present, and merges with what has gone before to establish our present reality. The current situation, the way things are at present, then, is the immanent reality with which he is concerned. Transcendence, on the other hand, can be understood as that which *should be*. Transcendence, although in Creation, is not historical, and is never realised or made concrete. It consists of the situation's ideal, its perfect possibility, what should happen (in fact what God, apart from human free will and sinfulness, would make happen) but which in a fallen world is not realised. This transcendent ideal is what history *would* be if there were no such thing as sin. It is more than just an idea, however: substantially, the ideal in Niebuhr's thought consists of some kind of abstract force, constantly present and actively relating to the moment.[19] It is more than a set of rationally-discernible, eternal laws useful for guiding moral behaviour. Niebuhr sees this transcendence as something dynamic, effective and powerful, existing regardless of human perception or understanding, intrinsically moral and at one with God, yet essentially a part of this (immanent) realm of being rather than God's. It only exists in relation to historical reality, consisting of its ideal possibility, of God's perfect intention for any given moment. It is this which sets the standard for any given situation, providing a sense of what could be. This ideal can be contrasted with the actual situation to reveal its ideal possibility, and so provide the means by which the world can be judged moment to moment.

---

[19] *BT*, pp. 276-7, 284-6.

It is this transcendence which confronts the actual, challenging it to aspire and strive towards a higher, more holy level of existence.

> The kingdom of truth is consequently not the kingdom of some other world. It is the picture of what this world ought to be. This kingdom is thus not of this world, in as far as the world is constantly denying the fundamental laws of human existence. Yet it is of this world. It is not some realm of eternal perfection which has nothing to do with historical existence. It constantly impinges upon man's every decision and is involved in every action.[20]

As we have already noted, Niebuhr is unclear about the status of this transcendent ideal. Sometimes he identifies it with the Logos. Where this occurs, his position seems to reflect something we find in Bonhoeffer's *Ethics* (pp. 162-3, 167), whereby morality consists of participation in the divine perfection of Christ. At other times, though, Niebuhr presents this transcendent ideal in terms of the Kingdom of God.[21] Perhaps these notions are not distinct when we consider that, for Niebuhr, the Logos is the power (and therefore the authority, or Kingdom) of God. Still, this unclear status is unsatisfactory, making an important aspect of his thought opaque and, at the very least, leaving him open to misunderstanding, and at worst, revealing an unsettling tendency towards concepts perhaps more Platonic than strictly biblical concerning the structure of reality at the foundation of his theology (see below). Whatever the status of this force, however, it is the basis of Niebuhr's moral philosophy as the source of universal moral ideas. It is also the source of power by which they can be carried out, although only to a limited degree within history: it is by the influence of these ideals that humanity becomes inspired to strive towards greater things, working hard to implement reforms which will improve our world and make it more like it should be. The influence, however, is one way. Whilst the transcendent ideal challenges, uplifts and eventually fulfils the historical reality by the power of God, historical being exerts no significant influence on the transcendent. The ideal remains out of reach, an 'impossible possibility' to quote his famous phrase from *ICE*. Despite its close and powerful connection with fallen existence, for Niebuhr, the ideal maintains a constant distinction and inviolability from the immanence with which it connects.

CONSIDERATIONS

With Niebuhr presenting this dualist cosmology of transcendence and immanence, it is necessary to consider the ontological status of these realms, particularly the posited transcendence. His position raises certain

---

[20] *BT*, p. 277.
[21] E.g. *CPP*, p. 25.

Doctrinal Motifs in Niebuhr's Theology 81

questions regarding the realms' true nature, and how they can be interrelated in this (or indeed any) way. A great deal of his theology revolves around this transcendence-immanence dualism, with an epistemology based on myth, symbol and paradox to connect them. As mentioned earlier, this draws heavily on Berdyaev's *Freedom and the Spirit*, which Niebuhr read prior to completing *BT*;[22] but unlike Berdyaev, Niebuhr's deep aversion to metaphysics results in an insufficient clarity for determining the ontological status of these realms, and how they may relate to each other. It is necessary to consider these matters, particularly the question of boundaries and the mechanisms which make communication between the realms possible.

The nature of the transcendent realm
First, then, it seems that his position has uncomfortably close ties with a Platonist-style cosmology, based on the Forms. It seems that he has in mind a similar kind of semi-transcendent realm, filled with non-historical perfections which exerts its one-sided influence upon an inferior, corrupted material realm. Joseph Haroutunian's charge of Platonism, then, can be regarded as accurate and perceptive.[23] A charge of supernaturalism may also be levelled, since he posits a powerful realm out of reach and influence of humanity, but with a strong effect on the human realm. This must raise the question of whether this really is a Christian cosmology at all or whether in fact, underneath, Niebuhr's thinking is more like a Platonic-deist position, with his final emphasis being on impersonal forces and a humanity striving to reach perfection. Certainly there seems little, if any, biblical support for what he is saying here.

Second, there is the question of the being of the transcendent realm. How does it actually exist? Niebuhr nowhere makes the ontological status of the transcendent realm specific, a factor which perhaps reflects his general aversion to metaphysics. This is problematic since it leaves important questions regarding the nature and operation of this realm unanswered. Apparently this realm consists of the ideal possibility of *this* world. If this is the case, then it should be related in being to the Creation and seen as an extension of it. At times, though, such as in the important passages we have noted, Niebuhr identifies it with the divine Logos. Therefore it should be seen, not as a part of Creation but rather as something of the being of God. There is a further way Niebuhr seems to see this ideal possibility: as the intended will of God for history. Here its status is less ontologically blurred than the Logos position, since it is then clearly something in the mind of God. At the same time, it exists *in respect to, or only in reference to*, the Creation. In this scenario the source of its being is in the mind of God, and therefore the divine realm, but it arises in relation

---

[22] Fox, p. 179.
[23] Fox, p. 183.

to the cosmos, consisting of what God would have it be. This position also has the advantage of connecting the ideal with God's omnipotence to give it the powerful and uplifting character Niebuhr attributes to it. In turn, however, this raises other questions. First, there is the matter of the possibility [or rather impossibility] of living up to this ideal, and the consequences this has for the culpability of humanity for its sinfulness. If this possibility 'hovering over every situation' is the will of God; and if the definition of sin includes failing to obey or live up to God's holy commands; and if humanity's existence and history constantly falls short of the ideal that God has in mind for the moment; then effectively, human history is constantly falling short of that ideal, and is therefore in a constant state of sin. This, in fact, may well be sound Christian doctrine, in terms of humanity constantly failing to live up to the demands of God's holiness, and also fits well with Niebuhr's understanding of the Fall, in which a shortfall from the ideal occurs moment to moment.[24] But there is the question of how this situation arose in the first place. There is a serious danger here that, unless a historical event of the Fall is included, this situation of constantly falling short is precisely as God created it from the beginning. If this is the case, then to be human is to fall short – effectively a 'Fall into particularity' since Creation and 'falling short' must come at the same moment in human history. This must be so unless a previous era of sinlessness, of living up to the ideal, occurred first; in which case Niebuhr must include a doctrine of some kind of historical event in which the first falling short happened. If some kind of historical Fall occurred, then we can consider the state of constantly falling short as a humanly-derived situation, arising as a consequence of a previous generation destroying the situation God originally created in which no falling short occurred. But Niebuhr stays well clear of such a doctrine, presenting the Fall in terms of an ahistorical 'myth' reflecting something of the moment. It must be then that in Niebuhr's theology the historical situation is as it has always been. This means that, essentially, the situation of constantly falling short is as God created it to be; and therefore, humanity was created in a state of sinfulness, incapable of 'not-falling-short' since that is how the human situation is and always has been. Despite his best efforts, there is this 'Fall into particularity' underlying his theology, since human history always has, and always will, fall short of the 'ideal possibility' of each moment. Niebuhr's fudging of the issue by stating the origin of sin to be a mystery, or 'paradox', is unacceptable; all this does is mask the unpalatable conclusions his philosophical doctrine leads to, and provides no solution to the question of how evil could have arisen in the first place without it coming from the creating act of God himself.

---

[24] See the section on Myth in Epistemology Part 2, 'Myth, symbol and paradox' below for further elaboration.

There also arises the matter of revelation. If this ideal is the will of God, then human knowledge concerning it becomes a matter of perceiving divine revelation through (sinful) human understanding, unaided by the Holy Spirit. This is not so problematic for Niebuhr because first, he does not claim that human understanding of revelation is perfect (in fact quite the opposite); and second, he does not separate the perception of divine revelation from other forms of knowing. Consequently it is at least consistent for him to posit the general human understanding of, for example, the ideal of justice, comprehended through the conscience, by Christian and non-Christian alike.

Despite its problems, not least of which are those due to Niebuhr's own inconsistency, viewing the ideal possibility as the will of God seems to work reasonably well. Certainly the possibility exists that God has some intention for the world, which, being perfect while we remain sinful, implies a shortfall of the ideal. Furthermore, the concept of the ideal being God's will *for that situation* corresponds well to this position that the ideal 'hovers over every situation as its ideal possibility'. This implies a constantly changing, powerful moral force intentionally-defined: a suitable description of the will of God. If Niebuhr does have the will of God in mind, this might solve some of the key questions regarding the transcendent realm. Where does it exist? In the mind and will of God. How did it arise? Through the holy will and intention of God drawing his Creation towards its salvation. What does it consist of? The holiness of God, enforced by his will and providence and conditioned by his love, would form the substance of its being. This model therefore provides an attractive solution to the question of ontological status for the transcendent realm.

Yet this is still not satisfactory. Niebuhr does not explicate such a position; in fact he seems rather to regard the transcendent realm as something along the lines of natural law,[25] as an in-built moral order which forms a part of the structure of the natural world. He is very critical of the Catholic concept of natural law; [26] but mainly because first, he sees the Catholic position as failing to grasp the unpredictable freedom of human consciousness,[27] which leads it to make overly simplistic statements on moral issues based on a static concept of humanity and history; and second, because of the Church's tendency to affirm the given political order, whereby it confuses the political system with an eternal, divinely

---

[25] Lovin, pp. 107-13; Harland, George, *The Thought of Reinhold Niebuhr*, (New York: OUP, 1960), pp. 29-32.

[26] As Paul Ramsey notes in *KB*, pp. 80-92. However, Ramsey is careful to point out that Niebuhr has an ambiguous attitude to the Catholic doctrine of Natural Law, sometimes being very critical but at others giving 'strong commendations' in its favour (p. 80).

[27] Harland, pp. 31-2.

sanctioned moral order.[28] He saw this in his own era with the Catholic defence of Franco's Fascist state in Spain. However, the actual concept of reality itself having a natural moral structure of some kind is compatible with his own thought, prompting Lovin to apply the label 'ethical naturalism' to Niebuhr's type of moral Realism.[29] So while the model of the divine will might be simpler for Niebuhr's ideal realm, and works better with his concept of Logos, in fact this would be too straightforward to correspond to the position Niebuhr holds.

It seems, then, that Niebuhr holds two ideas regarding transcendence, which he does not take sufficient trouble to define and differentiate thoroughly. On the one hand lies the idea of the divine will of God impacting upon history, challenging, judging and redeeming the sinful world of humanity through divine encounter. This might be broadly identified with the concept of Logos, although with reservations.[30] At the same time, he posits a natural transcendence, part of the natural order, which likewise consists of what the world should be and so challenges, judges and sets the standard for history. The crucial difference, perhaps, is that the natural transcendence does not necessarily bring with it the power required to carry out its moral requirements, depending instead on human vitality to establish such things as justice. Thus with the Logos, the saving grace of God is linked to the will and power of God, while the 'natural law' is more concerned with judgment and inspiring human power. Again, though, Niebuhr is not explicit on this distinction, and it should be made with caution. It is also the case that, even if this distinction between divine will and 'natural law' is valid, Niebuhr's weakness in the realm of metaphysics gives rise to confusion and imprecision when considering this area and which type of transcendence he has in mind, and this is a serious shortcoming in his theology. This reflects, perhaps, his ambiguous relationship with liberalism: determined to break away from it (so establishing the infinite qualitative distinction between Creator and created) yet still deeply influenced by some of its basic concepts, and allowing such ideas as natural transcendence to slip through.

The relation between transcendence and immanence

Niebuhr's use of dualist cosmology in this way presents other problems, particularly concerning the relation between the realms of transcendence and immanence. In the absence of an explicit ontology, the boundaries between the two types of existence, and therefore the mechanism of their inter-relatedness, are unclear. If the realms really are separate orders of existence, how can the transcendent judge and redeem immanence in the

---

[28] *NDM I*, p. 234; Bennett in *KB*, p. 56; Harland, p. 32.

[29] Lovin, pp. 105-7.

[30] Particularly that the Logos is the ground of Creation's being, and therefore must be more substantial than God's will for history alone.

way Niebuhr describes? Niebuhr makes use of the concepts of myth, symbol and paradox to bridge the gap, yet gives no discussion of how, for example, a symbol may be potent in bringing judgment and power to change. There is also the matter of the influence being one-sided. If only the transcendent realm has influence, the situation again lapses into a kind of deist Platonism, where God/the ideal realm remains detached, immutable and unaffected by those of us residing in the Creation. Niebuhr reacted aggressively to the charge of Platonism but it is in fact a genuine concern. Also, one of Niebuhr's goals is to give meaning and significance to human activity within history, albeit to a limited extent. With this cosmology, though, Niebuhr ends up placing the locus of history, in terms of what *really* counts, in the transcendent realm. It is the transcendent realm which judges, influences and forms the ideal to which the inferior Creation should aspire. The result is that he deprives historical events of their value and significance when they are juxtaposed with the eternal.

A further matter concerning the distinction between the transcendent and immanent should be mentioned here. In Niebuhr's theology, God is certainly active in history and therefore intimately involved in Creation. The same is true of the transcendent ideal. The question is, therefore, how can decisive lines be drawn between the being of the transcendent (be it God or 'natural law') and the being of the immanent? The relationship seems to be so very intimate that a clear line cannot be drawn, since the ideal consists of the ideal possibility of *that situation*. How can the possibility of a situation, particularly a sinful situation, exist without that ideal being so intimately related with its sinful counterpart that it becomes contaminated? Furthermore, if the holiness of God is intrinsic to the divine transcendence, yet so closely related to sinful reality, is there not a problem with God's involvement with sinful reality to such a close level, particularly if the biblical concept of wrath is invoked? Once again, Platonism rears its head, with different forms of transcendence forming a hierarchy of being to keep the purity of the divine separate from the decay of the Creation.

Part of the answer to this question of relation can be given in terms of Niebuhr's epistemology of myth and symbol, whereby it is possible to construct an understanding of these types of communication which includes a one-way effect and in-built defence against sin. The Atonement may also have some bearing on the matter. An important part of this picture, however, concerns the third cosmological dualism Niebuhr employs, to which we will now turn.

Two realms of Power: the Kingdom of God and Kingdom of the world

This third dualism is the area of cosmology in which morality emerges most clearly, since for Niebuhr only two forms of power exist, divine power and human power.[31] It is an underlying concept in Niebuhr's understanding of historical existence that, for him as with others in the history of Pragmatism, reality is defined by power. This means that, for something to exist at all, it must have the power to sustain itself in the natural world, able to resist factors in its environment which are able to destroy it and so deprive it of its being. This broad concept applies equally to all areas of life, as much in the realm of society as the natural realm in which humanity lives. Thus it is necessary to have the power to exist to continue existing; and in this sense power is a cosmological category, a matter of being.

Niebuhr identifies two forms of power at work in the cosmos.[32] The first is divine power, the power of God. It is by the power of God that all Creation comes into being and is sustained. Ultimately, then, it might be thought that all power is divine power. However in fact, for Niebuhr, while all power must come from God, human power is distinct: it is corrupted by human sinfulness. The identity of divine power is this: it is intrinsically holy, and so contains no contradiction between power and goodness.[33] In divine activity, there is no possibility of corrupt, self-seeking or immoral behaviour. It is not destructive of anything good, and is characterised by harmony.[34] This type of power is present, not only in the Godhead, but throughout the cosmos, the only exception being the sinful human realm. Since power defines existence according to this scheme, the intrinsically moral nature of God is matched by the intrinsically moral nature of the cosmos, and God is active in the cosmos in the form of his own holy power, which is the power of the Logos. Thus all of the natural world is in harmony with the will of God, under his sovereign authority without conflict or resistance against his purposes. In the realm of the Kingdom of God, it is divine power which defines and sustains existence.

The human realm is distinct from this model of power. In the human realm, while it is still power which defines reality, human power has become corrupted by the anxious self-consciousness and so has a different identity. Here power has lost its ethical nature. Consequently, human power does not sustain goodness but actually contradicts it. In Niebuhr's theology, human power (in the form of the will-to-power) is intrinsically

---

[31] This area of his theology bears a certain resemblance to Luther's doctrine of Two Kingdoms. Luther presents the picture of two realms which exist side by side, one being the Kingdom of God, made up of true believers, the other being the Kingdom of the world, made up of non-believers. The former conform to exceptional levels of morality, while the latter, vicious and barely restrained, require the secular authorities to control them. Cf. 'Temporal Authority: To What Extent it Should be Obeyed, 1523', *Luther's Works*, ed. by Jaroslav Pelikane and Helmut T. Lehmann, 55 vols (Philadelphia: Muhlenberg Press, 1952-86), XLV, pp. 75-130.

[32] *BT*, Chapter 14.

[33] *NDM II*, p. 22.

[34] *BT*, pp. 180-81

hostile to moral goodness. This means that it is necessary to choose between existence and morality in human circles. To pursue moral ends such as love and self-sacrifice is to invite exploitation and ultimately annihilation by the virile forces of the hostile wills-to-power present in the human situation. Apart from existing in the state of grace, where a person depends on God's power for existence, the person must act immorally, selfishly and aggressively to survive. To do otherwise is to invite destruction, in fact crucifixion, even as Christ himself, taking the route of selflessness, was crucified.

> The kingdom of God must still enter the world by way of the crucifixion. Goodness, armed with power, is corrupted; and pure love without power is destroyed...pure goodness, without power, cannot maintain itself in the world. Its ends on the cross. [35]

Human power, therefore, is intrinsically sinful, and since for Niebuhr power defines reality, it may be stated that human existence itself, according to Niebuhr's theology, is intrinsically sinful.

This intrinsic sinfulness has far-reaching consequences for the human realm; for it means that a sinful corrupted evil force exists in the midst of God's kingdom of power. The power of God, however, shares his divine attributes, not least of which is his holy antipathy to sin which results in destructive wrath. Concerning the sinful human realm, therefore, not only is God wholly and destructively opposed to it; his whole Creation is so too.[36] The holy power of God, active throughout Creation, responds aggressively and destructively to humanity. In a position strongly reminiscent of Romans 1: 18-32, Niebuhr establishes a Creation which is powerfully hostile to the evil of human sin, perhaps in the way that a healthy body is hostile to an invading disease.

> Mankind does not destroy the law of life by violating it. It operates in history, if in no other way than by destroying those who violate it.[37]

> The judgement of God is always partly the effect of the structure of reality upon the vitalities of history which defy that structure.[38]

An outer limit is set for this human defiance of the divine will by the fact that God's power, revealed in the structures of existence, leads to the

---

[35] *BT*, pp. 185, 177.
[36] *NDM I*, pp. 151-3.
[37] *BT*, p. 190.
[38] *NDM I*, p. 153.

ultimate self-destruction of the forms of life which make themselves into their own end by either isolation or dominion.[39]

Creation itself participates in the divine wrath of God, by being implacably hostile to sinful humanity and its corrupting influence. This includes history itself, as the dialectic movement of the power of God by which God exercises judgment on the nations and destroys them.

In this, then, we have another indication of a solution to the problem of evil. One of the major causes of suffering in this world is that the natural world is consistently, constitutionally hostile to us; not because Creation is itself evil but on the contrary because it is innately holy and reacts violently to corrupt sinful humanity. The hostile environment is hostile because of human sinfulness.[40]

CONSIDERATIONS

It is necessary to state that, while Niebuhr makes his distinction between divine and human power in a fairly simple and straightforward manner, in fact this is a complex issue and one which Niebuhr does not take sufficient trouble to clarify. In the difficult moral dilemmas of the real world, how should we draw the line between the power of God and the power of humanity, and between the purposes and activities of God and those of humanity? To take an example from the Old Testament, the violent, imperialist forces of king Nebuchadnezzar are clearly seen by the prophets as carrying out the judgment of God against Jerusalem. Is this divine power or human power at work? If divine power, then it occurs only by the actual activities of human beings, and using methods which are amongst the most horrific encountered in human history; if this is human power, then the biblical texts must be discounted, and furthermore Niebuhr's own understanding of the catastrophes of history as God's judgment is discredited. This same matter emerges in the question of human power working with divine power to overcome evil, which is a vital part of Niebuhr's response to the problem of the will-to-power in human existence. If God is working to establish justice, and human beings are consciously (or unconsciously) striving to carry out the same task with him, are they really in contradiction to his divine power? And if not, then it is very difficult to distinguish between God's activity and human activity when they are working together. A significant part of Niebuhr's agenda involves either people living through the power of God, or striving to achieve ideals such as the law of love or the Kingdom of God, which God is activity working towards through humanity. Finally, the question of living by faith, of

---

[39] *FH*, pp. 27-8.
[40] Genesis 3: 17-18 comes to mind here: 'Cursed is the ground because of you; through painful toil you will eat of it all the days of your life. It will produce thorns and thistles for you, and you will eat the plants of the field.'

Christ's power working in the individual which is discussed later in the section on Salvation, becomes problematic when Niebuhr's strong distinction between human and divine power is maintained.

A second matter concerns the difficulty of making a clear distinction between being and power, especially if the Nietzschean and Pragmatist views that will and power define existence are taken on board. It is not easy to distinguish God's power from his being, especially in areas of the divine nature such as omnipotence in which the power of God is expressive of an aspect of the divine being. Even if it is possible to draw a distinction between God's will, holy, loving, and intimately involved in Creation, and God's being, it would be a difficult distinction to make and Niebuhr makes no attempt at it. Again, this reflects this weakness in the areas of metaphysics and logic. Without a more detailed exposition of his understanding of human and divine power, and the distinction between them, Niebuhr again opens himself to difficult theological situations, and problems with consistency.

Having outlined Niebuhr's cosmology, and discussed some of its implications, we will now turn to one of the most important areas of his thought, his anthropology, and consider with it a matter which is, for Niebuhr, very closely related: the sinfulness of humanity.

Anthropology and sin

Introduction

We have already seen how Niebuhr's theology is influenced by various schools of thought; furthermore that his theology is set within a cosmological framework based on three types of dualism, Creator and created, transcendence and immanence, divine power and human power. One of his most important contributions to modern theology was his anthropology. This was radically shaped by his overriding quest to form a modern and realistic response to the existence of evil.

Niebuhr came to the conclusion that the suffering and evil of his time, which he observed arising from human action, could not be explained by the anthropology then holding currency in theological circles. The idea of intrinsic human goodness, prevalent in the dominant liberalism, could not account for the human behaviour he had witnessed. At the same time he had been impressed by instances of outstanding selflessness amongst his fellow men. This meant that in his opinion a doctrine of absolute depravity could not be sustained.[41] Niebuhr wanted to formulate a new concept of human nature which could recognise the reality of human evil, but would not result in an excessively pessimistic dismissal of human endeavour. Finding both liberalism and Barth's Neo-orthodoxy lacking, he established his own 'Biblical'[42] anthropology which would do justice to both the limitations of human nature, but also its possibilities. His first task, in the face of liberal 'optimism' regarding human goodness, was to firmly establish the existence of human evil as a real force integral to all human endeavour. Following this he could then establish realistic possibilities of what humanity might still be capable of, in terms of goodness and the role we play in achieving some forms of salvation, most importantly overcoming the effects of evil to achieve a level of justice and peace in society.

Humanity 'Created in the Image of God'

Niebuhr's main task therefore is to deal effectively with the existence of human evil. To do this he must pinpoint its source, explain how it might emerge, and accurately describe its nature. It might then be possible to provide a suitable response to its powerful effects.[43] Niebuhr begins this task with the first of the three dualisms we considered in the earlier section, Creator and Creation. Separating all Creation from its God, Niebuhr lays the foundation for his anthropology, establishing humanity in its entirety within the context of the temporal, natural, finite reality of the cosmos;[44] a cosmos, furthermore, which is intrinsically good. This not only dismisses the rationalist and, to a large extent, liberal tendencies to exalt certain aspects of humanity such as the faculty of reason, beyond their true status; it also bestows sanctity on the material aspects of human existence. This creates a level basic status of being whereby all aspects of created humanity are seen as valuable, being the work of God, but none immortal or even divine. Hence the source of evil cannot be in created finitude, particularity

---

[41] Niebuhr has a somewhat ambiguous attitude towards 'total depravity'. In *NDM I* he affirms something close to it, stating that 'it is not possible to exempt "reason" or any other human faculty from the disease of sin' (p. 293; also p. 140). Elsewhere he explicitly rejects the doctrine (*CPP*, p. 38), claiming that it is too absolute in its condemnation of humanity. Perhaps a distinction could be made between 'total depravity', in which every aspect of humanity is affected by sin but some degree of goodness remains, and 'absolute depravity', in which every aspect of goodness in humanity has been destroyed. In this case Niebuhr could be said to subscribe to total depravity, but not absolute depravity.

[42] His own phrase, *NDM I*, pp. 140-1. See also, *NDM 1*, pp. 1-18, *BT*, pp. 301-2; *MMIS*, pp. xxiv-v.

[43] *NDM I*, pp. 140-1.

[44] *NDM I*, pp. 12-6.

or materiality, but must be located elsewhere.[45] Furthermore, the nature of reason is thus established, in the tradition of Marx, James and the existentialists, not as some kind of pure and abstract force, eternal and divine, but as proceeding from material existence and therefore as organically related to natural life and its requirements. Thus Niebuhr's cosmology forms the foundation of his anthropology and also his epistemology. He sees a humanity radically conditioned by God as the Creator, with the individual as a cohesive unit and, like all Creation, entirely dependent upon God for existence.

With this unity as the foundation of his anthropology, Niebuhr identifies two aspects of human constitution corresponding to the second cosmological dualism we identified, of (natural) transcendence and immanence. On the one hand there is material human finitude, the aspects of humanity which participate in physical, natural realm.[46] On the other, the infinite, humanity's unique, self-conscious, transcendent spiritual nature.[47]

Thus humanity is a 'citizen' of two realms, participating in the natural physical world, yet transcendent to it, the finite and infinite together.[48] This is Niebuhr's idea of humanity 'made in image of God'[49] – 'made', and therefore a natural part of Creation; 'in the image of God', and therefore personal, moral, self-conscious and able to relate to God and in fact made to live in relation with him. It is this dual nature, of humanity being both nature and spirit, which forms the main concept of his anthropology, built on the foundation of our ultimate status as being created.

> To the essential nature of man belong, on the one hand, all his natural endowments and determinations, his physical and social impulses, his sexual and racial differentiations – in short his character as a creature imbedded in the natural order. On the other hand, his essential nature also includes the freedom of his spirit, his transcendence over natural process and finally his self-transcendence.[50]

The content and the means of relation between the two epicentres of human personality are crucial for Niebuhr's understanding of the limits and possibilities of humanity, and more importantly still, his presentation of the source of the problem of evil. Niebuhr's theology is shaped by his agenda to produce an answer to the problem of evil; and it is with this dual status that his answer begins to take shape. It is by being both natural and spiritual, finite yet having the unique self-conscious, transcendent freedom

---

[45] *ICE*, pp. 77-8.
[46] *NDM I*, pp. 16, 179-81.
[47] *NDM I*, p. 287.
[48] *BT*, p. 292; *CPP*, pp. 155-7.
[49] *NDM I*, pp. 14, 161.
[50] *NDM I*, pp. 286-7.

that the worst in human nature, the will-to-power, emerges. How does this happen?

For Niebuhr, the human person is, on the one hand, a natural being, subject to all the vicissitudes of historical existence: finite, dependent upon God, relatively fragile when compared with the dangerous elemental forces surrounding him. In this sense humanity is a natural creature, deeply involved in nature's processes as all other creatures are. However, these qualities of finitude and humanity's involvement in them are not in themselves evil or the source of evil.[51] Unlike rationalist prejudices against matter and particularity, for Niebuhr material finitude or particularity itself is not evil. Neither is the transcendent dimension of humanity, including the rational faculty. Contradicting the 'naturalists',[52] Niebuhr is determined to acknowledge the goodness and importance of the rational, spiritual aspects of humanity, which are the basis of humanity's uniqueness and distinction from the animal kingdom.[53] This is not to bestow divinity upon the spiritual-rational elements: Niebuhr defines human transcendence not in terms of the infinity of God but rather as awareness of the infinite and nature of God, and of various absolutes within the historical realm, such as the ideal of the law of love; also an endless ability to imagine future possibilities, to survey the world, and to form general concepts. Niebuhr's concept of human infinity therefore is concerned with standing apart from temporal limits and material finitude and rising towards that which is not-limited (the infinite) and not-temporal (the eternal),[54] and is not identifiable with any divine quality.

For Niebuhr, then, both elements, the natural and the transcendent, the finite and the 'infinite', must be present in any proper understanding of human nature.[55] To ignore or deny either one must result in a wholly deficient understanding of human nature, seeing humanity as merely a sophisticated animal or else a divine being trapped in a corrupting body. Both approaches, in Niebuhr's view, have seriously detrimental consequences; but most seriously for him, neither view, whether 'naturalist' or 'idealist/rationalist', is capable of recognising the real human state and therefore the depth of the source of human evil.[56] Moreover, each hands responsibility for evil over to God, since the source of evil is placed in some aspects of God's creation of humanity. Niebuhr is determined to protect the key Christian doctrines of God's intrinsic goodness and the

---

[51] *NDM I*, p. 161; Kroner in *KB*, p. 188.

[52] Niebuhr's label for those he perceives as attempting to deny the transcendent aspects of humanity and reduce our existence entirely to categories of the natural realm. Cf. *NDM I*, pp. 72-9.

[53] *BT*, p. 235.

[54] *NDM I*, pp. 266-7.

[55] *NDM I*, pp. 3-4.

[56] *NDM I*, pp. 132-4.

goodness of Creation; and he is equally determined to identify the real source of evil, which is in humanity itself. From these two requirements Niebuhr's approach to anthropology arises, conditioned as it is by his quest to find a sufficiently substantial source for the root of evil, which must lie, not in some contingent or separable part of human existence, but in the very heart of humanity and its existential position. It is to this that we will now turn.

Anxiety: the source of sin and the will-to-power

We have presented Niebuhr's understanding of the human person in terms of a dual nature founded upon the unified ontological status of being-created. We must now consider how this constitution gives rise to human evil, particularly in the form of the virile force, the will-to-power, which Niebuhr identified as the perpetrator of so much of the evil he observed, from Detroit to Nazi Germany.

For Niebuhr, then, it is humanity's actual nature which sets up the situation by which the possibility of sin emerges. It is neither finitude nor transcendence alone which give rise to sin, but rather the unique combination of the two in humanity. While sin arises from self-conscious freedom, it is not only that freedom, created by God, from which it emerges,[57] nor the involvement in the natural order, itself also intrinsically good. It is the being of humanity as both free and finite which forms the grounds by which sin becomes possible, and thence evil.

> Man is mortal. That is his fate. Man pretends not to be mortal. That is his sin. Man is a creature of time and place, whose perspectives and insights are invariably conditioned by his immediate circumstances. But man is not merely the prisoner of time and place. He touches the fringes of the eternal.[58]

As we discussed in the third cosmological dualism, it is power which defines reality, the power to resist and overcome opposing destructive forces and so maintain integrity of being in a hostile world. Humanity, along with the whole of nature, exists in a cosmos of elemental forces, vast (in fact effectively infinite in contrast to humanity) and dangerous.[59] In this world of infinite threats, infinite in terms of variety and potency when compared to humanity, a defence is needed to prevent annihilation: power sufficient to resist the forces opposing human existence. Ultimately, the power which death itself has to destroy the living organism is the final,

---

[57] *BT*, pp. 28, 294.
[58] *BT*, pp. 28-9.
[59] *BT*, 95-8.

absolute threat which each individual faces, and which in human terms is impossible to defeat.

This threatenedness, of course, is common to all creatures. It is in terms of its unique self-conscious freedom that humanity stands alone. This outstanding quality, as being made in the image of God, means that the human person is not only threatened as all creatures are, but is uniquely aware of the fact of that precariousness. Through self-conscious freedom, the existing person can rise above moment-to-moment existence and look beyond it to become acutely aware of the future terror it may face. Unlike other creatures, then, humanity does not simply live in the moment, concerned only with its immediate future and environment; on the contrary, transcending mere existence, the self becomes aware of the vast dangers of the cosmos, and also the sheer finiteness and limitations of the human self.

> [B]oth man's involvement in nature and his transcendence over it, must be regarded as important elements in the situation which tempts to sin. Thus man is, like the animals, involved in the necessities and contingencies of nature; but unlike the animals he sees this situation and anticipates its perils.[60]

It is this knowledge, arising from its status of participating in two realms, which makes the person anxious.

> In short, man, being both free and bound, both limited and limitless, is anxious. Anxiety is the inevitable concomitant of the paradox of freedom and finiteness in which man is involved. Anxiety is the internal precondition of sin. It is the inevitable spiritual state of man, standing in the paradoxical situation of freedom and finiteness. Anxiety is the internal description of the state of temptation. It must not be identified with sin because there is always the ideal possibility that faith would purge anxiety of the tendency toward sinful self-assertion.[61]

As was noted earlier, Niebuhr's concept of anxiety in some ways corresponds to Kierkegaard's. Unlike Kierkegaard however, Niebuhr conceives anxiety not as a response to the self's possibilities and the arising self-responsibility, but rather in more practical, even Pragmatic, terms.[62] For Niebuhr, anxiety emerges from the physical insecurity of being threatened by the forces of natural existence, and also the psychological consequences of final annihilation which renders the whole of life's achievements ultimately meaningless. It is humanity's actual situation of being

---

[60] *NDM I*, p. 194. See also p. 190, and *ICE*, pp. 86-7, 94.

[61] *NDM I*, pp. 194-5.

[62] As we saw in the section on William James, pp. 105-6.

threatened by the perils of the world, and being acutely aware of this fact, which gives rise to insecurity and anxiety.

The whole human state is insecure, therefore, and anxiety emerges from the awareness of this. As we have seen in the quotation above, however, the anxiety itself is not sinful. Niebuhr is very clear on this matter. The danger Niebuhr is seeking to avoid is thinking that, if this is the created human state, and anxiety is sinful, humanity must have been created sinful. One of the strengths of Niebuhr's position, and also one of his key goals, is that his presentation of the situation of humanity explains how sin arises for all humanity, yet this universal quality is not built into its created being. The position he is trying to establish should, he hopes, provide a way of establishing human culpability for its sin, even while the ability to avoid that sin remains out of human reach.

Such is Niebuhr's attempt to restate the doctrine of original sin. In fact, an important part of Niebuhr's agenda is his development of Kierkegaard's reinstatement of the Christian concept of sin, particularly the oft-ridiculed doctrine of original sin.[63] Niebuhr himself is unequivocal regarding the doctrine of original sin, acknowledging its apparent absurdity,[64] whilst vigorously maintaining its validity and powerful insight.[65] His justification for the doctrine is not that it is rationally coherent, but that it is indispensable for the comprehension of human nature, and with it the problem of evil.[66] This sits well with his Pragmatism: the very usefulness of the concept guarantees its acceptability, rather than any lack of conflict it has with accepted or supposedly rational ways of thinking. Indeed he lambastes the pacifist wing of the liberal tradition's rejection of it, along with its consequently insipid interpretation of the Cross, as equally absurd.

> [M]ost modern forms of Christian pacifism are heretical. Presumably inspired by the Christian gospel, they have really absorbed the Renaissance faith in the goodness of man, have rejected the Christian doctrine of original sin as an outmoded bit of pessimism, have reinterpreted the Cross so that it is made to stand for the absurd idea that perfect love is guaranteed a simple victory over the world, and have rejected all other profound elements of the Christian gospel as "Pauline" accretions which must be stripped from the "simple gospel of Jesus." This form of pacifism is not only heretical when judged by the standards of the total gospel. It is equally heretical when judged by the facts of human existence.[67]

---

[63] Kroner in *KB*, pp. 182-5.
[64] *NDM I*, pp. 256-60.
[65] *CPP*, pp. 4-7.
[66] *NDM I*, p. 264.
[67] *CPP*, pp. 5-6.

Returning to the matter of anxiety, then, it is clear that anxiety itself is not sinful; rather, it is only the grounds by which sin may occur. It will be recalled that it is the essential powerlessness of the self in the face of powerful dangerous forces which makes the self anxious. God, however, the loving father, is all-powerful. Hence, while anxiety may produce sin, it is possible to be anxious yet turn immediately to God and trust in his providence for security against the forces of nature.[68] The 'infinite' threats of the environment are in fact infinite only in terms of the variety of possible future threats, and 'infinite' in power only in relation to human fragility; indeed, the truly infinite power of God far outweighs them and is ample for salvation from its destruction. Thus, through dependence upon God, anxiety may be transformed into a state of blessedness and sin avoided. Indeed, this is Niebuhr's model of the life of Christ: truly human and therefore open to anxiety, yet totally dependent upon God, obedient to him, and so sinless.[69]

Consequently, each individual person has the possibility of remaining sinless since the emerging human personality, in becoming anxious, is able to turn to God and so escape sinless. This, however, never actually happens. Each person prefers to turn away from God and, in pride seek security through personal means. Yet the possibility is there; hence for each person, sin is an individual event of turning from God and striving to become secure through the self's resources. This means that each person becomes responsible for the state of sin in which all humanity shares, as security is sought apart from God. This is one of the most interesting aspects of Niebuhr's doctrine of sin, in which he combines the universality, indeed inevitability of sin, with personal responsibility. Whether a choice really exists where 100% failure occurs is a matter for debate; but using the concept of possibility, Niebuhr produces a plausible explanation of the concept that sin is inevitable yet not necessary, and so the individual is responsible for the situation he finds himself in.

Despite the possibility of righteousness, then, the total trust necessary for complete (sinless) dependence upon God is an unattainable ideal.[70]

> The ideal possibility is that faith in the ultimate security of God's love would overcome all immediate insecurities of nature and history...The freedom from anxiety which He [Jesus] enjoins is a possibility only if perfect trust in divine security has been achieved. Whether such freedom from anxiety and such perfect trust are actual possibilities of historic existence must be considered later.[71]

---

[68] *NDM I*, pp. 195, 268.

[69] See Chapter 3, Salvation and the Power of God, 'The example of Christ'.

[70] *NDM I*, pp. 306-8.

[71] *NDM I*, p. 195.

[T]he root and source of all undue self-assertion lies in the anxiety which all men have in regard to their existence. The ideal possibility is that perfect trust in God's providence ("for your heavenly father knoweth what things ye have need of") and perfect unconcern for the physical life ("fear not them which are able to kill the body") would create a state of serenity in which one life would not seek to take advantage of another life. But the fact is that anxiety is an inevitable concomitant of human freedom, and is the root of the inevitable sin which expresses itself in every human activity and creativity...That is the tragedy of human sin. It is the tragedy of man who is dependent upon God, but seeks to make himself independent and self-sufficing.[72]

Paradoxically it is the fact of sin which makes the ideal of total trust impossible to realise.[73] The nature of human sin is that it turns from God; in turning from God the total dependence upon God which would overcome anxiety and transform it into serenity becomes impossible. Indeed the turning from God is itself sinful, being rebellion against him. Thus sin itself consists of separating the self from God; and this in turn increases anxiety. And so it is by being sinful and turning from God that sin arises. This must have begun somewhere presumably; or in the first instance perhaps sin exists only as a possibility before becoming actualised through choice, following Kierkegaard. This concept of actualisation might provide a solution for the question of how sin first arose. Niebuhr himself prefers to resort to naming the ultimate origin of sin as a paradox:

The actual sin is the consequence of the temptation of anxiety in which all life stands. But anxiety alone is neither actual nor original sin. Sin does not flow necessarily from it. Consequently the bias toward sin from which actual sin flows is anxiety plus sin. Or, in the words of Kierkegaard, sin presupposes itself. Man could not be tempted if he had not already sinned.[74]

One may, in other words, go farther back than human history and still not escape the paradoxical conclusion that the situation of finiteness and freedom would not lead to sin if sin were not already introduced into the situation.[75]

---

[72] *CPP*, pp. 12-3.
[73] *NDM I*, pp. 266-70.
[74] *NDM I*, p. 266.
[75] *NDM I*, p. 270.

This position is frustrating, however, since it leaves the matter of the source of sin open, an unanswered question.[76] Unless a specific explanation for the source of sin is given, unacceptable alternatives are difficult to refute: either that evil created itself, a dualism along Manichaean or Zoroastrian lines whereby both God and evil, Light and Darkness are self-creating, self-sustaining forces; or that God created sin as a part of humanity, a position Niebuhr is determined to avoid. Niebuhr's failure to give a better account on this matter than he does weakens his position.

Security and the will-to-power

We have seen that for Niebuhr the origin of sin is anxiety, arising from insecurity, and sin itself begins in turning away from God. How does this progress to sinful behaviour?

For Niebuhr, the locus of the event of sin is the act of gaining power for the self, in competition with others, in order to become secure against the terrors of existence.[77] It is the attempt, repeated constantly, to overcome the fragile temporal nature of human finitude in order to deal with the physical forces of existence and the ultimate threat of death, which carries with it the destruction and consequential deprivation of meaning for everything which humanity deems significant. In pursuing power, the self attempts to reach a situation which is impregnable to the threats of historical existence. This is sinful in three ways, each of which is a form of defiance against God and his precepts.

The first of these occurs in terms of humanity rejecting the provision of God's power, which could make it secure against the forces of existence. Proud of its own abilities and determined to maintain autonomy, the sinful self rejects the promises of God to provide all that is needed for existence, and instead seeks to carve its own place in the world on its own terms. Niebuhr defines sin in terms of rebellion against God,[78] and that consists of rejecting the provision of God and his promises of salvation and seeking to set up a state of existence separately and independently from the providence of God.

This rejection of God's promise is followed by a second kind of defiance, the determined rebellion against the divinely-established limits of human existence. The creaturely qualities of temporality and finitude given by God in his wisdom and sovereign power are rejected by the self, which seeks eternal life for itself. This is where Niebuhr applies Promethean tragedy as his model of the self's defiance against a divine statute, resulting in judgment and the self's destruction. If sin is to be defined as rebellion

---

[76] A point picked up by Robert L. Calhoun, 'Review of The Nature and Destiny of Man, Vol I: Human Nature', p. 479.

[77] *BT*, pp. 94-5.

[78] *NDM I*, p. 17; *ICE*, pp. 95-7.

against God, then defying the natural limits of life set by God, as Adam and Eve are described as doing in the Fall account, can be understood as sinful.

The third form of defiance consists of breaking divine commandments, most crucially the law of love, in order to pursue the agenda of gaining power for the self.[79] Human power is finite, while the forces of existence are comparatively infinite. This means that to become secure any given individual must acquire infinite power; but with human resources being limited, each person (and group) is engaged in a competitive struggle for what power there is, with survival itself at stake. The whole of humanity, therefore, in Niebuhr's perspective, is engaged at some level in an aggressive drive for power, trying to gain the resources needed to become invulnerable to the vast forces of nature through a vast variety of means, varying from manipulation to outright thuggery.

> He seeks to protect himself against nature's contingencies; but he cannot do so without transgressing the limits which have been set for his life. Therefore all human life is involved in the sin of seeking security at the expense of other life. The perils of nature are thereby transmuted into the more grievous perils of human history.[80]

It is this constant war, whereby the stronger members of society exploit and destroy their weaker counterparts for the sake of power, which is the source of the evil Niebuhr had observed and became determined to deal with theologically. This struggle, directly opposing the divine commandment to love others as oneself, is the epitome of sin.[81] Apart from giving rise to the evil prevalent in society, the egoistic drive, in proudly rejecting God's provision for salvation, attempts to overcome the divinely set limits of creatureliness, and in doing so breaks the law of God and creates a whole catalogue of sins. Niebuhr labelled this drive for domination the 'will-to-power', making use of Nietzsche's phrase as we discussed in the section on Romanticism.

The will-to-power as the identity of sin

Niebuhr sees the problem of evil, therefore, in terms of the effects on human nature of being anxious emerging in the drive for power which is the will-to-power. If the problem of evil is to be overcome (for it is a *practical* issue) the will-to-power must be dealt with effectively. Indeed, this is precisely the task he is engaged in, and his whole theology revolves around it. Identifying the will-to-power, in more or less the form Nietzsche presented it, as the source of the problem of evil, Niebuhr's agenda

---

[79] *NDM II*, p. 58.
[80] *NDM I*, p. 194.
[81] *NDM I*, p. 17.

becomes that of how to deal with it effectively. This task shapes his epistemology, Christology and doctrine of salvation as well as the ethics of Christian Realism. It also determines his concept of sin, and his understanding of the tragic state of human existence. Before we consider some of these matters, we must take a moment is spell out his anthropology in terms of the will-to-power.

We have already noted that Niebuhr employs the dualism of the natural with the transcendent in the context of his anthropology. More specifically, this natural aspect of human existence must be seen in terms of the human self as a will-to-power, with the transcendent element consisting of an attached and integrated self-consciousness. The will-to-power is then, strictly speaking, not a natural phenomenon. Rather, the natural will-to-live of normal creatures is disrupted in the person by humanity's unique self-consciousness. The anxiety of the self transforms the will-to-live, which all creatures have, into the obsessive, aggressive will-to-power as the self seeks infinite power to overcome its vulnerability.[82] While the will-to-live may reside within the harmonies of nature, the will-to-power cannot be content, striving beyond its God-ordained, natural limits and seeking to dominate and extract power from those around it. Thus the will-to-power breaks the harmonies of nature in its divinely-established order – part of its sinful activity; and this reflects the fact that humanity is more than just a natural being, that its sinfulness emerges from its place 'at the juncture of nature and spirit'.

But while the will-to-power is sinful, and the source of evil, it is not itself entirely evil. It is a nucleus of energy, organically related to other wills-to-power, and with social impulses.[83] Thus it is possible for the will-to-power to be turned to good use. It is, essentially, a powerful force. Thus Niebuhr, within his scheme of salvation, will seek to condition the will-to-power through certain forms of epistemology in order to harness its power for the task of establishing justice. This task is aided by the second aspect of human existence, the transcendent self, which is the weaker, but more morally-inclined epicentre of the person. Through self-consciousness, the person becomes aware of other selves beyond the will-to-power, and also of transcendent realities such as the law of love and the requirements of justice.[84] Thus, for Niebuhr, there are moral resources within the individual. This is important since he is determined to recognise the possibilities for human goodness, albeit within the context of human sinfulness.

---

[82] *BT*, p. 103; *CPP*, pp. 156-7; *CLCD*, p. 21.

[83] *MMIS*, p. 25.

[84] Lovin correctly describes Niebuhr as a moral realist on this basis (pp. 12, 22), since Niebuhr's position includes ideal possibilities which exist apart from the realities of normal life in some kind of transcendent realm.

Doctrinal Motifs in Niebuhr's Theology

Of the two aspects of human nature, however, it is the will-to-power which is dominant. For Niebuhr, along with James and Marx, reason is not a pure, objective force distinct from the existing self but rather proceeds from the material being, employed by it for the task of survival.[85] This means that reason, and in fact the self-conscious faculty generally, serves the will-to-power, not vice-versa. The will-to-power uses reason, and also the ideals the self-consciousness seeks to act under, for its own hidden agenda of aggressive power seeking.[86] Thus despite on occasions appearing to act for selfless and generous motives, all human endeavour is tainted by the egoism of power acquisition, whether or not the person realises it or is prepared to acknowledge it; and this is Niebuhr's main doctrine of original sin.

Original sin as pretence

We have seen how the anxiety of the self emerges in the will-to-power. One of the two main aspects of the sin of the will-to-power, we saw, was the determination to overcome finitude and temporality in order to become secure against the forces of nature, time, and ultimately death which God ordained to maintain the limits of creaturely existence. One aspect of the will-to-power's agenda, therefore, is to transform its finite and temporal being into something absolute: eternal and infinite, secure against the ravages of history. This is the imperial ambition of the ego, which sets itself up against God and his precepts, and seeks to make the self divine.[87] In the course of doing this through the egoistic acquisition of power and in defiance against God, the sin and thence evil of the world increase. Reversing Romans 5: 12-14, Niebuhr asserts that death leads to sin, not sin to death.[88] It is the final, destructive power of death which gives rise to anxiety and the will-to-power. Thus, for Niebuhr, sin is not so much a problem created by finitude, but almost the opposite: the refusal to acknowledge the true finiteness and limits of humanity, and claiming divinity for some aspect of the self.

> The real evil in the human situation, according to the prophetic interpretation, lies in man's unwillingness to recognise and acknowledge the weakness, finiteness and dependence of his position, in his inclination to grasp after a power and security which transcend the possibilities of human existence, and in his effort to pretend a virtue and knowledge which are beyond the limits of mere creatures. The whole burden of the

---

[85] *NDM I*, pp. 36-8, 120-21.
[86] *MMIS*, 44-7, 245; see also the section in Chapter 3, Epistemology Part 1: 'Negative aspects of reason'.
[87] *CPP*, pp. 156-7, 183, 206.
[88] *NDM I*, pp. 187-9.

prophetic message is that there is only one God ("I am the first, and I am the last; and beside me there is no God" Is. XLIV, 6) and that the sin of man consists in the vanity and pride by which he imagines himself, his nations, his cultures, his civilizations to be divine. Sin is thus the unwillingness of man to acknowledge his creatureliness and dependence upon God and his effort to make his own life independent and secure.[89]

Claiming the universality of the will-to-power, Niebuhr uses it to establish his doctrine of original sin, or the sinfulness common to all humanity. Original sin begins with the will-to-power, present in each person, seeking divinity for the self through the acquisition of power. Yet as we have noted, there are certain moral elements in human nature which, though not necessarily dominant, nevertheless exert a significant influence upon the person. Amongst these qualities, primarily found in self-consciousness, is the desire to act morally,[90] and perhaps more tellingly, the need to give the appearance to others of acting morally. Since all wills-to-power are in competition, to openly act egoistically is usually self-defeating, since the self can then be quickly identified as a threat to others and then censured. However, to appear to be acting selflessly when actually acting egoistically works in the opposite manner. Others, seeing apparently selfless activity, applaud and even support it, perhaps perceiving this will-to-power to be a source of benefit to them. Thus a devious disguise of moral behaviour, when in fact egoism is occurring, is effective for the agenda of the will-to-power. This is Niebuhr's main concept of original sin, which he identifies as 'pretence' – disguising the egoistic activities of self behind high-sounding ideals, rational arguments and noble causes.[91] In pretending to act in the general interest, or for Humanity, or the long-term good, the self is able to pursue its ends without excessive interference, utilising moral justifications for its activity.[92]

But this pretence is not only towards other people; it also occurs internally. Self-deception takes place between the will-to-power and the self-consciousness.[93] It is possible, indeed it regularly happens, that the will-to-power disguises its activity not only to others but also to its own self-consciousness, which also might intervene in the agenda of power acquisition if the will-to-power's activity became too blatant. It is necessary, in the internal make-up of the person, for morality to play a recognisable role in the self's activity. The self-consciousness, though less powerful than the will-to-power, exerts sufficient influence for the will-to-power to have to conform to some extent to its requirements in even the

---

[89] *NDM I*, pp. 147-8.
[90] *MMIS*, pp. 25-32; *CPP*, pp. 157-8.
[91] *BT*, pp. 28-34.
[92] *MMIS*, pp. 40-4.
[93] *MMIS*, pp. 44-7.

most depraved of people if its agenda is not to be severely hampered. Thus the role of pretence begins at the deepest level: for the will-to-power to act according to its nature it must dress up its activities in the semblance of moral action, appearing to the self to be serving some higher purpose than its own egoism.[94]

> In analysing the limits of reason in morality it is important to begin by recognising that the force of egoistic impulse is much more powerful than any but the most astute psychological analysts and the most rigorous devotees of introspection realise. If it is defeated on a lower or more obvious level, it will express itself in more subtle forms. If it is defeated by social impulse it insinuates itself into the social impulse, so that a man's devotion to his community always means the expression of a transferred egoism as well as of altruism. Reason may check egoism in order to fit it harmoniously into a total body of social impulse. But the same force of reason is bound to justify the egoism of the individual as a legitimate element in the total body of vital capacities, which society seeks to harmonise...The egoistic impulses are so powerful and insistent that they will be quick to take advantage of any such justifications.[95]

> The rational forces, which seek to bring this energy, in which self-consciousness has focused the primal dynamic of all life in one particular point, seem weak indeed, when compared with the force arrayed against them. They are all the more inadequate for having no impartial perspective, from which to affect human action. They always remain bound to the forces they are intended to discipline. The will-to-power uses reason, as kings use courtiers and chaplains to add grace to their enterprise.[96]

In this way, masquerading plays a vital role in Niebuhr's understanding of sin, and also therefore, salvation. Part of his response to the will-to-power involves the task of unveiling its true purposes, stripping egoism of its pretence and forcing the will-to-power to knowledge of its real agenda. This occurs through a confrontation, at best with God but also with less exalted forms of transcendence.[97] Self-awareness therefore plays a key role in his doctrine of salvation, and for him is the first stage of dealing with the will-to-power. Through becoming aware of the true state of its supposed altruism, the self may take steps to counteract the worst effects of its drive for power. For Niebuhr, recognising the deceitfulness of the will-to-power

---

[94] *BT*, pp. 32-8.
[95] *MMIS*, pp. 40-1.
[96] *MMIS*, p. 44.
[97] *NDM I*, p. 140.

is absolutely necessary for salvation, and thence for the possibility of genuine moral action. Consequently, understanding the will-to-power yields the criteria by which he evaluates other schools and thinkers. This was what was behind his rejection of liberal Protestantism. Its optimistic view of humanity was wholly incapable of recognising the real nature of humanity as the will-to-power, and therefore could not explain the problem of evil which emerged in his lifetime. Likewise Marxism: his devastating critique was based on the fact that Marxists, so aware of the 'ideological taint' of their rivals, were blind to their own egoistic influences; and it was this blindness, in Niebuhr's view, which made them 'children of light',[98] essentially naive regarding their own human nature. This in turn meant that they failed to see their own agendas for power, and also the agendas of those around them, and so, rather than ushering in a new era of peace and justice, the result of their revolution was actually the oppression of the communist regime.[99]

Original sin, for Niebuhr, therefore consists of the use of reason and objective ideals by the will-to-power to mask and justify its own interests. By rationalising its choices, presenting what is actually a matter of self-interest in terms of the well-being of others, a moral veneer is laid over unacceptable activities to make them pass moral censorship both within the person and without. If the self can produce a plausible argument that the fulfilment of its own inclinations would be obedience to the law of love (the accepted norm of humanity, Niebuhr holds) then it can go ahead with its agenda without inhibition. The power of moral censorship, though weaker than the will-to-power, is sufficiently influential to make its satisfaction essential for the successful pursuit of the agenda of power acquisition.

There is a second way in which this pretence emerges. As noted earlier, a key part of the self's work to give itself security involves its attempt to deny the true limits of its temporality and finitude. One means of overcoming finitude is to acquire the identity of a being far greater than itself, and which can sustain the impression of greatness, even divinity. Through self-consciousness, the self becomes aware of the whole of its environment, the totality of its surroundings.[100] If some kind of merging occurs with that totality, then its own limits, the limits of finitude, lose their definition and thereby perhaps their power to limit the self to finitude. In this merging of identity, the finite self, by participating in the identity of the group, may regard itself as having something of the attributes of the far greater entity – class, race or nation – in which it participates. From this it is possible to gain for the self an impression of greatness and power derived from the greatness and power of the collective in such a way that it can

---

[98] *CLCD*, p. 29.
[99] *NDM I*, p. 50.
[100] *NDM I*, p. 18; *BT*, p. 29.

deny its own weakness, dependence and insignificance.[101] In turn, the corporate identity with which the self identifies has sufficient greatness, power and longevity to establish god-like pretensions and so emerge as a kind of deity, to be served and worshipped by its participants, very much as Rome became, with its own mythology and a god-emperor to be worshipped as the embodiment of the empire. So by participating in the life and identity of the god-like group, the god-like qualities of that group can be appropriated by the self in such a way that the illusion of the self as having those qualities can be supported. This is Niebuhr's doctrine of pride,[102] or better, hubris, as Tillich notes:[103] the attempt by humanity to elevate itself to the status of the gods, refusing to acknowledge the true limits of the self, in arrogant rebellion against its own finite reality.[104]

> Sin is rebellion against God...man makes pretensions of being absolute in his finiteness. He tries to translate his finite existence into a more permanent and absolute form of existence...they always mix the finite with the eternal and claim for themselves, their nation, their culture, or their class the centre of existence ...man is destined, both by the imperfection of his knowledge and by his desire to overcome his finiteness to make absolute claims for his partial and finite values. He tries, in short, to make himself God.[105]

This pretence of divinity consists of attempting to make the particular, temporal, finite creature of the self into something resembling the eternity and infinite greatness of God himself. And this attempt is the expression of the agenda of the will-to-power to give itself permanence, a state of security against elemental forces surrounding and threatening it.

Niebuhr's doctrine of original sin, therefore, revolves around pretence. The will-to-power makes use of certain aspects of self-consciousness to carry out its agenda of power seeking, first by gaining sufficient power for itself to attempt to defy the God-given limits of creaturely existence under the guise of moral behaviour; second by using the transcendent capacity of self-consciousness, which enables it to survey the world beyond itself, to blur the distinction between the finite self and greater forms of being and so set itself up as a form of god, with the appearance of divinity and indestructibility. Through these two prime methods the self seeks to deny its finitude and, through power and pretension, transcend its historical limits and secure itself against the dangers of existence. In Chapters VII and VIII of *NDM I* Niebuhr describes the means by which sin, in the form of pride,

---

[101] *NDM I*, p. 105.
[102] *NDM I*, pp. 198-220.
[103] In Landon, p. 38.
[104] *NDM I*, p. 130; *FH*, p. 121.
[105] *ICE*, p. 95.

emerges in the quest for power, and in the pretence of the self claiming a greater status for the self than mere creatureliness.[106] Here, Niebuhr draws on the idea of making the self's agenda divine, even the representation of God himself. The self's knowledge, judgments and activities are designated perfect, absolute in decree, unconditioned by finite understanding or human frailty.[107] In this case the self, in pride, overlooks its finite and egoistic nature and sees itself as the servant of God, engaged in carrying out the divine will. Merging the agenda of the will-to-power with the work of God in this way, the self regards itself as the vehicle for God's activity (or some equally exalted idea). Regarding its own crusade for 'truth', 'justice' and 'righteousness' in this way, the will-to-power has a justification for dealing ruthlessly with its opponents, who it comes to regard as being the enemies of God himself, and therefore demonic, if they stand in its way.

> Moral pride is revealed in all "self-righteous" judgments in which the other is condemned because he fails to conform to the highly arbitrary standards of the self. Since the self judges itself by its own standards it finds itself good. It judges others by its own standards and finds them evil, when their standards fail to conform to its own. This is the secret of the relationship between cruelty and self-righteousness. When the self mistakes its standards for God's standards it is naturally inclined to attribute the very essence of evil to non-conformists.[108]

Thus, through pride, the will-to-power denies the nature of its sinful, conditioned agenda and through this removes the moral constraints which would be necessary to inhibit its egoistic quest for power since, in serving God, such restraints must be irrelevant, even demonic, if they restrain the 'divine' work.

Clearly, then, Niebuhr's understanding of sin is heavily biased towards the idea of pride, and with it the concept of the will-to-power as the central factor in human nature. This means that other, perhaps more subtle forms of sin, are given a secondary status, and in some works even ignored altogether.[109] This is particularly the case with certain sins often identified with femininity, most importantly sensualism, the passive absorption into dominance perhaps more common than aggressive self assertion in women. This has attracted criticism from feminist theologians, most famously Judith

---

[106] Particularly pp. 191, 198-216.
[107] *NDM I*, pp. 194, 207, 211-16.
[108] *NDM I*, p. 212.
[109] E.g. *MMIS, CPP*.

Plaskow.[110] Also, problems prevalent in the oppressed such as apathy, fear or even despair, highlighted by Liberation theologians coming from an impoverished social sphere, are passed over.[111] Both sets of critique argue that Niebuhr's concept of sin is inadequate, being so heavily biased towards the powerful, male-dominated Protestant culture of the US that its relevance for less affluent circles is limited. Indeed some argue that his influence is actually negative, attacking self-assertion so vigorously that the necessary task of standing up to aggressors by the weak is compromised by him.[112] Those experiencing oppression, it is argued, should be encouraged to assert themselves, rather than being criticised for doing so. Henry Clark attempts to respond to these criticisms on Niebuhr's behalf, arguing that Niebuhr gives weight to other types of sin apart from domination, most importantly the sin of sensualism (pp. 164-71). Lovin also attempts to argue this, stating that although Niebuhr seems to trivialise sensuality, in fact he holds just as deep a commitment to recognising this danger, and only fails to develop it fully.[113] Clark's argument is vigorous, but his conclusion is not entirely persuasive. Niebuhr simply devotes too little of his writings to other ideas of sin apart from the will-to-power. Lovin's approach is more convincing, reflecting the presence but lack of development of alternative ideas of sin. The important point for us, however, is that this overall bias of Niebuhr's towards sin as dominance reflects the fact that his theology is an attempt to deal with the problem of evil in the form of the will-to-power. Whatever other subtle sins exist, Niebuhr's theological agenda concerns the disastrous consequences of the will-to-power which he observed in his formative years. This is what concerns him; anything else, however important for others, is basically irrelevant to him. Thus the very validity of Plaskow's (and others') critique, as well as Lovin's defence of Niebuhr's treatment of sensuality, can be pressed into serving the our argument; for if Niebuhr's agenda is to deal with the will-to-power then one would not *expect* him to be interested in other forms of sin.

Sin and the tragic human state

Having seen how Niebuhr understands the emergence of sin and its nature as will-to-power, we now consider its effects on the actual human situation. Clearly the most obvious effect of sin, for Niebuhr, was the evil he perceived in the aggressive activities of Henry Ford, Hitler and others, and

---

[110] Plaskow, Judith, *Sex, Sin and Grace: Women's Experience and the Theologies of Reinhold Niebuhr and Paul Tillich*, (Washington D.C.: University Press of America, 1980).

[111] As Rasmussen notes, pp. 19-20, 32-3.

[112] Clark, Henry, *Serenity, Courage and Wisdom: The Enduring Legacy of Reinhold Niebuhr*, (Cleveland, Ohio: Pilgrim Press, 1994), pp. 154-7.

[113] On pp. 143-47 in respect to *NDM I*, pp. 242-55.

so this was his preoccupation. However, a more subtle effect is also recognised by him, that of turning the exalted human state of being created in the image of God into a tragedy. This emerges in three ways.

First, and most important, Niebuhr employs the Promethean model of tragedy to describe the effects of the will-to-power on the human situation.[114] Here, the will-to-power's battling defiance against God-given limits of finitude consists of breaking holy decrees, which in turn brings down the judgment of God. The human situation becomes the Titanic rebellion against all boundaries of prudence, reasonableness and the vast powers of God's Creation which will inevitably bring disaster.[115] This dramatic defiance is doomed, since it consists of defiance against God himself, and thus it seals its own fate through its very struggle – a classic case of tragedy, where, like Oedipus, it is the actual attempt to defy Fate which brings about its fulfilment. This is not the tragedy of Hardy or Hamlet, where pitiful individuals struggle against overwhelming malevolent forces.[116] It is the will-to-power's attempts at self-assertion against its own finitude which brings about its downfall. By defying God, the will-to-power becomes sinful and thence tragic.

> In the Promethean myth the hero is not a man at all but a demi-god who defies Zeus for the sake of endowing mankind with all the arts. In this myth we come very close to the Christian conception of the inevitable guilt of pride which attaches to the highest human enterprise. Man becomes guilty of "hybris" and arouses the jealousy of God. But since God is conceived as only just and not loving he is something less than just. He is vindictive. The Promethean tragedy, in other words, recognises the perennial self-destruction of man by his overreaching himself.[117]

Not only does this set humanity against God in a struggle it cannot win, since God's power really is infinite; it also cuts itself off from the same infinite power which would overcome its finitude, particularly in the face of death. Furthermore, in becoming sinful, humanity finds itself attacked if anything more vigorously by the powers of the cosmos which, being holy, seeks to eradicate humanity from within it in accordance with the holy purposes of God. Thus the attempt of the will-to-power ends in tragedy as the fate it defied – being destroyed by the destructive forces of nature – is hastened to its conclusion by the very activity of the will-to-power.

---

[114] A matter already noted in the section on Romanticism, particularly 'Niebuhr's Concept of Tragedy'.
[115] *BT*, pp. 160-61.
[116] *BT* pp. 156-7.
[117] *BT* pp. 160-61.

This brings us to Niebuhr's second motif of tragedy, the cycle of the will-to-power's self-destruction within human society.[118] It is the will-to-power's agenda to become secure through power, and this is carried out by some members becoming strong enough to dominate others. This, however, results in oppression and injustice, a matter which in time prompts a revolt by the oppressed against their masters resulting in the ruling class being overthrown. In this way the oppressors are destroyed: exactly the situation they were attempting to avoid; and this defeat came about by the very means they employed to prevent it. In turn, those who were oppressed become the new masters; but they find themselves carrying out the same drive for power as their old rulers. Again, in time this provokes a second revolt from those they have come to oppress, and the new rulers are overthrown, to be replaced by their old slaves, and so on. This soon becomes a cycle of tragedy and destruction brought upon itself by the will-to-power.

The third motif of tragedy Niebuhr brings to our attention concerns the very source of human greatness, our self-conscious, self-transcendent spirit. It is this spirit which is the source of the creative vitality which lies behind our greatest achievements. But this same spirit also gives rise to humanity's evil.[119] As a creature made in the image of God, the human self can rise above finitude and, through imagination and inventiveness, create tremendous new possibilities. It is this capacity which gives rise to 'Progress', the advance of science, art and literature which is to humanity's credit. But it is this same capacity which transforms the natural will-to-live into the malevolent will-to-power, the source of evil and the means by which humanity is estranged from God, judged and destroyed by God's power. Furthermore, because of the influence of the will-to-power, this same inventiveness is channelled into evil means, creating more effective methods to wage war against others and achieve dominance. Thus, even as the beneficial effects of self-consciousness impact on history, so also do its terrible consequences. In tragedy it is often the very greatness of the person that brings about his own destruction, having exceptional powers which lead him to defy Fate, anger the gods, and bring down their judgment upon him. Likewise for humanity, it is our greatest quality, 'being made in the image of God' which is the source of our troubles. The consequence for human history is that rather than enjoying a steady progress towards Utopia, evil actually increases with human progression, creating the terrible levels of war and destruction which have occurred in the 20th-century.

Tragedy therefore plays a major role in Niebuhr's understanding of sin, reflecting his perception that the will-to-power itself is essentially a tragic force, doomed by its very nature to destruction. The fact that its agenda is self-defeating then poses an important question for Niebuhr. Clearly the

---

[118] *MMIS*, p. 11; *BT*, pp. 103-5.
[119] *BT*, pp. 161-2, 202-3; *NDM I*, 11-2; *CLCD*, p. 46.

will-to-power is power-orientated, since the problem it faces - being powerless in a dangerous world - is essentially a power issue. If power is necessary for existence, and this is how we were created, then the self's quest for power is legitimate. Yet the actual attempt by the self always ends in self-defeating sinfulness, not only because of the nature of individual wills-to-power, but also due to the whole identity of human power which has formed under its influence.[120] It seems that the whole realm of human power, then, is tragic, doomed to a tragic fate. In that case, how can anyone be saved? What route can be taken that will provide the power necessary for existence and the ultimate overcoming of death, without it slipping into the ways of the will-to-power? The problem is not only created, but also compounded by the nature of the will-to-power, which almost by definition precludes the appropriation of God's power which could, and should, provide salvation. We will consider Niebuhr's answer to this question shortly. Prior to that, we will consider some of the consequences of Niebuhr's anthropology and doctrine of sin.

Considerations

The first question which must be asked is whether Niebuhr's concept of sin marries well with accepted Christian ideas in this area, with particular attention paid to the relevant biblical texts. On consideration, it seems that while the issues of anxiety, security and dependence upon God are important biblical and doctrinal issues, they do not take the prime position Niebuhr allocates them, particularly when compared with matters such as idolatry, faithlessness towards God and the refusal to accept the gospel of Christ. As Carnell continually points out, Niebuhr is closely, perhaps too closely, wedded to Kierkegaard. In this matter, Niebuhr provides an account of human life which is useful and interesting, but lacks biblical support. In fact it might be argued that Niebuhr's theology is less concerned with the Bible's message regarding the nature of sin than with modern philosophical or psychological theories as the source of his understanding. There is too much psychology and too little reference to biblical texts in Niebuhr's account, and this must questioned.

A second question we can ask here is, Is his account true to human experience? While the will-to-power may be the response to insecurity of certain kinds of people under certain circumstances, surely this is not always the case. The response to overwhelming odds can also be despair, apathy and hopelessness, an indifferent lethargy or simple resignation to the future. The idea that the *universal* human response to threatenedness is the will-to-power does not carry weight, since there are too many examples of oppressed people continuing their existence, not to emerge as aggressive

---

[120] For further discussion on Niebuhr's view of power see below, the section on Christian Realism, 'Power and justice' and 'Considerations'.

Doctrinal Motifs in Niebuhr's Theology   111

victors but as broken and timid victims; and this on both the individual and corporate scale. It seems that something more than aggression is necessary to maintain resilience of spirit during long-drawn-out times of oppression. Furthermore, the means by which this resistance is maintained might be better expressed in terms of a hope for outside intervention – most importantly, from a biblical perspective, the salvation of God. It is often hope based on a higher power which provides an effective response to overwhelming odds, not some element of the victim's own nature such as the will-to-power. In this case the critique of the Liberation theologians may be very close to the mark, that Niebuhr's concept of sin is too much the expression of his personal experience of a minority of affluent individuals to be applied generally.

A third point, related to this, is the question of whether life really is concerned with the struggle for power. To some extent this probably holds true; but Niebuhr's reductionist approach, employed very effectively in some areas to cut directly to the main issues at stake, here lets him down, and his perception of human existence lacks breadth. Again, this may be reflective of his engagement in powerful circles; but surely human life is more than a concern for personal well-being and survival? It is dangerous to argue a single point through the whole of Niebuhr's theology and then accuse him of reductionism (although he uses this approach himself on various occasions); yet Niebuhr's preoccupation with the will-to-power and its effects does seem to present too coarse an understanding of humanity than really does it justice. While certain areas of life such as big business and politics do seem to conform to Niebuhr's model, other areas such as family life, Christian fellowship or the arts, whilst still human activities and therefore tainted with sin, are more than just exercises of the will-to-power. But perhaps this is Niebuhr's point: that underlying such civilised activities lurks the will-to-power – more subtly than its more obvious manifestations perhaps, but still present. This reflects his major contribution in this area, a doctrine of original sin which can be quickly applied to any human situation and found relevant. Indeed this may also help to deal with the second point made above: even the oppressed live according to the demands of survival, and while they may be powerless, the desire for power is ever-present. Marxism failed to see this, and this was a fault which resulted in its idolising of the proletariat, since the Marxists assumed that the absence of power was synonymous with the absence of the lust for power. Niebuhr's analysis here must surely be correct. Even so, perhaps an analysis of sin which had taken biblical texts and well-established Christian doctrines as its starting-point, rather than experience and existentialism, would have given a broader and richer understanding of the matter.

Niebuhr's main contribution in the area of analysing sin, therefore, is to have set up a modern doctrine of original sin which draws upon recent insights into psychology, epistemology and the nature of power. Such a doctrine cannot be dismissed as easily as traditional ideas concerning material particularity might be.[121] Like Kierkegaard, Niebuhr presents an essentially psychological, rather than ontological theory regarding the origins of sin. This means that he can place the source of sin not in created finitude, nor in the rational faculty, but in the centre of the human personality. This is important since it means that humanity is not created evil by God, but rather only has the possibility for evil through its anxious state. It also means that Niebuhr affirms human life, including its transcendent elements, without giving total affirmation to any individual human capabilities. This is an important achievement, as Lovin states (pp. 133-5), not least since his opposition to liberal theology involved reducing the status of human qualities from the semi-divine. This also means that he can give humanity a (limited) role in his scheme of salvation, since some level of value is still given to human activity. Most important, though, is the fact that Niebuhr, in providing a workable contemporary understanding of sin, placed a Christian anthropology, including a fully fledged doctrine of sin, back into mainstream thought, a fact reflected by the extent to which Niebuhr's analysis was taken on board by the general secular world.[122] The usefulness of Niebuhr's anthropology, and the accuracy of the analysis it provided, was for him the ultimate proof of its validity.

Two final points should be made in respect to Niebuhr's doctrine of sin as the will-to-power. One is that, by making the will-to-power the locus of his anthropology and the source of sin, Niebuhr places human sinfulness right in centre of the person. Sin is not incidental to human existence, to emerge only in isolated areas of human life. For Niebuhr, sin is the act of the whole person,[123] and so affects every area of human life and activity.[124] It is impossible to separate humanity from sinfulness; and this is important in his agenda to dismiss liberal ideas of human goodness, which he felt had failed to account for the depth of human evil and so made Western society so much more vulnerable to its effects. This also means that egoism and the conflicts it produces are to be expected and countered.[125] Rather than expecting to build Utopian societies, the modern mindset is to become more realistic, identifying its task more in terms of dealing effectively with human sin, and what can be achieved in a world conflict-ridden by nature. Thus 'Christian Realism' can take a significant long-term role in the social agenda.

The other, and last, point is that Niebuhr's understanding of human nature as the will-to-power strongly influences his whole understanding of

---

[121] Lovin, pp. 131-2.
[122] Davies, D.R., *Reinhold Niebuhr: Prophet from America*, (London, James Clark, no date), p. 43.
[123] Grenz and Olson, p. 104.
[124] *NDM I*, pp. 293-7.
[125] *ICE*, p. 71.

human power itself. This emerges in his cosmological dualism between human power and divine power, where he cites the identity of human power in terms of its contradiction with goodness. Seeing human power in terms of the will-to-power, the more positive aspects of power, 'power-to' rather than 'power-over', as Hinze puts it,[126] are sometimes overlooked. This has a particular bearing on his approach to the use of power in society and politics, a matter for discussion in the later section on Christian Realism.

Salvation and the Power of God

Introduction

We have seen that, for Niebuhr, the basic nature of sinful humanity can be identified as the will-to-power: an aggressive, egoistic and power seeking drive for security. Furthermore, it is this crucial aspect of human nature which is the source of the problem of evil. For Niebuhr, salvation must therefore consist of dealing effectively with this element of humanity: salvation firstly in the traditional sense of the word, i.e. the matter of redeeming the individual from the consequences of sin before a holy God; but also salvation in a broader sense, consisting of saving humanity from the results of its sinfulness in terms of historical evil and suffering. The first, which may be seen as the matter of personal, or individual salvation, is the subject of this chapter. The second is the matter of dealing effectively with the will-to-power in the political or corporate sphere and consists of the approach often called Christian Realism. This will be discussed in a later section.

The task of salvation: Sinful humanity before a holy God

1. THE HUMAN SITUATION

Niebuhr identifies the primary problem of salvation as the question of how a holy God will overcome and destroy the sin in an intrinsically sinful humanity, without destroying humanity in the process.[127] We have seen that Niebuhr places the source of sin, not in some contingent or historical element of humanity such as the material body, ignorance, or some kind of political system, but in the very centre of human being – the self-consciousness. The same human quality which is humanity's crowning

---

[126] Hinze, Christine F., *Comprehending Power in Christian Social Ethics*, (Atlanta: Scholars Press, 1995), pp. 4-5, 64.

[127] *NDM II*, pp. 44-5.

glory, 'being made in the image of God', the source of humanity's personality, uniqueness and creativity, is also the source of the problem of evil. Consequently, the taint of the will-to-power emerges within all human achievements, since all activity is engaged, to some degree, in the will-to-power's drive for power. Human striving, no matter how idealistic its supposed end, is in part a disguise for the self's agenda for power-seeking in order to overcome its own God-given finiteness. This sinfulness, in its rebellion against God, permeates the whole of human nature, activity and achievement.

2. The 'Prophetic Question': Can God be Merciful as Well as Just?

The judgment of God

In contradiction to human sinfulness stands the holiness and justice of God. These qualities are intrinsic to the nature of God himself, and all his Creation.[128] Sinfulness, as defiance against God-given finitude emerging in acts of pride, selfishness and greed, transgresses the Law of God which is itself an expression of that holiness.[129]

For Niebuhr, the justice of God is well attested to biblically, and forms the principle of interpretation of history which emerges in the prophets.[130] In the history of Israel it is the judgment of God which brings about disasters such as the Flood and most importantly the Exile. He understands the catastrophes of history not to be random events or the work of a capricious or vindictive deity, but the inevitable consequences, on a grand scale, of divine action against human sinfulness.[131] As humanity attempts to over-reach itself, denying its God-given limits and setting itself up in proud (supposed) self-sufficiency, it violates the God-given limits of humanity, and also the God-given Law which is an expression of God's holiness, and prompts God's righteous judgment and punishment in return, which breaks all human pride and pretence. For Niebuhr, the prophetic message is that the meaning of history itself, with its rise and fall of civilisations, consists of God's ongoing work of judgment against, and the destruction of, sinful humanity..

> The catastrophes of history by which God punishes this pride, it must be observed, are the natural and inevitable consequences of men's effort to transcend their mortal and insecure existence and to establish a security to which man has no right... The serious view which the Bible takes of this sin of man's rebellion against God naturally leads to an interpretation of history in which judgment upon sin becomes the first category of

---

[128] *NDM I*, p. 151.
[129] *NDM II*, pp. 58-9.
[130] *NDM I*, pp. 150-51.
[131] *NDM I*, p. 149.

interpretation. The most obvious meaning of history is that every nation, culture and civilisation brings destruction upon itself by exceeding the bounds of creatureliness which God has set upon all human enterprises. The prophets discern this fact of judgement most clearly in regard to Israel itself.[132]

This God stands over against man and nation and must be experienced as "enemy" before he can be known as friend. Human purposes, insofar as they usurp the divine prerogatives, must be broken and redirected, before there can be a concurrence between the divine and the human will.[133]

God's judgment therefore forms the first stage of the divine strategy for dealing with the will-to-power. In destroying the historical achievements of the will-to-power, God brings home the fact that the agenda of the will-to-power, in terms of self-seeking power acquisition, is self-defeating, a tragic failure. Not only is finite human power inadequate to stand against the vast threats of the universe; the sinfulness of the activity itself results in God's answering wrath and destruction. God's work of revelation, then, is more than simply a matter of knowledge: it also consists of expressing his holiness through destructive acts against human sinfulness. The judgment of God brings home the truth, in full force, that security from the vicissitudes of history is unattainable by human means; and this confronts human pride, shatters its pretension and exposes its claims to eternity and divinity for a sham.

But the terrific events of judgment by God pose a great question: is God merciful as well as just? If so, how will he demonstrate this mercy? Most importantly, can the compassion of God be shown to humanity in any substantial way without the justice of God being compromised?[134] Justice as the expression of God's holiness demands the destruction of evil, and therefore of sinful humanity which is the source of evil in history. In carrying out this justice though, the love and mercy of God towards humanity is precluded. This is Niebuhr's famous 'prophetic question',[135] discussed and applied particularly by Harland: how is it possible to reconcile the mercy of God with the justice of God?

The mercy of God

It is by sweeping away the supposed achievements of the will-to-power that the judgment of God prepares the way for the mercy of God. This is the answer to the prophetic question. For genuine, eternal salvation to occur it

---

[132] *NDM I*, pp. 149-50.
[133] *FH*, p. 103.
[134] *NDM I*, pp. 141-2.
[135] *NDM II*, pp. 28-35.

is necessary to draw not on the finite powers of humanity but on the infinite power of God. Salvation is ultimately a matter of security, of making the anxious self-consciousness invulnerable against the forces of nature. This is what the person desires above all else, and it is the intention of God to bring this about. However, the state of sin has created problems for this situation beyond the basic necessity of natural survival, and these must be dealt with in addition to the basic problem of security. The main problem here is the serious matter of human sinfulness and God's answering justice. How may God deal with human sinfulness without destroying humanity, since sin is so much a part of everything that is human, and not only overcome sin but provide the power to the person necessary for security and existence? The destruction of the achievements of the will-to-power exposes humanity's true frailty, but does nothing to alleviate the anxiety which results from that frailty. Yet the holiness and justice of God cannot be compromised. The question of salvation, then, is not how will God destroy sin, but rather how will God overcome the evil which is present in everything human right up to self-consciousness itself, in a way which will enable the power of God to bring salvation and security? For justice to occur, all that is necessary is the destruction of humanity; but for salvation to occur as the revelation and activity of the love and mercy of God, humanity must somehow be separated from the sin which is deeply ingrained in its nature, and provided with a means existing in the power of God and apart from the will-to-power. This is a far more difficult matter.[136]

For Niebuhr, the matter of sin is a matter of power, since it is the lack of power, answered by the will-to-power's egoistic quest which results in evil, suffering and offence against God. The matter of salvation, then, is also power-based: first in terms of the individual, to be given power to be secure, and also to have the consequences of sinning against God dealt with; second, for society, to be able to fight effectively against the constant results of the will-to-power which creates suffering and injustice. At this point we are concerned with Niebuhr's analysis concerning the source of the will-to-power, and the way in which God deals with sin in the individual to bring about salvation. The social aspects of this matter will be discussed later. The question at this point rather is this: how, according to Niebuhr, can God deal with sinful humanity in a way that is more than judgment and destruction? How is God's mercy, and his love for the race that he created in his own image, to be expressed in a way which brings salvation without compromising the demands of God's actual nature as holiness and justice? For Niebuhr, the answer to this prophetic question is the work of God's grace in the sinful person, which is made possible by Christ's life, death and Resurrection.

---

[136] *NDM II*, p. 30.

The basis of salvation: Niebuhr's Christology

Paul Lehmann, in his chapter in the *KB* volume, argues that Niebuhr's theology was Christological from the start.[137] His argument is not entirely convincing; however by the time Niebuhr wrote *NDM*, his thought clearly did centre on the life of Christ, and particularly the events of the Cross and Resurrection. This does not mean that Niebuhr's early theology lacked a Christology; in fact Niebuhr held Jesus in high esteem from the beginning. The point is that Niebuhr's early Christology is very much in the liberal tradition. As Rasmussen points out, Niebuhr's idea of Christ, discussed particularly in *REE* (1934), approximates to Troeltsch's inspired religious poet.[138] At this stage Niebuhr sees Jesus, like Paul, as a hero of the faith: a remarkable teacher expressing his deep insights through myth, paradox and impossible ideals; a remarkable man who became a symbol of God's acceptance of human intentions for St. Paul.[139] Separate from the 'historical Jesus' is the Christ of faith, a symbol or mythological expression of the eternal in history, the possibilities and limits of humanity, which establish a relationship between all human reality and the ideal of God.[140]

At some point, this 'low' Christology began to change, such that by the time he wrote *NDM I*, in 1941, his theology had become far more Christocentric and orthodox. To some extent Niebuhr's mature Christology shows signs of its origins, most importantly in terms of seeing Christ and the Cross as symbols.[141] One aspect in particular remains the same: Niebuhr discusses Christ primarily in terms of his humanity. Jesus is the archetypal man, the 'impossible possibility' of human perfection;[142] Christ's main significance is the example he sets for us in terms of trusting God completely and relying on the methods and power of God to overcome human fragility and anxiety, as we shall see shortly. This trust results in the Cross – but also the Resurrection, in which the power of God replaces the will-to-power as the means of sustaining existence.[143] Yet there are substantial differences in Niebuhr's later position. Christ is the revelation of God, the appearance of the eternal in time, fully God as well as fully Man, the Incarnated Logos who enters history.[144] The paradox of the Incarnation does not point to its impossibility, but rather the truth of an infinite God who becomes finite Man.[145]

---

[137] Chapter 11 of *KB* (pp. 251-80), especially pp. 254-8.
[138] Reinhold Niebuhr, pp. 25-6.
[139] *REE*, pp. 133, 211, 279-82.
[140] *REE*, pp. 287-8; *ICE*, p. 25.
[141] *NDM II*, pp. 76-9.
[142] *CPP*, p. 3.
[143] See 'The example of Christ' below.
[144] *NDM I*, pp. 29-30; *SNE*, p. 136.
[145] *BT*, pp. 13-4.

There is, then, a substantial change in Niebuhr's position on Christ. We contend that this change coincides with Niebuhr's growing perception of the depth of the problem of human sin, and in fact reflects the consequences of that dawning recognition. It was his growing understanding of the seriousness of the will-to-power which soured his relationship with liberalism, as he began to realise that human attempts to deal with the will-to-power would not work. Gradually, the virulence of the will-to-power forced him to see the impossibility of the task humanity set itself, to overcome the consequences of its own sin without God. Thus, the problem of evil, in the form of the will-to-power, darkened his perception of life, and this emerged in his tragic vision of the hopelessness of the sinful human state. In recognising this tragedy, he could critique any school of thought which looked to human means to overcome the problem of evil, particularly for him liberalism and then Marxism; but furthermore, this made the question of salvation all the more crucial; for if humanity could not save itself, where could its salvation come from? Increasingly therefore, Niebuhr began to see the problem of evil in terms of divine, not human, power for salvation. In response to this, Niebuhr's focus becomes the power of God rather than humanity – his movement from liberalism to his so-called Neo-orthodoxy. He is still interested in the human element of the equation, and this emerges in his Christian Realism which focuses on the role humanity plays in dealing with evil; but the foundation of his concept of salvation lies with God, and this is reflected in his emergent Christology. As the depth of the power of sin emerges, so the necessity of Christ's work comes to the fore. In understanding the crisis of sin, Niebuhr turns to the Cross to bring in the salvation of God.

What is worth stressing, then, is that Niebuhr's Christology is shaped by the problem of evil in the form of the will-to-power. His understanding of the will-to-power is what prompts him to develop his Christology, in order to provide an effective response to it. This also means that his Christology is primarily messianic-functional, not logos-incarnational, as Wolf states in *KB* (p. 237). Equally – typical of his Pragmatic approach – Niebuhr is concerned with the practical consequences of Christ and the Cross for us, not its metaphysical aspects. This also means that Niebuhr's Christology is not systematically developed; and that Niebuhr expounds his doctrine in terms of Christ showing us the way to God, and from there, concentrates on the illustrative importance of the Cross. As a theological methodology, especially when compared with Barth's thoroughly Christocentric approach, Niebuhr's approach may be considered less than satisfying. It can be considered too narrow an understanding of the importance of Jesus, that being limited to the example of his Cross and Resurrection, rather than being a function of the events of the Incarnation which culminate in the Cross.

The means of salvation: The work of Christ on the Cross

We have considered something of Niebuhr's Christology and noted how it developed from the necessity of providing a response to the will-to-power. We will now consider his doctrine of the Cross and Resurrection and show how it developed from the same agenda. In the course of this study though, we have noted Niebuhr's understanding of the nature of Christ is presented primarily in terms of revelation and symbol – a point we will develop more in due course. Consequently, it is to be expected that his understanding of the Cross will follow this pattern, and this is the case to a high degree. Underpinning this is his doctrine of Atonement, based on the actual event of the Cross and followed by the bodily Resurrection of Jesus.

1. THE CROSS OF CHRIST: THE REVELATION OF GOD'S JUSTICE AND MERCY

When we examine Niebuhr's mature theology, we find that he considers the events of the Cross and Resurrection to be central to the Christian faith. In particular, it is through Christ's work on the Cross that the salvation of humanity from its sinfulness is accomplished. In *NDM* and *CPP* particularly, we find a strong emphasis on Christ's work of salvation. In *CPP* he states

> For the Christian Faith holiness is ascribed only to the God who is the Creator, Judge and Redeemer of the world. The world is made and sustained by Him. Its historical realities are thus the fruits of His creative will. The world is judged by Him. Its sins stand under His divine judgement. The world is redeemed by Him. Without His grace mediated though Christ, human existence remains a problem to itself, being unable to escape by any effort of its own from the contradictions of a sinful existence. (pp. 203-4)

> Our gospel is one which assures salvation in the Cross of Christ to those who heartily repent of their sins. It is a gospel of the Cross; and the Cross is a revelation of the love of God only to those who have first stood under it as a judgment. (p. 210)

It is the Cross that forms the basis of salvation. It shows the way in which the mercy of God is extended to sinners in a way which does not compromise the justice of God. Thus the Cross answers the 'prophetic question' of the relation between God's justice and mercy; for in the sacrifice of the Cross, the holiness and justice of God are satisfied, not by humanity bearing the consequences of its sin, but by God paying the price in our stead.¹⁴⁶ The transgressions against the holiness of God, carried on through history by sinful humanity, are atoned for by the death of Christ, by Christ making the supreme sacrifice of his own life in accordance with the will of God. In doing so, the integrity of the judgment of God in relation to sin within history is maintained. The Cross reveals the seriousness of sin, the fact that sin has tremendous consequences, since it takes the death of God himself to overcome the effects. Sinfulness is not some minor matter, to be put aside easily or removed by political re-organisation or improved education. Sin requires so much to deal with it that its mastery is beyond all human means. From this arises Niebuhr's understanding of the tragedy of humanity. Humanity is forced into despair by the seriousness of sin. 'The knowledge that sin causes suffering to God is an indication of the seriousness of sin. It is by that knowledge that man is brought to despair.'¹⁴⁷

The Cross as the death of God also indicates the rightness of the divine Law. The Law is not arbitrary, easily dismissed or ignored. It is the nature of God which sets the Law, and the nature of reality itself, including the divine person, is affronted by humanity's sin. Consequently the acts carried out by humanity have genuine and irretrievable consequences. In this, Niebuhr maintains the significance of historical activity: whatever God does in response to sin, the nature of sinful acts as transgressions against God's holiness are real and have real consequences, which are overcome only by the sacrifice of God's own Son on the Cross.¹⁴⁸ This indicates a most robust doctrine of sin, reflecting perhaps Niebuhr's clear understanding that sinfulness is no abstract matter, but rather emerges in the great evils of history which he observed personally.

While the Cross reveals the judgment of God, it also becomes the supreme expression of God's mercy. It is *God* in human form who bears the punishment of sin, not humanity. Through the events of the Cross, God extracts justice for the transgressions of the Law, but he himself pays the price. This shows the paradox of God's freedom over, but not from, his own Law.¹⁴⁹ The Law still stands, and in fact must stand, since it reflects the eternal holiness and justice of God himself. Its demands, though, are carried out not against humanity, but against God. So, while the justice of God is satisfied, it is the mercy of God which actually prevails. The death of the Second Member of the Trinity in human form fulfils the Law on humanity's behalf, even though the requirements of the Law, demanding a standard of holiness to the level of God himself, are too heavy ever to be carried by sinful humanity. The Cross is the answer to the prophetic

---

[146] *NDM II*, pp. 47, 58-9, 106-9.

[147] *NDM II*, pp. 58-9.

[148] *NDM II*, pp. 58, 108, 219.

[149] *NDM II*, pp. 58, 69.

question of how God can maintain his justice while also showing perfect mercy.

It can now be made clear why the absence of a substantial doctrine of the Incarnation is problematic for Niebuhr. It is because the mechanics of the Atonement as God's justice and mercy depend heavily on the nature of Christ as man and God together: man as representing humanity, God as bearing the consequences of sin.[150] Niebuhr's 'symbolic' presentation of the Incarnation is just too insubstantial to carry the weight of a fully attested doctrine of Atonement such as the one he delivers. In fact, despite so many key Christian doctrines, Niebuhr's exposition of the Atonement covers just a few pages of *NDM II* (pp. 56 - 60). Niebuhr's primary interest in the Cross is that it reveals the work of God in history, and also shows the mechanics of salvation in terms of how the Christian should respond to God in order to be saved from the sin of the will-to-power. Compared with the profundity of Niebuhr's analysis and consistent unmasking of sin, this understanding of the Atonement must be declared something of a disappointment.

2. CHRIST AND POWER

It has already been made clear that, for Niebuhr, the questions of sin and salvation revolve around the matter of power. It is the anxious self-consciousness in its quest for power which emerges as the marauding will-to-power, which is his model for sin. So salvation consists of the appropriation of infinite divine power by the person in order to become secure. This matter of power in his ideas of sin and salvation naturally carries through into his understanding of the Cross of Christ. Where Niebuhr is concerned, the question of salvation is essentially the question of how the power of God can be appropriated by the person. It is here that the events of the Cross, and most importantly the example of Christ, are of first importance to him. For Niebuhr, the Cross is an event which uniquely demonstrates the possibilities of human faith which itself is the means by which God's power works in the person. Niebuhr's understanding of Christ, therefore, revolves around Christ's moral choice to elect the way of self-sacrifice rather than the will-to-power's egoism; and it is this choice which brings Christ to the Cross but, from there, to the Resurrection also. How does this work?

---

[150] Edward J. Carnell notes Niebuhr's lack of a solid doctrine of Atonement, and the fact that it follows from a weak Christology, (*The Theology of Reinhold Niebuhr*, (Grand Rapids: Eerdmans, 1951), p. 159). Carnell's criticism, though, is based on his analysis of Niebuhr's Christology and his argument that it makes the sinlessness of Jesus impossible, and so no Atonement could have occurred. It is debatable whether Carnell does full justice to Niebuhr's position on Christ, though, as he takes a generally hostile approach to him, and perhaps tends to over-emphasize his doctrinal failings.

Power and goodness

In the cosmology section of this chapter we considered the three dualisms which Niebuhr establishes, the third of which was the dualism of power. Niebuhr presents two models of power: divine power, in the 'Kingdom of God', in which power and goodness work together; and human power, the 'Kingdom of the world', in which goodness and power contradict each other. The contrast between these two models is necessary to understand his doctrine of the Cross and Resurrection.

It must be remembered that, for Niebuhr, it is power which defines existence. For existence to continue, it is necessary that the existing being has the power to oppose the natural forces of the world which can destroy it. To lose power is synonymous with destruction – hence the will-to-power's obsessive drive for power to make itself secure. In the divine realm, power and goodness work together in such a way that it is natural, and indeed necessary for existence, to act morally, that is, in conformity with the holiness of God. Anything acting immorally contradicts the holiness of God and therefore the power of God; and so the power of God turns against it and destroys it. In the realm of God, then, moral action is integral to existence; and since the power of God is infinite, moral activity is not only necessary for survival, but carries with it the resource of infinite power, which makes security in a finite world natural.

In the Kingdom of the world the opposite is the case. Here the identity of human power is dominant, and this is the will-to-power. The will-to-power is intrinsically sinful, and by its very nature as egoistic and proud is opposed to God and his holy Law. Consequently, in this realm power opposes goodness. Where morality and power meet, power dominates and forces moral compromise. For survival to be possible, power is necessary; yet behaving morally is to oppose power (in the form of the will-to-power) and so face destruction. Because of the nature of the will-to-power, in the human realm goodness is only possible where power is disavowed, while power is only possible when goodness or moral action is abandoned. The person is therefore faced with the stark choice: behave morally, and be destroyed by the surrounding will-to-powers which will take advantage of honesty, trust and forgiveness; or behave as a will-to-power and so survive temporarily but in doing so contradict God's holy Law and ultimately be destroyed by God's judgment. Furthermore, this is an ongoing problem since to change society power is required; but in serving power, the person becomes corrupted, having to compromise and lie, cheat or even murder in order to wrestle power from his opponents, and in doing so, become indistinguishable from the evil the person is trying to defeat. The problem of history, then, consists of this battle between good and evil, and the essential impotence of the good; and it is this situation which makes divine intervention necessary. Humanity, so conditioned by the will-to-power, is incapable of bringing about change for itself to come into line with the holiness of God, and so, without God, is doomed to God's judgment and divine retribution.

While this contradiction between power and goodness exists in the human realm, that realm itself is finite, and also penetrated by the power and activity of God. Therefore, within the 'Kingdom of the world', the Kingdom of God is at work. Furthermore, the identity of power in the Kingdom of God is very different from human power, being both moral and infinite. Most importantly, it is possible under certain circumstances for the power of God to work in the individual. Where this occurs, the moral, infinite power of God replaces tainted, finite human power to carry the person beyond the tragic situation of human sinfulness into the redeemed state of security, where the infinite power of God in its moral purity can easily withstand the finite powers of historical existence, including death itself. This is what happened with Christ on the Cross followed by the Resurrection.

The example of Christ

Niebuhr's model of Christ's sinless humanity revolves around Jesus' dependence upon God for the power to exist.[151] Like all people, Jesus experienced anxiety in the face of the forces which opposed him during his earthly life. Unlike other men, however, Jesus' response to this was not to seek power egoistically for himself at the expense of God's holy instructions, but rather to depend, in total trust, on the power of God to sustain him. This presents the ideal perfection of faith which, though it is *de facto* impossible for sinful man, remains an ideal possibility.

> The ideal possibility is that faith in the ultimate security of God's love would overcome all immediate insecurities of nature and history. That is why Christian orthodoxy has consistently defined unbelief as the root of sin, or as the sin which precedes pride. It is significant that Jesus justifies his injunction, "Be not anxious" with the observation, "For your heavenly Father knoweth that ye have need of all these things." The freedom from anxiety which He enjoins is a possibility only if perfect trust in divine security has been achieved. Whether such freedom from anxiety and such perfect trust are actual possibilities of historic existence must be considered later. For the present it is enough to observe that no life, even the most saintly, perfectly conforms to the injunction not to be anxious.[152]

Christ's moral choice, therefore, consisted of trusting in the power of God as the source of his power. For him this meant turning aside from his natural drive for power in obedience to God; and it was this choice, of

---

[151] *NDM I*, pp. 195-8, 304-9.
[152] *NDM I*, p. 195.

sacrificing power (to exist) to serve God which resulted in the Cross. '[P]ure goodness, without power, cannot maintain itself in the world. It ends on the Cross.'[153] 'The Kingdom of God must still enter the world by way of the crucifixion. Goodness, armed with power, is corrupted; and pure love without power is destroyed.'[154] Just as Christ's obedience and moral action resulted in the Cross, so the Cross is apparently the inevitable end of all those who follow Christ and choose goodness over power. Following Christ in this way is the act of faith: trusting in God's power, and his way of working, rather than the will-to-power's more obvious route of seeking power for the self. The Cross of Christ, therefore, shows the initial consequence of trusting in God, which is death as the person who chooses goodness over power is destroyed by the powers of the world.

Niebuhr identifies this stage of salvation with the Suffering Servant.[155] Under historical conditions, the decision of self-sacrifice, of acting morally, particularly in line with the law of love, results in the destruction of the Messiah since, in opposing power through goodness, (human) power is abandoned and the Messiah suffers and dies. This symbol of the Suffering Servant corresponds to the general historical situation in which love in this world does not conquer evil but in fact is destroyed by it. Thus the liberal hope that love carries with it its own power to overcome evil is naively optimistic.[156] The true end of love, in the kingdom of the world, is the Cross. This means that the norm within history is not triumphant love, symbolised by the Son of Man, but the suffering love represented by the Suffering Servant.[157] Sin may have been overcome at the Cross, but only 'in principle', i.e. its destruction is guaranteed, but is not realised in history. Love triumphs over evil only at the end of history, at the Eschaton, where God's power finally overwhelms and replaces human power.[158] Consequently, within history, love has no rational justification: there is no reason to act self-sacrificially and live according to the law of love, because, alone, it results in death. It is only by the transcendent power of God breaking into history that love can exist,[159] sustained by a power separate from this world. This means that, for Niebuhr, the transcendent ideal of sacrificial love, the love which *God* has, is necessary for love to exist within history at all.[160] The power for love to exist in the kingdom of the world is simply absent. The transcendent power of God, therefore, is

---

[153] *BT*, pp. 177-8.
[154] *BT*, p. 185.
[155] *NDM II*, pp. 46-53.
[156] *NDM II*, p. 47.
[157] *NDM II*, pp. 46-7, 50.
[158] *NDM II*, pp. 50-4.
[159] *NDM II*, p. 92.
[160] *NDM II*, p. 71.

needed to complete the historical existence of love, and even make it possible.

Following Christ

Christ's choice, then, of obedience to God at any cost, sets the example for humanity, and reveals the choice that individuals should make when faced with the dilemma of acting morally verses acting to survive. It also makes clear the cost of that action, not presenting a sentimental or romanticised ideal, but rather makes clear the destructiveness, in human terms, of such a choice. By choosing God's way of working rather than the will-to-power's, tragedy results, the Cross, on which Jesus Christ the man is destroyed. But while the abandoning of human power for goodness is lethal for the human self, that same act makes way for a different power to enter into the person, the power of God. This power, being infinite and in conformity with God's holiness, overcomes human finitude, including death, and establishes a new, eternal existence. Through the Cross, new life is bestowed upon Christ who emerges as the second Messiah figure, the Son of Man, the eschatological figure for whom divine authority, holiness and power combine. It is through the self-sacrifice of Christ, with his trust in God's method and power in contradiction to human means, that the Cross results. But while death is the initial consequence of this, it is followed by the new life of the Resurrection by the infinite power of God. Through this, as well as achieving the Atonement, Christ sets the example which others can follow, showing how the tragedy of the human situation is overcome by trusting in the power of God. It is the example of Christ which makes it possible for others to take the same choice that he did with confidence, since God's activity is now revealed and, like Christ, we can expect our faith and choice of self-sacrifice to be rewarded as Christ's was. Thus Christ's Resurrection is the foundation of our hope, since, like Christ, when we follow God we can expect first 'death to self', but then 'life to God'.[161]

Christ, therefore, illustrates the way in which God works to overcome the human state of sinfulness as the will-to-power. The Cross and Resurrection make Christ 'the first of many brothers',[162] in that, by following Christ's example of choosing goodness over power, his followers will experience 'crucifixion', since the world of the will-to-power will destroy the person. The crucifixion is essentially the abandoning of human power as the will-to-power and choosing to trust the power of God instead. Casting the self upon the power of God is an act of faith, of trusting God and his promises instead of the self's agenda. The response given by God is to take up the person, replacing the human power with infinite and perfect divine power. Hence, like Christ, the believer's death (to self) is followed by the 'Resurrection' – the new self in the infinite power of God. The event of

---

[161] See the discussion below on Niebuhr's interpretation of Galations 2:20, pp. 222-4.
[162] Romans 8:29.

The grace of God: wisdom and power

For Niebuhr, it is by the grace of God that sinful humanity is redeemed from its tragic state of sinfulness.[163] He describes the work of grace as a two-stage process: first the 'wisdom' of God comes, bringing in the truth of the person's situation as a finite creature before God; second, grace as the 'power' of God comes, replacing the human will-to-power as the means of existence. We will consider these two aspects of grace in turn.

1. GRACE AS THE WISDOM OF GOD

We have seen that, for Niebuhr, the source of sin lies in the anxious self-consciousness. It is the anxious self, aware of its finitude in a world of vast threatening powers, which seeks to make itself secure by grasping at power (the will-to-power) and setting itself up as a being (supposedly) immune to the forces which threaten it. This attempt at self-sufficiency, intimately associated with proud defiance against God, emerges from anxiety and develops into pretence, as the self identifies its own agenda with the ideals of humanity and uses them as the justification for acting egoistically. Hence pride and pretence, in Niebuhr's scheme, are the expressions of sin, while the source of sin lies in the very centre of humanity, in its actual self-consciousness.

If sinfulness arises from the anxious self-consciousness, and emerges through an agenda disguised by ideals, it is to be expected that Niebuhr will likewise address the problem of sin through the self-consciousness. Most importantly, it is the true state of finiteness which forms the foundation of sin, followed by the self's consciousness about finiteness which emerges in anxiety. This proceeds by the self's attempts to disguise or overcome that finiteness through power, in order to become secure; and it is this false state of pretence founded on (supposedly) self-sufficient pride which must be overcome. The first stage of salvation then, consists of overcoming that pretence. It is by the collapsing of the false facade of finiteness-overcome that God begins to reach the source of sin which is the finite, anxious self. The overcoming of pretence is necessary first because it is an attempt to defy or rebel against God, and as such is intrinsically sinful and destined for the judgment and destruction of God; but second, because it is a false position, inadequate for true salvation, and in fact the tragic means by which the person is actually condemned and destroyed. The tragedy of the

---

[163] *NDM II*, Chapter IV.

will-to-power is that it brings about the very destruction of the self which it was supposed to prevent.

Cutting through the pretence, God is able fully to expose the true state of the self, and from there, deal with its insecurity. Only in dealing with the source of sin itself can sin be overcome. In a state of truth, the anxious self, stripped of its comforting pretences, stands naked before God in its finitude, and it is this self in its real state which is the beginning of the possibility of salvation. For sin to be dealt with, it is necessary for the self to understand its true nature, the hopelessness of its attempt to overcome both its finitude and the sin which emerges from finitude, and as a result to throw itself upon the mercy of God. The truth, therefore, specifically in respect to self's real nature and position, is the starting point for salvation in Niebuhr's theology.

Saving knowledge through divine encounter

The revelation of truth is the first stage, then, of the work of grace. This is grace as 'wisdom': the realisation of its true situation by self-consciousness, which is brought about by an encounter with God. Thus the work of salvation begins with judgment, whereby the reality of the self is exposed by God and judged sinful, and then has its presence removed by God's power. This starts with the destruction of human achievements by the catastrophes of history, which make manifest the fact of humanity's true inability to become secure apart from God. The 'wisdom' of God therefore, is not an abstract matter, but rather a living truth, brought home to the person through historical events. Precisely this moment of judgment is the means by which God prepares the way for his acts of salvation.

The wisdom of God, then, is first brought into the consciousness by the acts of God in history which destroy sources of human security which seem to provide alternatives to the power of God. Thus, experiences of disaster are actually historical manifestations of the encounter between God in his holy power, and sinful humanity. In this encounter, the presence of God contradicts the existence of sin. At its harshest level, this results in the kinds of catastrophes which the Old Testament describes, particularly in reference to the destruction of Israel at the hands of the Babylonians.[164] But for Niebuhr, this broad encounter between God and humanity is also the first moment in the event of grace. The encounter is a matter of judgment to begin with, yet it is through this encounter that repentance becomes possible, followed by God's holy power replacing human power.

In order that the person be saved, it is necessary to surrender the agenda for power so as to live by the power of God. This however, is extremely difficult for the person: in fact it is impossible, since it is effectively an act

---

[164] *FH*, pp. 124-33.

of suicide: an act in which the person's whole possibility of existence is abandoned. This goes so far against the person's natural agenda that it is simply impossible to achieve unaided.[165] Furthermore, the self-consciousness is surrounded by all manner of pretences set up by itself and those around it to justify its own belief in its immortality and essential goodness. Overcoming those pretences is impossible, at least without God, since they are necessary for the self to feel safe and so avoid anxiety. Removal of one barrier will just result in the creation of another by the self to protect itself, perhaps accompanied by a renewed vigour in the will-to-power to give itself still more reason to believe itself secure.

For salvation to occur, it is necessary to deal with this situation. The wisdom of God therefore, consists of a decisive divine revelation which cuts through the disguises and pretences of the self to make it realise its true vulnerability and therefore its final dependence upon God.[166] This realisation must come from outside the self, and in fact comes from God. Furthermore, the revelation must be of a sufficient potency to shatter the self's pretensions effectively in order for the truth to emerge. In Niebuhr's scheme this occurs through divine encounter at the personal level.[167] It is in the actual presence of God that the true state of the person emerges with tremendous force. It is in being confronted by God in some way that humanity sees itself in context. It is in contrast with God's holiness and infinite power that human sinfulness and finitude fully emerge. 'Man does not know himself truly except as he knows himself confronted by God. Only in that confrontation does he become aware of his full stature and freedom and of the evil in him.'[168]

It is this experience which strips the self-consciousness of its pretences and forces it to stand naked; and also to realise the hopelessness of its own quest for power and therefore deceitfulness of the agenda of the will-to-power. It is a divine confrontation which makes salvation possible.

> If a man does not know the truth about God, who is more than an extension of his self (a truth to be known only by faith), he cannot repent of the premature and self-centred completion of his life around a partial and inadequate centre. But it can be, and has been, argued with equal cogency, that without repentance, that is, without the shattering of the self-centred self, man is too much his own god to feel the need of, or to have the capacity for, knowing the true God. The invasion of the self

---

[165] *NDM II*, p. 118.
[166] *BT*, p. 142; *NDM II*, p. 121.
[167] Hofmann, pp. 104, 109-10, 138.
[168] *NDM I*, p. 140.

from beyond the self is therefore an invasion of both "wisdom" and "power", of both "truth" and "grace".[169]

We can now see that self-understanding is integral to Niebuhr's scheme of salvation. This is to be expected if self-consciousness is the starting point of sin. It also means that knowledge, particularly self-knowledge, is essential to Niebuhr's whole theology. Humanity knows itself by knowing God, and in knowing itself, salvation comes about. In the section on epistemology we will discuss more fully the vital role knowledge plays in Niebuhr's theology. For the event of salvation, however, he considers a specific type of knowledge. It is not only a matter of realising one's true nature: this may occur in any pseudo-religious situation. The strongest evidence of Niebuhr's essential orthodoxy – despite its weaknesses – is this clear recognition of the desperate nature of the human plight highlighted by the holiness of God. Salvation is not simply a matter of recognising one's own finiteness, but of seeing the sinfulness of the will-to-power's agenda and the total impossibility of overcoming the will-to-power without the grace of God. The encounter with God produces not just understanding but repentance, and it is this which makes it possible to overcome the will-to-power and replace it with divine power. It is by recognising the total unacceptability of the self's agenda, and all that this agenda has done, that the self feels the horror of the will-to-power, and the desire to be rid of it, which is necessary as a precursor for God doing exactly that; and it is the contrast between the sinner and God, realised by encounter, that brings this riddance about.

The first moment of the work of grace, then, is grace as the 'wisdom' of God: the bringing home of the truth of the person's situation in its finitude and sinfulness. This is an event of judgment: judgment in the sense of divine destruction of human pretence, and also as self-judging, in that the self sees itself clearly in the light of revelation and can see its utter sinfulness and hopelessness. The wisdom of God therefore, especially in the individual, is a matter of knowledge.

But knowledge alone is not sufficient to save.[170] All this first moment does is make the self aware of its true state. The resources necessary to overcome this state are absent from grace as 'wisdom'. In his typical distancing from rationalism, Niebuhr is clear about the fact that the rational, self-conscious faculty is impotent before the force of the will-to-power.[171] Knowing alone does not give the self the power to overcome the will-to-power and become sinless. Following the encounter with the transcendent perfection of God, the self is still totally dependent upon the grace of God for salvation, and the second moment of grace is grace as the power of God.

---

[169] *NDM II*, p. 104.

[170] *NDM I*, pp. 274, 279.

[171] *NDM I*, p. 275.

2. GRACE AS THE POWER OF GOD.

Following the encounter with God's perfection, the grace of God as wisdom has prepared the way for the grace of God as power. Having been stripped of its pretences, the self stands alone in repugnance at its own will-to-power yet, as finite, still anxious and needing power to survive. In this state it is ready to sacrifice its own will-to-power and self-seeking agenda, and throw itself upon the mercy of God. When this occurs, the grace of God as power will enter the existence of the person and re-establish it as it should always have been, living in community with God and others in the power of God. How does Niebuhr describe this second stage?

Divine power *in* humanity

Niebuhr presents grace as power in two ways. First it is the power of God *in* humanity. When the person is ready to abandon the self's agenda, he has reached a position of repentance. It seems that, for Niebuhr, repentance is the situation in which the person is open and willing to let go of the self's will-to-power and all that it stands for, and seek God instead.[172] This position is only possible through an encounter with God, wherein the true plight of the self becomes apparent in such a way that the person feels such revulsion at the will-to-power that it is prepared to do anything to be rid of it. The contrast between the will-to-power and the holiness of God is made manifest only in the presence of God. In this moment, the self is able to reject its self-seeking agenda and turn to God; and this is the event of salvation. Salvation indeed consists of rejection of the will-to-power in favour of the power of God. Therefore it is essentially an event of power. In jettisoning the will-to-power as the means of survival, the self becomes totally dependent upon the power of God instead and releases itself from the sinful egoism and evil of the will-to-power. Escaping the will-to-power in this way means that the person escapes the influence of the force which contradicts the power and goodness of God. In theory at least, therefore, it is possible now for the person to live in conformity with the will of God and so avoid sinful rebellion.

---

[172] Note that this understanding of repentance leaves open the question of whether or not the event of salvation is a single, unique event or an ongoing series. It is equally possible that Niebuhr has in mind one cataclysmic 'shattering of the self' followed by repentance and turning to God; or a continual series in which the agenda of the will-to-power is overcome but regains ascendancy, to be challenged and overcome by divine encounter once more. Either way, this makes renewal rather than eschatological fulfilment the principle of hope in Niebuhr's theology, as Langdon Gilkey notes ('Reinhold Niebuhr's Theology of History' in *The Legacy of Reinhold Niebuhr*, ed. by Nathan Scott, (Chicago: University of Chicago Press, 1975), pp. 36-62 (p. 55)). Thus Niebuhr places the locus of faith not in the Eschaton, to which he allocates primarily symbolic significance, but in the imminent activity of the power of God in the believer.

Doctrinal Motifs in Niebuhr's Theology

This new life consists of a state of total dependence upon God. It is solely by the power of God that the self can now exist, since it has ceased to live for itself as the will-to-power, and so equally has ceased to strive to attain the power to exist for itself. The person now has to 'live by faith', in the true meaning of the phrase since it is only by continuing to appropriate the resources of God for the self, provided by God in his grace, that continual existence is possible;[173] and this is a state of faith since all the person has to live by is the power of God, provided afresh each day.

This day-to-day supply of resources to the person is the work of grace as the power *in* the person.[174] It is by this power that the person continues to exist. More especially it is the holy, infinite and perfect power of God that is at work, and not the mean, impoverished power of the will-to-power. Life in the power of God, therefore, is not only a matter of survival but of fulfilment, restoration and sanctification.[175] The power of God in the person which is the 'Holy Spirit'[176] gives the person the resources needed to make the person what he or she should be, and in fact should have been, before sin marred the 'image of God'. This not only ensures the continuing existence of the person after the rejection of the will-to-power; it fulfils him beyond the limits of sinful self-centredness by the power of God.[177] As Cornelison says,

> For Niebuhr, then, God's transcendence is understood is terms of a confrontation between the will of God and the will of the human. When this is apprehended in faith, this confrontation becomes judgment and causes a person to recognise his or her inability to find complete fulfilment in the created world. It breaks the vicious circle of self-centeredness by revealing the source of fulfilment to be outside of the self. Once this fact is apprehended, the person's purpose and intention are set in the direction of Christ as norm. Because the source of this apprehension is God, Christ's perfection is "imputed" to man from without. (p. 43)

> According to Niebuhr, God has resources of love, wisdom and power which are available to humans and which enable them to become what they truly ought to be. (p. 42)

The effect of grace as power-in therefore, is that the person is carried beyond his own limits, not in a sinful, Promethean defiance of God-given

---

[173] *NDM II*, p. 103; Cornelison, pp. 41-2.
[174] *NDM II*, p. 102.
[175] *NDM II*, pp. 103, 107.
[176] *NDM II*, pp. 102-3, 124 (Niebuhr's quotation marks).
[177] *NDM II*, p. 102.

boundaries, but rather by the power of God carrying it beyond the self into selflessness, serving God and the community from a new relatedness to God in a way impossible for the old will-to-power.[178] Grace as power-in, therefore, or as the 'Holy Spirit', consists of the completion or fulfilment of the person through the power of God to live a life of selflessness and relatedness to God through the work of divine power.

For Niebuhr, this is the mercy of God which follows from the judgment of God. The judgment of God makes the mercy of God possible since it prepares the way for the sinner to throw himself on God's mercy and depend on divine power for existence rather than the will-to-power. In doing so, God overcomes the sinful element in humanity; for by this process the anxious self-consciousness is dealt with in such a way that the sinful will-to-power is jettisoned and replaced by divine power. If we recall the task of salvation, it was exactly this: to remove and destroy the sinful aspects of humanity without destroying humanity itself. In replacing the will-to-power with divine power, this is precisely what has happened: the sinful element is removed at its source, and replaced by Godliness. But most crucially, the effect of this development is in fact complete salvation. Not only is the sinfulness removed, ensuring the ongoing presence of God; the anxiety which gave rise to it can now be dealt with. The power of God which replaces the will-to-power is not tragic, but eternal.[179] It does not end in destruction, since there is no contradiction between God at work in the person and the infinite power of God at work in the cosmos. Hence judgment and destruction are avoided. Still more crucial, however, is that the power of God, unlike human power, is infinite. The vast cosmological forces might seem infinite in comparison with humanity, but in fact are no match for the power of God. Indeed, even the power of death itself is to be overcome by the power of God – a truth symbolised by the Resurrection,[180] first of Christ, then of those who have followed his example of complete dependence on the power of God for salvation. It is through the infinite power of God, and that alone, that the person becomes secure in the face of historical forces,[181] and therefore the power of God is what is required to save: first from the judgment of God, second from the temporal finitude which ends in death. And it is by following the example of Christ, dying to the self and its egoistic struggle to survive, that we are resurrected in the infinite power of God which, ultimately, secures us from the powers of history and even death itself.

It is now clear that Niebuhr has a very practical attitude to the spiritual matter of grace. Living by the power of God is a straightforward matter of maintaining existence day-to-day. This brings the matters of grace and

---

[178] Hofmann, p. 111.

[179] *BT*, pp. 118, 297.

[180] *FH*, pp. 149-50.

[181] *BT*, pp. 96-8; *CPP*, p. 12; *NDM I*, pp. 306-8.

salvation right down to the problem of living daily in the presence of God through faith. Living by faith is a matter of the sinful person obtaining the resources needed to live out the righteous life, and to have the limits of finitude which give rise to anxiety overcome not by human defiance but by divine grace. This also means that the widely held criticism of Niebuhr,[182] that he has no adequate doctrine of the Holy Spirit, must be treated with caution. Niebuhr presents God's involvement with the person primarily in terms of grace and power, rather than as the active Third Person of the Trinity. This has certain implications, most dangerous of which is that he comes very close indeed to reducing the Holy Spirit to an impersonal power – a matter we will discuss later. However, he clearly has a very definite idea of how God works within the life of the individual believer, and this should not be overlooked. In his description of the power of God at work in the person, he provides a substantial and coherent account of the work of God in the believer, and the life of faith, and while this falls short of a properly developed doctrine of the Holy Spirit, the concept of an intimate and personal involvement of God with the believer is not omitted.

It is important at this point to state clearly that grace as 'power-in' is only the first part of Niebuhr's description of grace as power. Up to this moment it might be thought that Niebuhr holds a romanticised view of salvation, in that, having experienced grace as wisdom, then grace as power-in, the force of sin is dealt a terminal blow and, in Niebuhr's theology, the person goes on to live an unhindered life of selfless devotion to God and to others. This is definitely not the case. The second stage of grace as power makes this clear, which is grace as power over humanity.

Divine power *over* humanity

Grace as power-over humanity reflects the fact that, despite the replacement of the will-to-power with divine power as the main source of power, the sinful self remains to some extent.[183] The will-to-power is delivered a mortal blow, as it were, but lingers on to disrupt the person's existence for as long as the person is alive. This means that, regardless of one's best efforts, and the ongoing work of the power of grace in the sinner, the ravages of the will-to-power leave permanent disfigurements in the nature of the person which are never quite overcome, at least till physical death followed by bodily Resurrection occurs. This means that God's role of judgment, in which he exercises power over the sinner, continues after the initial event of salvation, as does the work of grace as forgiveness. The 'new self', living in the power of God, is never fully completed, reflected in

---

[182] See King, Rachel Hadley, *The Omission of the Holy Spirit From Reinhold Niebuhr's Theology*, (New York: Philosophical Library, 1964), particularly; also Plaskow (pp. 81-2, 158), Lehmann (*KB*, p. 277), Cornelison (pp. 58-9) and Grenz and Olson (p. 111).

[183] *NDM II*, pp. 104-7, 125-7.

the fact that, for Niebuhr, the Resurrection is an eschatological event standing beyond history, and is not a historical possibility. The 'old self', the will-to-power, continues to exert its influence, bringing about selfish acts which transgress the divine law of love and so require forgiveness. Thus sin is broken 'in principle but not in fact',[184] a phrase which evoked considerable criticism. Yet surely this is an accurate account of Christian life even after the redemptive experience of being 'born from above', when, despite living by the grace of God, sinfulness continues to exert its influence. Perhaps, once more, Niebuhr's rhetorical style results in badly phrased statements which capture attention but leave him vulnerable to misunderstanding. What he is discussing is this matter of ongoing forgiveness and dependency on God, not only for existence but forgiveness and justification also. This reflects the fact that our dependence upon God for our salvation is an ongoing matter, and not a once-executed event. For Niebuhr, grace consists of a new power of righteousness, and also pardon for the inevitable failure to live up to the standard of this righteousness which is actually the perfection of God himself. Thus holding grace as the power of God *in* humanity, and the power of God *over* humanity in tension, Niebuhr brings out the complete ongoing dependence of the person upon God's grace for life and salvation.[185] This is the 'paradox' of grace: that sin has been conquered, but also the ongoing mercy of God is needed to deal with the continuing presence of sin.[186] Dependence upon grace in these terms also means that, while we are fully dependent upon God for salvation, it is necessary to continue to repent, and continue to rely on God for the power to exist in an ongoing manner. This further means that pride and pretension are prevented from re-emerging: the ongoing existence of sin demolishes any religious pretence of achieving self-perfection, and maintains the realisation that it is only through the grace of God that existence continues to be possible. In these terms, grace as wisdom as well as power continues to play a vital role in the life of the believer as the true state of human sinfulness is revealed over and over again, resulting in continual dependence upon God for forgiveness and power.

> Yet whatever "newness of life" flows from the experience of repentance and faith is, when governed by true Christian faith, conscious of a continued incompleteness and a certain persistence of the strategy of sin. For this reason the peace which follows conversion is never purely the contentment of achievement. It is always, in part, the peace which comes from the knowledge of forgiveness.[187]

---

[184] *NDM II*, pp. 106, 125.
[185] *NDM II*, p. 122.
[186] *NDM II*, p. 104.
[187] *NDM II*, p. 104.

Doctrinal Motifs in Niebuhr's Theology

The event of salvation: life in the power of God

GALATIANS 2.20 IN *NDM II*, CHAPTER IV PART III

Having discussed Niebuhr's doctrine of grace, we are now able to analyse his exposition of Galatians 2.20 in *NDM II*, pp. 112-30, a key text in which he describes the event of salvation in three successive phases.

1. 'I am crucified with Christ'

Here, the encounter of the self with the wisdom of God is brought out. In being confronted by the divine presence, the true centre of the universe, the sinful self-consciousness comes to realise its true state. Its self-centredness and aggressive will-to-power are exposed and contradicted, resulting in the person's self-image and pretence being irrecoverably shattered and destroyed.[188] Out of this comes the desperate dependence upon the mercy of God which is the mark of true repentance and, from there, the hope of new life in God.

> The self in this state of preoccupation with itself must be 'broken' and "shattered" or, in the Pauline phrase, "crucified"...The self is shattered whenever it is confronted by the power and holiness of God and becomes genuinely conscious of the real source and centre of all life. In Christian faith Christ mediates the confrontation of the self by God; for it is in Christ that the vague sense of the divine, which human life never loses, is crystallized into a revelation of a divine mercy and judgment. In that revelation fear of judgement and hope of mercy are so mingled that despair induces repentance and repentance hope.[189]

2. 'Nevertheless I live'

From this shattered state, the self is recreated by the power of God in conformity with the divine purposes. Most importantly, this new state corresponds to the ultimate law of life, the law of love; thus the new person, by the grace of God as power-in, begins to live a new life of relatedness to God and to others.[190] This new life completes the self rather than annihilates it. In contradiction of mystical religions, and also the demonic control of the collective social organisations such as Fascism or communism,[191] true salvation consists not of the destruction of individuality but rather its fulfilment. If true humanity, essential humanity, consists of self-consciousness, standing above and apart from the self, then by the power of the Holy Spirit the new self is able to rise above the demands of the ego and

---

[188] *NDM II*, pp. 112-3, 118.

[189] *NDM II*, p. 113.

[190] *NDM II*, p. 114.

[191] *NDM I*, pp. 72-98; *NDM II*, pp. 114-7.

genuinely serve God and others. In transcending the self then, the new person becomes more fully human than before, when it was trapped within the agenda of the will-to-power. Again, the change is incomplete, and the will-to-power still exerts its influence; but there is a fundamental change in the approach to life, where the basic principle which governs the life of the person changes from being self-centred to God-centred.[192]

3. 'Yet not I; but Christ liveth in me'

The completion of the event of salvation is the new life experienced as the life in Christ. Here, the person lives through the power of God, 'Resurrected' as Christ was, and now living in the 'righteousness' of Christ.[193] It is in this third section particularly that Niebuhr discusses grace as power, both in humanity and over humanity. The 'yet not I' indicates the intrinsic sinfulness of the person – a sinfulness which continues to exert its effect, even in the new life: the denial of self and turning to Christ is an ongoing necessity.[194] Niebuhr thus includes the matter of grace as 'power-over' humanity, in terms of God's power to judge and humanity's consequent need for forgiveness, in this section.[195]

At the same time, it is Christ's power which is now at work in the person, the 'Resurrection' power of God in which goodness and power coincide rather than contradict each other, therefore allowing existence to continue beyond judgment and death. In the 'Resurrection' of the person, the power of God carries existence through: first, in this world till death; second at the Eschaton, symbolised and fore-promised by the Resurrection of Christ, in which the power of God takes over completely from the power of the world.

> To understand that the Christ in us is not a possession but a hope, that perfection is not a reality but an intention; that such peace as we know in this life is never purely the peace of achievement but the serenity of being "completely known and all forgiven"; all this does not destroy moral ardour or responsibility. On the contrary it is the only way of preventing premature completions of life, or arresting the new and more terrible pride which may find its roots in the soil of humility, and of saving the Christian life from the intolerable pretensions of saints who have forgotten that they are sinners.[196]

---

[192] *NDM II*, p. 106.
[193] *NDM II*, pp. 119, 307.
[194] *NDM II*, pp. 118-9.
[195] *NDM II*, pp. 123-30.
[196] *NDM II*, p. 130.

TAKING UP THE REVELATION OF CHRIST

It is now clear why Niebuhr holds an understanding of the Cross in terms of revelation rather than Atonement. For him, it is necessary for Christ to show us how God works if we are to take the apparently suicidal step of abandoning power for goodness. The choice of goodness, followed by the death of the self, is necessary for our salvation, since without the power of God we are doomed to judgment and destruction. But without the Resurrection of Christ, as well as the Cross, the course he advocates is simply out of the question. If power is the primary necessity of life, there is simply no sense in taking the route of the Cross, of self-sacrifice in love, unless the Cross is followed by the Resurrection. It is the Resurrection of Christ therefore, which reveals the true nature of God's work, his faithfulness in response to trust demonstrated by this mighty act.

Hence, the Cross and Resurrection are primarily events of revelation for Niebuhr. They are symbols of the work of God, the work which carries on throughout history but is hidden by the huge variety of historical events which arise from God's work. The Cross and Resurrection, then, are unique, in that they unequivocally reveal exactly how God works in relation to humanity and in particular with respect to the task of overcoming sin. Niebuhr's position is that the whole of history is conditioned by the activity of God working out his redemptive scheme for humanity.[197] The Cross and Resurrection therefore reveal what God is doing generally, and from there, the actual meaning of human history.

> History is conceived meaningfully as a drama and not as a pattern of necessary relationships which could be charted scientifically. The clue to the meaning of the drama is in the whole series of revelatory events, "God's mighty acts," culminating in the climax of revelation in the life, death, and resurrection of Christ. In these mighty acts the mysterious design of the sovereignty which controls historical destiny is clarified.[198]

It is by looking at the Cross that we understand not only the seriousness of sin, and the depth of the problem of human sin, but also the way out of our tragic situation and the cost of our salvation. In this way Niebuhr maintains a strong sense of the seriousness of sin, particularly in terms of the price God paid to overcome its power, but also in terms of the constant battle against sin for the believer, even after salvation. Nowhere in his theology is the strength of the will-to-power underestimated; and from there the cost of overcoming that force is understood. Following his understanding of the problem of evil as the consequence of the will-to-power, Niebuhr can explain why even the 'righteous' suffer. Following Christ does not simply solve life's problems. On the contrary, the way of

---

[197] See Hofmann, pp. 117-9.
[198] *FH*, p. 27.

the Cross is a way to suffering. But evil is defeated in the end, not because of some element of humanity – or the world – naturally and inevitably overcoming evil, but because of the power of God, which works in the heart of the believer to bring about new life in Christ on the other side of the Cross.

Considerations

On this doctrine of Christ and salvation thus explained, a number of points should be made at this time.

The first is that the position described here is Niebuhr's mature position, expounded in *CPP*, *NDM* and *FH* particularly. During his early years his outlook was more liberal, not only in his Christology as already discussed, but also in the matters of grace and salvation.[199] As we have seen, the development of Niebuhr's thought reflects his deepening understanding of the intractability of the will-to-power and therefore the necessity of an external factor, namely the grace of God, to enter the situation and deal effectively with this form of sin. Just as his understanding of Christ, the Cross and Resurrection grew out of the necessity of providing a theological answer to the will-to-power, so did his perception of grace as wisdom and power. Thus his whole theology can be seen to have been shaped by the agenda of dealing with the will-to-power.

This situation has a major drawback, however. As we discussed in the section on sin, Niebuhr's viewpoint only corresponds to certain types of sin, particularly the proud self-assertion of dominant males. Since his doctrines of Christ and salvation are shaped quite directly by the model of sin as the will-to-power, these doctrines may be said to suffer the same shortcomings as his doctrine of sin, most important of which is that, while claiming universality, they are actually relatively narrow in perception and application. The correct approach to deal with the will-to-power may well be to have it shattered then rebuilt through divine encounter; but what of those who are already ' shattered', fragmented by disastrous experiences or overwhelming hardship? Do these also require shattering, or are they now ready for grace as power? If they are ready, does this mean that social structures of extreme poverty or prejudice are acceptable, even godly, since they carry out the work of God? And if the person is not yet properly prepared for grace as power, what needs to be done first? Is more 'shattering' necessary, or is some other work of grace, absent from Niebuhr's theology, more appropriate? Niebuhr, concentrating so much on the form of sin with which he is most familiar, gives no answer to these questions, and this is a significant failing since he does seem to claim universality for his position.

---

[199] See, for example, *REE*, pp. 281-4.

The same criticism may be applied to his doctrine of Christ. If Christ's life, death and Resurrection are to be seen in terms of overcoming the will-to-power, what relevance are these things to those for whom the will-to-power is not the primary problem? The example of Christ as the model for us to follow only works while the will-to-power is the main problem. What is the position for those for whom other sins, such as apathetic indifference to themselves and others, are the primary issue? Niebuhr might claim that the will-to-power is universal, through, for example, sensualism, but if this is to be a successful claim he needs to show how it emerges in a wide variety of sins which are not usually identified with the will-to-power, and how Christ's life, death and Resurrection provide the model to deal with them. As things stand, Niebuhr's theology is not sufficiently well-developed for this claim to stand.

A very different line of criticism concerns his position of the Cross as being primarily illustrative. As we have discussed here, for Niebuhr, the prime function of the Cross seems to be to reveal the way in which God works, with particular reference to God's response to the sinner repenting and throwing himself upon the mercy of God in order to live by divine power. For Niebuhr, the Cross shows the way to the Resurrection; it also exposes the tragedy of sin, the contradiction between power and goodness in the human realm, and the way in which God carries us 'beyond tragedy' into new life by his grace. Ultimately it reveals the means by which God's judgment is reconciled with his mercy. In Niebuhr's theology, these illustrations are the primary functions of the work of Christ, while the traditional orthodox matters of Incarnation and Atonement are secondary, though present. He sees Christ, the Cross and Resurrection in terms of representations of divine, eternal truths and the means by which the transcendent realm of God breaks into history. It is in this sense that Christ is the self-revelation of God – not so much as God Incarnate, but more as revealing the heart of God, his mercy as well as his justice, and his way of dealing with humanity. Thus he holds a 'Christological' theology, in so far as, for him, the Cross forms the principle of interpretation for history and the supreme revelation of God.

This is a dangerous position to hold. First, it throws up deep-seated problems for the doctrine of the Incarnation. If Christ, the Cross and Resurrection are to be seen in terms of illustration, it has to be asked how much difference would be made to Niebuhr's theology if the divinity of Christ was removed? For Niebuhr, Christ's 'dual' nature is primarily a revelation of the transcendent ideal of love, an ideal which is an expression of God's nature, but not the actual divine nature itself.[200] This means that in Niebuhr's description of Christ, there is no systematic commitment to the

---

[200] *NDM II*, pp. 73-6.

Incarnation of God in the person of Jesus Christ.[201] Niebuhr makes some attempt to fill this void,[202] but his endeavours consist of little more than a set of short assertions and there does not seem to be any substantial argument to interpret or defend the doctrine. It is as if Niebuhr finds the doctrine of the Incarnation attractive, perhaps as part of his new 'Neo-orthodox' identity, but is not actually committed to the matter wholeheartedly. The result is that Jesus Christ becomes incidental to Christianity. If Christ, the Cross and Resurrection are essentially symbols, or worse still 'myth',[203] surely an alternative symbol might theoretically display the same information? Niebuhr is Christocentric in his mature theology, in so far as the Cross reveals the nature of reality, the law of love as the law of life etc., as Hofmann and Harland argue;[204] but with such a weak doctrine of Incarnation any divinely appointed symbol could achieve the same task. On this basis, it is the uniquely inspired religious poet who is crucified and then raised to life in the power of God, and any religious figure so chosen by God could have provided the same degree of revelation. This failing may be partly the result of his liberal heritage, partly also due to his functionalist approach which sets his agenda in terms of the practical consequences of Christ's life; and also his impatience with metaphysics generally. The consequence, though, is that these leave a necessary theological foundation under-developed in his position.

The second Christological matter, following on from the previous point, is that the lack of substance for the divinity of Christ, and the Cross as a symbol of God's work, deprives the theological areas of Atonement and justification of a substantial foundation. Niebuhr is able to describe the judgment of God, and the event of salvation, but the content of the doctrine of justification is lacking. Niebuhr places the righteousness of Christ in inverted commas, indicating that he sees this as an idea, a way of expression, but not the true nature of the status of the sinner before God.[205] This indicates that the righteousness of Christ is not to be taken literally, but rather is just a way of expressing a Christian idea. Presumably, then, another 'myth' would do the same job – human righteousness, perhaps? Considering the depth of his understanding of human sin as the will-to-power, it is disappointing that he fails to give an equally in-depth account of the doctrines of salvation which are needed to overcome that sinfulness.

---

[201] A point which is picked up and expounded vigorously by Carnell, pp. 144-65. Carnell gives a thorough critique of Niebuhr's theology from an orthodox perspective, with particular reference to the shortcomings in Niebuhr's Christology and the consequences of this for the rest of his theology.

[202] See particularly *NDM I*, p. 29.

[203] *BT*, pp. 13-24, 304.

[204] Harland, pp. ix-x; Hofmann, Hans, *The Theology of Reinhold Niebuhr*, trans. by L. Pettibone Smith (New York: Scribners, 1956), p. 128.

[205] *NDM II*, p. 108.

Perhaps there is a deep-seated appreciation of humanity here, emerging in a reluctance to acknowledge the unworthiness of humanity to take its place before God. Certainly the very positive role Niebuhr gives humanity in the fight to overcome the consequences of the will-to-power in society, which emerges in his Christian Realism, indicates a more humanist perspective than, for example, Barth might hold.

The third matter for consideration here is the much broader question of the status of the symbols, myths and paradoxes which emerge in his theology. If the Cross and Resurrection are essentially revelations, symbols of great transcendent realities, Niebuhr is in serious danger of depriving them of their substance, and even lapsing into docetism. Symbols are only the expressions of something else, happening or existing in another realm completely. If Christ's 'divinity' reveals the eternal in time, but is not *actually* the transcendent God, then the uniqueness of Christ is compromised, since another 'symbol' - another holy man, or Nature, or the Law - could also fulfil the same function. Furthermore, if Christ's divinity is just symbolic, then strictly speaking the death of Christ on the Cross should have no more meaning than the destruction of any other divinely appointed religious symbol. Again, Jesus is reduced to the uniquely inspired religious man of liberalism. A further point is that, if the crucifixion and its aftermath are basically revelations of God, symbols of his divine way of working, then the sacrifice of Christ, with all its pain and horror, loses its significance since the substance of the event lies elsewhere. Presumably, any symbol of God's activity would have done just as well provided the principle of dying to self then living to God was illustrated sufficiently well. The life, death and Resurrection of Christ become matters of identification, examples to follow, not the event of sacrifice by which we are made righteous before God. While Niebuhr mentions the Atonement, his discussion is so short that it cannot be taken as a thoroughly worked out doctrine.[206] Certainly he makes little reference to it elsewhere, since he sees the main issue of salvation as being the matter of living in the power of God instead of by the will-to-power. His whole account of the Cross lacks historical content and consequently substance. This leaves serious gaps in his understanding of the relationship between God and sinner, particularly in terms of the importance of the righteousness of Christ for our salvation, and not simply the example of Christ.

Niebuhr's use of symbolism, particularly in relation to the Cross and Christ's dual nature, is criticised again and again by his commentators.[207]

---

[206] Mainly *NDM II*, pp. 57-9 and 106-8, with some further discussion on pp. 46-7, 219-20.

[207] See particularly Daniel D. Williams in *KB*, pp. 207-10; Alan Richardson, 'Reinhold Niebuhr as Apologist', pp. 215-229 in *KB* (pp. 225-8); William John Wolf, 'Reinhold Niebuhr's Doctrine of Man', in *KB*, pp. 229-250 (pp. 243-8); Cornelison, pp. 58-60;

Presenting the Cross as a symbol empties it of its historical content. Wolf and Lehmann both go on to argue that Niebuhr's statement that sin is only overcome 'in principle', and not in reality, is the result of this failing since Niebuhr lacks any substantial historical event from which to assert the complete triumph of God over the power of sin.[208]

Epistemology Part 1: The nature of reason

Introduction

We have seen how, for Niebuhr, the main problem of human history, the source of evil in the world, arises from the darkest side of human nature, described by him as the will-to-power. We have also considered how overcoming the will-to-power is a work achieved not by human means but by the grace of God as 'wisdom' and 'power'. It is by the power of God replacing the will-to-power that human evil is dealt with and salvation achieved. We will now discuss the role that Niebuhr gives to epistemology in this work. First we will consider his perspective on reason, with its possibilities for overcoming the will-to-power and its limitations; second, the epistemological mechanisms, particularly myth, symbol and paradox which Niebuhr describes as integral to the work of salvation.

In considering the will-to-power, Niebuhr has become convinced that this dangerous and powerful element in human nature requires an equally powerful opponent to overcome it. In the past, the power of reason has often been considered – by theologians as well as philosophers – a suitable candidate for the task, sufficient to overcome humanity's passions. Niebuhr's perspective, however, is that this belief can no longer be sustained. He sees that reason is no match for the will-to-power, indeed that the opposite is the case. As we have already considered in a number of sections, it is the will-to-power which dominates and manipulates reason, not vice versa. An important part of Niebuhr's agenda, therefore, is to establish the true nature of reason as he understands it, and to demolish its claim to be a suitable means of dealing effectively with the will-to-power. This paves the way for his concept of salvation by the grace of God, as we have already discussed.

In our considerations of Niebuhr's cosmology and anthropology in this chapter, and Marxism and Pragmatism in Chapter Two, we have already touched on several key issues in respect to Niebuhr's understanding of reason. In the section on Marxism we saw how Marx views reason as

---

Durkin, pp. 150-2; Grenz and Olson, pp. 108-12. Only Hofmann accepts Niebuhr's illustrative Christ with barely a murmur: see pp. 118-39 and 204.

[208] Wolf in *KB*, pp. 243-5, Paul Lehmann in *KB*, p. 279.

essentially ideological, used by the ruling classes to justify the present social order and their own position of supremacy. In the section on Pragmatists we saw how, for James, truth is created in the situation, and so arises from concrete existence. We also saw how James considers the will to be the dominant force in the personality, using reason as a tool for survival. In the present chapter we have seen how, for Niebuhr, it is power which defines existence, not reason; and it is the will-to-power, not reason, which forms the locus of the personality; furthermore, that the will-to-power manipulates reason for its own ends. In all these considerations one factor emerges: Niebuhr has a 'low' view of reason, not only considering it to be inadequate as a means of controlling the will-to-power, but also dismissing any rationalist claims regarding its transcendent purity, objectivity, impartiality, and ability to maintain its integrity in the face of self-interest. How then does Niebuhr describe reason? What does he see as its positive and also its negative aspects, and what role, if any, does he give it to play in the task of overcoming the will-to-power?

Niebuhr's view of reason

THE POSSIBILITIES AND LIMITATIONS OF REASON

First, it must be stated that Niebuhr's primary interest in reason and rationality is negative. As part of his agenda of dealing with the will-to-power, it is necessary for him to expose the shortcomings of those forces which falsely claim competence in the area, to make way for the salvation of God, which alone is sufficient to overcome the will-to-power effectively. In the light of this he is generally dismissive of reason. In his cosmology it is power which defines reality, and this is a force upon which human reason has no particular bearing. Likewise with his understanding of human nature: the will-to-power is essentially a non-rational power, largely untouched by reasonableness and only interested in reason to the extent to which it can use it to further its aims of power acquisition. The consequence of this is that Niebuhr's concept of salvation has less to do with rational communication with or to the mind than with existential self-understanding brought about by encounter. The event of salvation is a matter of power: shattering disclosure followed by desperate dependence upon the power of God. In all these things, self-consciousness has something of a role to play, albeit a minor one of the mediator between the will-to-power and God; reason, and the rational faculty, very little. This means that Niebuhr's discussions of reason, rationality, and the idealism which attends it, tend to focus on exposing their shortcomings. In Niebuhr's view, reason is wholly inadequate to deal with the will-to-power, and its ages-long reputation as an impartial and powerful moral force needs a radical reassessment.

1. Positive aspects of reason

Niebuhr does not simply dismiss certain resources reason has to offer humanity. It is his intention to acknowledge the possibilities, as well as the limits, of humanity in terms of dealing with the will-to-power. Those resources which are valid, and available, he wants to make good use of; and this is partly what his Christian Realism is about: to describe accurately what humanity can (and can't) do for itself in overcoming the will-to-power. Hence, particularly in early works such as *MMIS*, he devotes considerable time to describing how rational resources can be employed to bring about certain levels of justice in society (Chapter 2). Continually, though, he returns to the fact that reason itself has a limited influence on the will-to-power. Reason cannot be expected to master or condition it to the extent that its power can be made good and employed unconditionally for the benefit of society.

In *MMIS* particularly we are given Niebuhr's perspective concerning the possibilities, and also the limits, of the rational faculty (pp. 27-35). Positively, Niebuhr considers how the rational faculty may enhance and increase those social impulses which do exist in the person through its self-transcendence. By being aware of the well-being of others, and also of transcendent ideals such as justice or the law of love, the mind is able to think through the consequences of its actions and compare its own activities with what it should be doing. From there it may influence the self's behaviour to bring it more into accordance with the principles of morality, justice and society. Also, the mind regulates the vital impulses of the person, subduing the more aggressive desires while encouraging those which will bring the whole self into line with moral principles. Finally, through the use of self-consciousness and self-transcendence, the rational faculty is able to analyse the motives and intentions of itself and others, and expose the hypocrisy and pretence which underlie supposedly moral behaviour. By such analysis, the dishonest use of reason to justify the social order or the self's aggressive activities can be exposed, depriving the perpetrators at least of their moral pretensions, if not the ability to carry out their activities. This depriving of moral armour helps give their victims the courage to defy them, as their pretensions of acting nobly are demolished and their actual egoism exposed.

In summary, Niebuhr states that

> [T]here are possibilities of increasing social justice through the development of mind and reason. It may extend social impulses beyond the immediate objectives which nature prompts; it may insist upon harmony in the whole field of vital impulses; and it may reveal all the motives which prompt human action and all the consequences which flow from it so that honest error and dishonest pretensions are reduced. The

development of social justice does depend to some degree upon the extension of rationality.[209]

Niebuhr, therefore, does give a positive role to the rational faculty. It is the employment of reason that reveals the misuse of reason. In depriving the will-to-power of some of its resources, its agenda is severely inhibited. But – and this is crucial – all these are insufficient actually to overcome the will-to-power itself. The use of reason may expose the pretensions of some people who claim to be acting for others when actually they are acting for themselves; but all this will do is diminish the effectiveness of that particular scheme which the will-to-power is employing at that time. It will not deal with the will-to-power's drive for power, nor its essential egoism. In time, other schemes will appear to carry out its agenda. The will-to-power itself is untouched by the power of reason. While the faculty of self-transcendence has its role to play in terms of mediation between the self and God (and other forms of transcendence), in terms of changing the will-to-power, and bringing about the long-term overcoming of evil which is the real task of salvation, reason and the rational faculty are powerless. Furthermore, it must be remembered that the activities of the rational faculty, even in exposing the shortcomings of the self and others, are tainted and conditioned by its own will-to-power. As we have seen in the section on anthropology and sin, Niebuhr is very clear that, as far as he is concerned, the rational faculty is strongly influenced by the will-to-power and cannot be considered dispassionate regarding matters of self-interest; and this is the case as much in apparently moral activities as with those which are more blatantly selfish. In the case of exposing the hypocrisy of others, it is a rival's agenda which is demolished, leaving the self unthreatened and its own position enhanced; and in critiquing the self, the more obvious and most easily censured activities of egoism are cut out, leaving more room for better, more subtle schemes. Reason, even in its apparently noble activities, really aids the self's agenda in the long-term. Thus the mind is the slave of the will-to-power, and while it may inhibit it occasionally, ultimately it will find itself used by the will-to-power to carry out its objectives of power seeking.

2. Negative aspects of reason

It is now clear that, even at his most generous, Niebuhr views the power of reason with suspicion. Drawing on the insights of so many of his teachers - Marx, James, Nietzsche, Kierkegaard, and also perhaps Freud - he considers the darker aspects of the self to be too powerful, and also extremely subtle. Reason itself, far from being the dispassionate, objective, almost divine power for impartiality and justice presented by the

---

[209] *MMIS*, p. 34.

rationalists, in fact must be seen as an expression of material interests.[210] At one point, Tillich castigates him for his 'low' view of reason, insisting that there are two forms of rationality, the type Niebuhr describes, and also a 'high' concept of reason, beloved by the philosophers, and that Niebuhr has confused the two.[211] However, Niebuhr's whole point is that there *is* no higher form of reason: all rationality is tainted by self-interest and so falls into the low, cunning variety. This forms part of his attack against those with rationalist tendencies, whether philosophers, liberals, Pragmatists or even Marxists: understanding, knowledge and education are not sufficient to overcome evil in humanity, and attempting to find salvation from evil in pure thought, or human wisdom, or projects of general education, will always fail. The self's perception of truth is simply too bound up with the self's agenda.

> [S]ince human personality is an organic unity of its vital and rational capacities, rational apprehensions are subject not merely to the limits of a finite mind but to the play of passion and interest which human vitalities introduce into the process. Knowledge of the truth is thus invariably tainted with an "ideological" taint of interest, which makes our apprehension of truth something less than knowledge of *the* truth and reduces it to *our* truth.[212]

Even the Marxists, usually realistic in their assessment of human nature, overlook this point, able to see the 'ideological taint' in the belief systems of their opponents, but not in their own. 'The Marxist detection of ideological taint in the thought of all bourgeois culture is significantly unembarrassed by any scruples about the conditioned character of its own viewpoints'.[213]

The limitations of reason now emerge. Reason, the mind and rationality are only minor players in the drama of the self's activities. The brain – itself material, situated in a material body with its threatened state of finitude – is the real source of rationality, such that reason arises from it. Indeed it is the mind itself which is most aware of that threatenedness, to the extent that, for Niebuhr, the self-consciousness gives rise to the will-to-power. It is by the mind being self-aware, aware of its finitude, that the self becomes anxious and seeks to gain power for itself. It is self-consciousness itself that transmutes the will-to-live into the will-to-power: and in that sense the mind can be considered intrinsically bound to the will-to-power, with the will-to-power being its protégé.

---

[210] *NDM I*, pp. 119-31.
[211] *KB*, pp. 37-8.
[212] *NDM II*, p. 222.
[213] *NDM I*, pp. 209.

The mind, in the first instance, then, cannot be considered as separate from the self's desires, innocent and distant from their aggression, but rather must be seen as their starting point. The passions, however, soon gain ascendancy, and make use of the mind to further the drive for power. Reason quickly becomes a tool of the will-to-power, used to probe future lines of action for the most effective for its purposes, and also to justify its activities where the need arises, presenting its egoistic, aggressive and manipulative actions in terms of selfless service and self-sacrifice in order to pass moral censure, both by itself and others. While self-understanding (in relation to God especially) plays its part in genuine, heart-felt repentance, reason alone can do little more than attempt to favour the more altruistic impulses of the self over those less socially acceptable. The mind is able to choose between impulses to some extent, but not actually generate them, so it is the passions which set the agenda for the self's activities;[214] the mind simply arbitrates between conflicting impulses to help direct the activity of the self. In participating in the realm of the will-to-power, however, the rational faculty is influenced by the power it is trying to manage.[215] Deriving its existence from the self, the mind's own well-being is too closely linked to the self and its agenda for survival for it to remain unaffected. The mind is easily bent to the desires of the self, and its main resource, the ability to reason, is employed, not for objective dispassionate analysis, but for self-interest and self-justification. The mind, as an expression of the self, is controlled by the self's agenda.

This means, of course, that the mind is not, and can never be, the means of resisting and overcoming the egoism of the self. Looking to the mind and its resource of reason to deal effectively with the will-to-power is simply naïve. It takes the power of God's existential encounter to do this. All reason can do, at best, is curb the worst activities of the will-to-power and try to direct some of its energy into projects which will benefit society as well as the self rather than the self alone. More often, though, the resources of the mind are used to further the ends of the will-to-power by furnishing its activities with the trappings of respectability. This is Niebuhr's doctrine of original sin, discussed in an earlier section, in which the self uses objective ideals to mask and justify its self-interested activity. The worst instance of this occurs when the mind employs absolute truth-claims to remove all restraint on the self, as we have already seen.[216] In this situation, the will-to-power is given *carte blanche* to act without the restraint, carrying out heinous crimes of intimidation, murder and insurrection to achieve its ends since, it convinces itself, it is acting on behalf of some high ideal, and humanity will benefit from the success of its projects in the long term.

---

[214] *MMIS*, pp. 40-1.
[215] *CPP*, pp. 103, 154-5; *CLCD*, pp. 50-4.
[216] 'Original sin as pretence', above; see also *NDM II*, pp. 225-9; *CLCD* pp. 102-4.

Thus Niebuhr sees that, far from being the resource best suited to overcome human evil, the faculty of reason provides no defence against it but on the contrary aids the will-to-power. Again, this forms an important part of his polemic against rationalist liberalism, and also the pacifism of his time, as he argues that a belief that humanity is essentially rational, and thereby able to settle its disputes justly and without violence by reasonable discussion, is totally naïve. The will-to-power requires a force beyond human means to deal with it - his doctrine of salvation by God's grace. In cutting reason down to size, Niebuhr makes it clear that no human means will be sufficient to deal with the will-to-power effectively, and, while reason has some part to play, is role must be limited.

The test of tolerance

Niebuhr's understanding of the dangers of reason, particularly the problem of absolutes, forms the basis by which he can assess the level to which people understand their true sinfulness. This assessment is 'the test of tolerance'.[217] A key stage in his account of salvation is the moment of self-understanding: the event through which the sinner becomes aware of their sin. At this point, the activities of the will-to-power come to light, and the person sees the depth of their egoism and its inescapability, and therefore their total dependence upon God for salvation. This is the first stage of grace, grace as 'wisdom'. While this appears most forcibly, and most effectively, in the presence of God, it may also occur, to some extent at least, through the natural self-consciousness, by which the self may see its actions in light of transcendent ideals such as the law of love and find itself wanting. This moment of self-understanding is necessary, Niebuhr considers, to avoid at least the most dangerous state of self-deception, the point at which one identifies one's own agenda in terms of an absolute. It is in understanding the nature of the will-to-power, and its manipulation of ideals, that one may realise its danger, and take steps at least to avoid the all-out 'holy war' against its opponents which characterises the will-to-power operating under the guise and inspiration of an absolute. For, in seeing the self's agenda for what it really is, i.e. an expression of the will-to-power, and not the quest for perfection that it imagines itself to be, the tainted agenda of the self cannot be confused with the absolute good it is supposed to be achieving. The partial, conditioned nature of the quest is recognised and with it, the partial, conditioned nature of the end result. In this case, partial success, influenced by the self's egoism, cannot be considered an absolute good justifying all manner of aggressive activities. Thus the demonic, self-righteous, unrestrained activism of an unconditioned will-to-power cannot be justified. In recognising the will-to-power and its

---

[217] *NDM II*, pp. 228-52.

use of absolutes, the most dangerous activities of the self can be restrained and the Holy Inquisitions and bloody revolutions of history's fanatics may be avoided.[218]

Niebuhr's means of assessing whether this understanding has occurred is the test of tolerance. The ability to tolerate the views of others, particularly regarding matters seen as vitally important by the self,[219] determines whether true self-understanding has occurred. Where it has, the self is able to recognise the true, partial, finite nature of its own understanding, and recognise that it does not have the final, complete and absolute truth. Therefore, other points of view on the same subject, though different, may also be valid. Here, the self is prepared to consider itself possibly wrong, and be open to other points of view. Certainly it will not consider itself purely right and its detractors purely evil and therefore to be eliminated. Those who have not been enlightened regarding the true nature of human knowledge, including its own truths, however, may well be tempted along these lines. The test, therefore, of whether a person has recognised his own sinfulness, and therefore his ability to act with restraint and with (relative) morality, is whether or not he can tolerate disagreement. Those who can are relatively safe, and can be entrusted with power since they are more likely to understand the nature of the will-to-power, and so take more trouble to resist its influence. Those who cannot have yet to realise the depth of the problem of their own sin. Their wills-to-power are less likely to be restrained; hence they should be resisted strenuously since the aggressive drive for power which is the will-to-power will wreak havoc given the chance.

Considerations

Niebuhr's analysis of the use of reason for disguise and self-justification is perceptive. Ultimately, however, the conclusion of his position must be a form of relativism. He has made it clear that, in his consideration, all human knowledge is sinful, partial, tainted by self-interest, and therefore presumably relative, conditioned by the context of power interests. He has even gone so far as to identify claims to objective knowledge as intrinsically sinful, in fact the definition of original sin since this is the means by which the will-to-power masks its activities. In the chapter of *NDM II* in which he presents the test of tolerance, he describes 'having the truth' as the claim of those who have yet to understand the effects of the will-to-power, and so are still dangerous, prone to fanaticism (pp. 221-3). Pretence, hypocrisy and manipulation are the true nature of claims to objective truth, and this applies to all areas of knowledge, from the rationalisation of action through to the interpretation of history. All areas

---

[218] *NDM II*, pp. 228-9.
[219] *NDM II*, pp. 246-8.

of knowledge and reason, for Niebuhr, are sinful, and it is impossible to achieve 'truth' at all.

In one sense this is a valid point, in that his analysis surely holds true for many events of history in which people have carried out terrible acts under the agenda of working for something they see as a greater good.[220] It also helps him put theology on a more equal footing with other academic disciplines.[221] Moreover, as one form of human knowledge amongst many, Niebuhr is able to reach out beyond theology's boundaries and draw on useful insights from non-Christian sources and make good theological use of them. Perhaps this calls for caution, especially when in Niebuhr's case it tends to be done at the expense of in-depth discussion of the relevant biblical and classical Christian texts, though one cannot deny the positive consequences for Niebuhr's theology.

However, it can be argued that, by relativising human knowledge in terms of its general sinfulness, Niebuhr makes one form of knowledge no greater, more objective or more valid than another. For him, all 'truth' is sinful, basically an expression of power interests, a tool of the will-to-power. Why, then, should theology, or even biblical texts, be seen as different from any other discipline or revered document? Furthermore, is theology, as the writings and belief system of the Church, a corporate body, essentially no different from the propaganda of the Nazi party? How can Niebuhr draw a distinction between them? Presumably all forms of 'truth' are to be understood as expressions of power interests, and so viewed with equal suspicion.

Niebuhr provides no epistemological criteria other than his 'test of tolerance' for assessing truth claims; and this alone is not sufficient. It may be suitable for giving some idea of whether those adhering to a belief system are aware of their own sinfulness, as Niebuhr perceives sin; but his concept of the matter is fairly narrow, as we have already discussed, and does not provide a broad enough understanding of sin, never mind provide a suitable foundation for epistemological criteria. Niebuhr needs a system of assessing competing truth claims, all of which will be tainted by the will-to-power (if his analysis is correct), but some of which will be more influenced than others, or more insightful, or (dare we say it) divinely inspired. A simple assessment of 'tolerance' does not provide this. Furthermore, it is necessary, according to his own position, actually to be intolerant in some ways if civilised society is to be maintained against the will-to-power. What is his advocacy of the use of coercion, so crucial in his Christian Realism, if not the forceful intolerance of certain destructive elements of humanity? Here we have a serious inconsistency, and once more it arises from his aversion to metaphysics. Niebuhr simply fails to set

---

[220] The current problems with Islamic fundamentalism in, for example, Egypt or Afghanistan might well come under this category.

[221] *NDM II*, pp. 238-9.

up the necessary criteria for assessing knowledge, and this is a significant weakness in his theology.

The end result of the situation is that, if all forms of knowledge are conditioned by power interests, presumably Niebuhr's own theology is conditioned in the same way.[222] This means that, without providing criteria for assessing truth claims, Niebuhr has no means of arguing that his theology is any more valid, insightful or useful than anyone else's, including those who contradict him at every point. He is defeated by his own argument. As Dennis McCann notes, Niebuhr's rejection of rationalism, without providing other criteria to take its place, deprives him not only of his means of assessing truth claims, but also the metaphysical foundation for his own views (p. 167). His own theology must be power-orientated, an expression of his own will-to-power, and therefore to be viewed with the deepest suspicion. What class interests really lie behind his work? What hidden agenda? The fact that Niebuhr himself overlooks exactly this point in respect to his own theology immediately disqualifies him by his own rules from the list of those we should listen to. Although his feminist and Liberation theologian critics overlook this angle, in fact their critique reveals exactly this point, that Niebuhr's theology is an expression of white, male, middle-class existence. Furthermore, in his ongoing criticism of liberalism and Marxism he reveals the very intolerance he views as symptomatic of those yet to realise that '*their* truth is not *the* truth'. Niebuhr needs an explicit epistemology, and his position is dangerously weakened without it.

Epistemology Part 2: Reaching the will-to-power effectively

Introduction

We have seen how Niebuhr's theology is essentially a response to the reality of human nature as he perceived it, summarised in the Nietzschean phrase 'the will-to-power'. The nature of the will-to-power emerges in his anthropology and doctrine of sin, and shapes his doctrines of salvation and Christology. Most importantly we have seen how the focus of his theology concerns dealing with the will-to-power in such a way that its malevolent characteristics are dealt a determined blow. His doctrine of salvation basically consists of demolishing or shattering the will-to-power, to make way for the entrance of the power of God. It is clear, however, from our

---

[222] Carnell states, 'Niebuhr, indeed, cannot be consistent in his skepticism, for his dialectical theology fairly bristles with finality claims...An absolute impasse must be admitted' (p. 241).

discussion of his view of reason, that the role communication must play in the event of salvation particularly, cannot be fulfilled by the rational faculty. Reasonableness is no match for the will-to-power, and reason is enslaved by it for the task of survival. Effective communication is necessary, though, if salvation is to occur. In this section of the chapter we will see how Niebuhr's theological agenda of providing a response to the will-to-power radically shapes his epistemology.

At this point we should recall one of the aspects of the will-to-power as Niebuhr perceives it: it is not rational, and cannot be governed by reason. In dealing with the will-to-power, therefore, normal methods of communication based on rational arguments, persuasive though they may be, will only fail. As far as Niebuhr is concerned, employment of reason for overcoming the will-to-power can at best only curb some of its excesses, and at worst, actually provide it with justification for its actions. Niebuhr's epistemology, therefore, revolves not around reason but other, non-rational forms of communication, particularly myth, symbol and paradox. These means of confronting the will-to-power are what Niebuhr emphasizes particularly. There is also another feature of Niebuhr's non-rationalist epistemology: it is his explanation of the successful communication of ideas too subtle for rational grasp. It is to this second aspect of his epistemology that we will turn to first.

Three roles for epistemology

1. THE REVELATION OF PROFOUND TRUTH

In our discussion of Niebuhr's cosmology, and also in the sections on Pragmatism and Romanticism, we gathered that, for Niebuhr, power defines reality. This is crucial because it is contrary to more rationalist conceptions of existence. For the rationalist, the rational is the real and the real the rational; hence reason accurately describes reality and thought can be used effectively for description and analysis, and also to bring about change. For Niebuhr this is not the case: it is (non-rational) power which constitutes existence. This means that, contrary to rationalist perceptions, the employment of reason for the task of uncovering the true nature of reality ultimately fails. To uncover the deepest truths, particularly those which reveal aspects of transcendent realities, other forms of communication are necessary. Rationalising such truths only leads to depriving them of their depth and power, oversimplifying and distorting the truth to fit into some artificial pre-set pattern.

In response to the perceived shortcomings of reason, Niebuhr presents an alternative epistemology as the means by which ultimate truth may be revealed. He gives more emotive types of communication such as myth, symbol and paradox as replacements for rational dogma in revealing true religion. Where the eternal, transcendent aspects of reality – the nature and will of God, the ideals of society, the possibilities of humanity – break through into the immanent realm, dogmatic expression fails to communicate them effectively. Myth, symbol and paradox, on the other hand, achieve this end. The nature of reality as power-based, non-rational and infinitely complex means that similar forms of revelation are necessary for its expression. In the revelation of transcendence, a different order of being from the cosmos emerges; thus normal forms of epistemology arising from the cosmos (including, for Niebuhr, reason itself) are inadequate to deal with it. For the expression of transcendent, eternal, infinite realities, particularly those concerning the nature of God, special forms of revelation are necessary. Here, for Niebuhr, the limitations of reason as part of the immanent, temporal, finite realm emerge most clearly; thus his 'low' view of reason complements his understanding of the cosmos in contrast to the transcendent realm.

> Every authentic religious myth contains paradoxes of the relation between the finite and the eternal which cannot be completely rationalized without destroying the genius of true religion.[223]

> Naturally rational theology has difficulty in bringing the paradoxes of this mythological conception into the canons of rationality. In both orthodox and liberal theology the profound mythological conceptions of the incarnation and atonement are rationalized and their profundity is endangered by canons of logic and consistency.[224]

Mythological thinking particularly is more profound than reason, and so more effective as a means of communication than its rational counterpart in this sphere. It is able to grasp reality in its true nature without distortion. Concepts such as Creation, Fall, Incarnation, Atonement or Eschaton cannot be expressed rationally since the systematising effects of reason distort the subject-matter.[225]

In Niebuhr's thinking epistemology has three points of relevance. The first concerned the effective communication of profound truths; the second is the event of divine encounter which brings salvation.

2. BRINGING DIVINE ENCOUNTER

In previous chapter sections, we saw how, for Niebuhr, the nature of sin, particularly original sin, consists of pretence, of carrying out the egoistic agenda of the will-to-power under the guise of selfless ideals. Integral to

---

[223] *ICE*, p. 24.
[224] *REE*, p. 287.
[225] See *BT* Chapter 1 especially; also *ICE*, pp. 24, 82-94; *REE*, p. 217.

the work of salvation is the overcoming of that pretence in such a way that the true nature of the person as finite and sinful, and so desperately insecure, can emerge. This can then proceed into repentance, throwing the self upon the mercy and power of God for salvation. For this to happen, however, it is necessary for the self to understand its true state. This is a matter of revelation since it involves the stripping away of pretence till reality emerges. Salvation therefore requires revelation: and this is a matter of knowledge.[226]

It is clear, however, that Niebuhr regards the power of reason, which might be seen as suitable for this work, to be inadequate. Reason is no match for the will-to-power, and it is equally impotent in the area of salvation. Consequently, more than rational dogma is required to bring about true, heartfelt repentance and thence salvation. The will-to-power is not rational; nor are the nature of reality and the being and activity of God. Communication that is effective for salvation must therefore consist not of logically derived doctrines, but of the shattering personal encounter with the power and transcendence of God. In this moment of salvation the self knows its true state and its total dependence upon God; and the experience, essentially mystical in nature, comes about through non-rational means.[227] Relating to God in a way which engenders new life is a matter of encounter, repentance, faith and commitment, not doctrine.

> The self is not related to God by sharing its reason with God and finding a point of identity with the divine through the rational faculty. The self is related to God in repentance, faith and commitment. All these forms of relation imply a certain degree of existential discontinuity with God. The self is always a creature, conscious of its finiteness, and equally conscious of its pretension in not admitting its finiteness. Insofar as it becomes conscious of its pretensions it is capable of repentance and a new life. The encounter with God is in short a dramatic one.[228]

As regards the matter of encounter, means of facilitating encounter are necessary; and if being is non-rational, then a non-rational form of communication must be used. Furthermore, the situation which brings salvation cannot be described rationally: the mystical event of a individual confrontation with God, the change in personal nature, in fact all the realities which collide at this moment are all non-rational by nature and defy rational systemisation. The event of judgment, therefore, and the metaphysical realities which lie behind it, such as the Atonement and the grace of God, lie outside the realm of reason; and this means that they cannot be described accurately by rational means.

---

[226] *NDM II*, pp. 66, 132.
[227] *ICE*, p. 99; *SDH*, p. 84.
[228] *SDH*, pp. 84-5.

The moment of salvation is also an event of power. With reason inimical to passion and vitality, using rational means of encounter and communication would not facilitate the event but rather inhibit it. The means of connection between God and sinner conforming in nature to the power which flows from one to the other, bringing judgment, repentance and new life, the process of salvation is aided, whereas rationalised dogma would stifle the experience and render it impotent. For the encounter to be effective it is necessary to set aside analysis and calculation and simply *be* in the presence of God. Employing rational criteria for the event detracts from it, depriving it of too much of its impact. It is essentially an existential encounter, a matter of being, which emerges in truth, power and salvation. Not only is the event essentially mystical; attempts to analyse it fail, and result in logical absurdity. Salvation itself, for Niebuhr, begins with self-knowledge, and for this to occur, effective means of communication which bring non-rational forms of reality to bear upon the non-rational will-to-power are required, and these must have non-rational elements themselves to work properly.

Besides these two aspects of Niebuhr's epistemology we should consider a third – the transformation of the will-to-power by transcendence so that its energy can be put to positive use.

3. MAKING USE OF THE WILL-TO-POWER

We have already considered how, for Niebuhr, the self consists basically of a nucleus of energy with an attached self-consciousness, with the latter playing a secondary role to the former. It is through the self-consciousness that the will-to-power is reached; but, as essentially opposed to reason, this is best and most powerfully influenced by forces which are likewise non-rational. The will-to-power can master reason, and so rational methods are unlikely to bring about a significant change in its nature and agenda and enable it to conform to such things as the will of God. Other forms of communication may be more successful.

Success in influencing the will-to-power is worth pursuing. As the cause of the evils of history, its power is beyond dispute. Furthermore, realistically, it takes power, force, coercion, to resist the will-to-power, establish justice and maintain the well-being of other, weaker members of society in the face of it. The power of the will-to-power, although naturally disposed towards egoism, can in theory be influenced and so turned towards better ends. Niebuhr's position is that, by effective manoeuvring, it can itself form that source of power to be used to stand against the wills-to-power of others. His point is that, in the will-to-power lies the very force necessary to battle with and, to a degree overcome, its own evil. Of course the success of this project will be limited, in effect consisting of no more than a balance of power between competing forces.[229] Niebuhr still regards this to be worth striving for, the best to be hoped for in a sinful world – an aspect of his Christian Realism. A valuable part of his theology which emerges here is that he gives a significant role to human energy and activity in the task of overcoming evil – a position which West and Diggins identify with Pragmatism.[230] Niebuhr is realistic about the limited effects of using the will-to-power to overcome itself; and this reflects his genuine insight into the depth of the problem of sin in humanity and so the ultimate impossibility of humanity overcoming its own evil. At the same time, though, Niebuhr can give this limited role to humanity to play in the task of salvation. Permanent, eternal salvation can only come from God; but temporal, provisional 'salvation', in terms of improving the situation for humanity within certain limits, is very much a human task. Niebuhr thus establishes two important theological positions, rarely combined: total dependence upon God for salvation, yet a positive role for humanity to play. This achievement is to be highly regarded, and worthy of more discussion than we have room for here.

Niebuhr therefore has a commitment to human energy and activity. To this end he employs his unusual epistemology in a third way, namely to bring about higher levels of vitality, in a more moral form than the will-to-power's natural egoism would otherwise provide. This revolves around providing the situation in which the self becomes aware of ideal possibilities impinging upon it in such a way that it is drawn towards them and becomes inspired to strive for their realisation.[231] The situation consists of encounter: the will-to-power is brought into relation with transcendent realities which activate it. One of the main examples Niebuhr uses is the Kingdom of God, 'an absolute society in which the ideal of love and justice will be fully realised'.[232] The dream of the ideal possibility draws the person towards it, giving inspiration to act, to fight against evil and oppression and to establish a better world. For Niebuhr, this excitement, leading to self-sacrifice, action and change, can only come about when the person is brought into contact with transcendent realities.[233] As we have seen, for Niebuhr, the non-rational forms of communication of myth, symbol and paradox are necessary for the 'coming close' of these forms of transcendence to the will-to-power in such a way that the ideals are communicated effectively. When this happens, the self's agenda is radically altered. Under the influence of the ideal, the goals and objectives of the person's agenda shift direction away from self-service into the

---

[229] *MMIS*, pp. 19-21, 270-2.

[230] See 'God, Freedom and Evil', in the section on William James above.

[231] *MMIS*, pp. 221-6.

[232] *MMIS*, p. 60.

[233] From the cosmological chart of Appendix 1, the second dualism, natural transcendence and also the transcendence of God.

service of the ideal. The shift is never complete – the person remains sinful, and in fact to some extent the ideal becomes the justification for the self's egoism (Niebuhr's doctrine of original sin) – but it is certainly significant, and directs new and substantial resources away from oppression and selfishness into justice and love. When this happens on a large enough scale, the force of the wills-to-power fighting for justice outweighs the force of the wills-to-power acting solely for their own ends, and society is changed for the better, most dramatically by revolution and war, but better by democratic means such as protest and effective vetoing.[234] Again, for Niebuhr, reason is not the means by which this happens.[235] It is by establishing a powerful relation between potent ideals and the will-to-power that the will is engaged in this way. For Niebuhr, it is not necessary for this effect to occur by means which would normally be regarded as religious.[236] However, he concentrates on religious concepts, such as the Kingdom of God or the nature of Christ mediated through myth and symbol, to describe how this powerful connection is made; and as is now clear, these are not rational but rather emotion-charged methods of communication. By working through identity, imagery and emotive symbols, such as embodiment of race in a monarch, the ideal society or the tragic hero, the transcendent possibilities of history are brought to the will-to-power through the self-consciousness in order to condition and inspire it. As connections between non-rational realms, these are essentially opposed to reason and resist rational interpretation. Their effect is real, though illogical. Myth, symbol and paradox provide non-rational power conduits between different forms of existence in a way which transforms the lower into something resembling the higher. They could be seen in terms of channels from a higher to a lower level, by which the potential energy flows down through the symbol from the transcendent realm to the immanent, activating the immanent to rise towards its ideal possibility.

Underlying this view of Niebuhr's is his cosmology of transcendence and immanence. We will now consider how this dualism sets up the activating tension between the real and the ideal which inspires the will-to-power to strive towards its ideal possibility.

---

[234] *MMIS*, pp. 250-6.
[235] 'Reason enables him, within limits, to direct his energy so that it will flow in harmony, and not in conflict, with other life. Reason is not the sole basis of moral virtue in man. His social impulses are more deeply rooted that his rational life. Reason may extend and stabilise, but it does not create, the capacity to affirm other life than his own.' *MMIS*, p. 26.
[236] He often discusses the Marxist dream of an equalitarian society, for example, in similar terms. However, Niebuhr also regards the post-revolutionary Utopian ideal as 'essentially religious' (*MMIS*, p. 61).

Setting up the tension of impossible ideal

In the cosmology section of this chapter we discussed how Niebuhr makes use of three types of dualisms. In the second of those, the distinction between transcendence and immanence, we saw how he identifies two orders of existence within Creation: one of which we see as the real – that which exists now, 'how things are'; and the other the ideal – 'how things should be'. For Niebuhr these are both substantial, 'real' in the sense that they exist; but while one consists of actuality, the transcendence above it consists of possibility, the ideal which the real should be and would be if it was not for human sin. In relation to the actual, there exists its ideal possibility, that which the actual should be, its very best.

The difference between these two realms forms the means by which the true nature of the real is revealed. It is in contrast to its ideal possibility, which 'hover[s] over every social situation as an ideal possibility',[237] that the shortcomings of the real are exposed. By being aware of what should be the case, what is actually in existence can be compared with it and judged. At each moment, therefore, as history unfolds, Niebuhr presents a situation of ongoing contrast, in which that which *is* is compared to that which *should be*, with the result that its failure to conform to its best possibility is exposed.

> The dimension of depth in the consciousness of religion creates the tension between what is and what ought to be. It bends the bow from which every arrow of moral action flies. Every truly moral act seeks to establish what ought to be, because the agent feels obliged to the ideal, though historically unrealized, as being the order of life in its more essential reality. Thus the Christian believes that the ideal of love is real in the will and nature of God, even though he knows of no place in history where the ideal has been realized in its pure form. And it is because it has this reality that he feels the pull of obligation.[238]

It is by being aware of these ideal possibilities that the person can judge circumstances, personal behaviour or the social situation and become aware of their shortcomings. Furthermore, in awareness of the ideal, the sheer value and greatness of what the real could be dawns on the self and energises it. Through the vision of the perfect society, the person sees society, with its selfishness, greed and violence, as it really is and is appalled. At the same time, and by the same vision, the dream of living in the ideal society, in which evil, injustice and misery have been banished, spurs people on towards achieving it.

---

[237] *CPP*, p. 25.
[238] *ICE*, pp. 18-9.

Doctrinal Motifs in Niebuhr's Theology

The crucial element of this situation is that the ideal world seems *possible*.[239] It is when it seems to be within reach that people are prepared to make the hard sacrifices necessary to bring it about. There must be a tension between what is and what could be, such that the difference is regarded as bridgeable. When the goal is perceived to be impossible, too far out of reach to be considered realistic, this tension is broken, resulting in indifference, apathy, even despair.[240] This forms the basis for Niebuhr's antagonism towards Neo-orthodoxy, which he perceives to be too pessimistic about the possibilities of (sinful) humanity and society within history. By emphasising sinfulness too heavily, he argues, Neo-orthodoxy makes the task of overcoming any of the effects of sin in society too great for humanity to achieve. The result is a lapse into indifference as the hopelessness of the task of self- and social- improvement emerges, and excessive dependence on God is engendered when in fact humanity itself has the power to make a difference. This is part of his critique of absolutes, in which the absolute nature of original sin particularly negates any finite human tendency to deal with the consequences of sin. The absolute nature of sin places the ideal possibility so far out of reach that the tension between the real and the ideal is broken, and the motivation for change is lost.

At the other extreme, it is possible to merge the real with the ideal prematurely, in such a way that the real is mistaken for its ideal possibility. This is the fault he perceives with liberal Protestantism and the doctrine of Progress, in which the Kingdom of God is thought to have already been attained to a substantial degree.[241] The prosperity and reasonable levels of justice attained in some societies result in those who benefit from it believing that the battle to realise the ideal has already been won. The sacrifices and hard choices needed to realise true social harmony are deemed unnecessary.

For Niebuhr, the task of successful ('prophetic') Christianity is to be seen in terms of maintaining this ethical tension. When Christianity becomes too strident in its denouncements of human failings, society loses heart and slides into indifference. On the other hand, the failure to denounce sin at all results in complacency, as people overlook their shortcomings and those of their society, and imagine that perfection has already been achieved. The contribution of religion is to establish the ideals of humanity in the first place, particularly through such impossible commands as those given by Jesus in the Sermon on the Mount, and relate society to them in such a way that the ideal is seen as possible but not actually achieved.[242] By setting up such absolute standards of personal and social holiness, relative human

---

[239] *ICE*, pp. 113-7, 126-31.
[240] *ICE*, pp. 114-6; *CPP*, pp. 193-6.
[241] *ICE*, pp. 20, 58, 126-8; *NDM I*, pp. 315-8.
[242] *DCNR?*, pp. 69-96; *ICE*, pp. 31, 130; *BT*, p. 246.

achievements are exposed and judged for their shortcomings, but at the same time the exciting possibilities of the ideal emerge and inspire people to strive harder in order to achieve them.

> The ethical fruitfulness of various types of religion is determined by the quality of their tension between the historical and the transcendent. This quality is measured by two considerations: The degree to which the transcendent truly transcends every value and achievement of history, so that no relative value of historical achievement may become the basis of moral complacency; and the degree to which the transcendent remains in organic contact with the historical, so that no degree of tension may rob the historical of its significance. [243]

Christ's teachings are for Niebuhr one of the most important sources of ideal possibilities. Central to Christ's position is the ethic of the Sermon on the Mount. On the one hand, these teachings are presented as direct, uncompromising instructions: 'If your right eye causes you to sin, gouge it out', 'If someone strikes you on the right cheek, turn to him the other also'. Jesus presents his instructions as actions intended to be carried out. They are *possibilities*, given to humanity for us to live up to. At the same time the actual task of fulfilling them is impossible.[244] Christ's teachings directly contradict the agenda of the will-to-power, which all human life is engaged in and which it is impossible for sinful humanity to escape from. They are wholly opposed to those prudential councils which expect a certain degree of moral self-sacrifice but fall far short of radically challenging the will-to-power's agenda in this way.[245] Highest on the list of Jesus' commands is the 'law of love' which is the law of life, bringing harmony between all people and nations: to love others.[246] This is the ultimate 'impossible possibility': possible, because Christ carried it out, and instructs us to do likewise; impossible, because the will-to-power which governs all human activity will never be overruled by human means to the extent that total, freely given self-sacrifice for others will occur.

According to Niebuhr, Christ recognised the impossible nature of the Sermon, even while he presented it as a possibility.[247] Its task is not to provide an ethic which we can adhere to comfortably. Rather, it is intended to reveal transcendence in relation to immanence: the ideal of what humanity should be doing, in order to expose the shortcomings of what it is actually achieving. The person then goes on to recognise the need for divine grace, for repentance and forgiveness for failure, and thence to living

---

[243] *ICE*, p. 19.
[244] *ICE*, p. 113.
[245] *ICE*, pp. 48-63.
[246] *ICE*, pp. 69-71, 117-22; *NDM I*, pp. 304-17.
[247] *ICE*, pp. 130-31.

in the power of God. It is through the revelation of such transcendence that the person comes to self-knowledge, repentance and forgiveness, and from there, seeking to serve God better and live by divine power instead of the will-to-power.

Myth, symbol and paradox

The task of religion, then, is to bring salvation – first to the individual through personal encounter with God; second, and in a less absolute way, to society, by influencing and directing the will-to-power in such a way that it is employed to overcome the effects of evil, to some extent, in this world. We have already seen how Niebuhr understands reality, power and the will-to-power primarily in non-rational terms. It now becomes a matter of seeing how he employs his distinctive epistemology for the task of relating the powerful elements which exist in the transcendent realms – God himself, history's ideal possibilities – to the will-to-power in such a way that the purposes of God are achieved.

As we have already discussed, Niebuhr employs the epistemological concepts of myth, symbol and paradox as the means by which these different forms of existence are correlated. First we will deal with myth and symbol, since Niebuhr often uses these terms interchangeably, and also because they serve a dual function of both revelation and inspiration. His idea of paradox is slightly different in that he tends to regard it primarily as a means of revealing transcendent truths too sublime for effective rational analysis, without the inspirational element. There is, however, a certain amount of overlap with these three types of expression, such that Niebuhr will sometimes describe the Kingdom of God, for example, as having a 'paradoxical' relation with the world. Largely this seems to be due to his loose use of the term, and so here the discussion of paradox has been narrowed down to the few cases where it can genuinely be applied.

1. MYTH

For Niebuhr, myth, like symbol, plays a dual role. Its primary function is to reveal realities from the transcendent realm within the immanent realm of human history. Myths reveal the eternal within time, the infinite within the finite, the Creator present within the Creation.[248] Through myth, understanding arises concerning matters which stand apart from the created realm. Such things include the true nature of the cosmos as the conscious work of a personal God who, though involved in his Creation, stands apart in being;[249] and it is by the Creation myth of Genesis that we come to know these things. As transcendent truths, myths express something of an existence which lies beyond normal human experience and therefore

---

[248] *ICE*, pp. 22-3, 93.
[249] *REE*, p. 200; *BT* pp. 7-8; *NDM I*, p. 143.

normal types of epistemology. It requires something different, more subtle than scientific reports or even philosophical discourses.

The first task of myth, then, is the revelation of transcendence to immanence. The second is to establish the ethical tension between the real and its ideal which is necessary to bring judgment and inspiration to humanity. Myths contain unresolved states of tension between situations which would otherwise fail to become related in an effective way.[250] Through myth, the self becomes conscious of its true nature and the substance of its existence, achievements and environment in a way which does not occur by any other means. Perhaps this is due to the interpretative nature of myth in which, rather than being presented with a logical argument, the person encounters the story, and identifies personally with the unfolding drama. This is particularly the case in tragedy, where an almost mystical identification of the observer with the events on stage provokes the passionate catharsis of 'pity and terror'. In the case of myth, the reader becomes personally involved in the plot, resulting in an individual interpretation of the events, personalisation of the consequences, and, through its power, an actual change in the person's life. Through myth, the existence of the ideal 'comes close' to the life of the person in such a way that the ideal is related to the person in a potent, personal, individualised way, impossible for more rational approaches to truth.

The Fall

Perhaps the clearest example of Niebuhr's view of myth is to be found in his treatment of the story of the Fall.[251] He clearly regards the status of the Fall as pure myth and without historical foundation.[252] In fact he goes so far as to criticise severely those who attempt to interpret any or all myths, including Creation, Fall and Eschaton, literally. Instead of an event of pre-history, the Fall is for him the moment-to-moment shortfall of the real in contrast to its ideal possibility. The Fall is act-centred, ahistorical, a matter of ongoing experience for each person throughout history. How does this work?

It may be recalled that, for Niebuhr, the concept of original sin relates to the self disguising its actions by pretending to act according to selfless ideals, when in fact it is acting selfishly. For him, then, there is a difference between the ideal which relates to the action, and the action itself; and this is essentially his position regarding the Fall. Prior to any given act, the self-consciousness becomes aware of the ideal possibility of that act, what the action should consist of in terms of altruistic self-sacrifice for selfless ends. It is this ideal which originally inspires the self to act, and remains the

---

[250] *ICE*, pp. 38, 44, 82-5, 93-4, 130.

[251] *ICE*, pp. 86-92; *BT*, pp. 10-3; *NDM I*, Chapter X, especially p. 284.

[252] *ICE*, pp. 100-1; *BT*, pp. 10-1; *FH*, pp. 33-4, 166.

justification for its activity throughout. However, momentarily, the self becomes aware of the wider implications of the act, particularly the advantageous and detrimental consequences for itself. In line with the agenda of the will-to-power, which constantly seeks its own security and well-being, the self considers the action it intends to carry out, not only in respect to its original idealistic intentions, but now also in respect of how the action might benefit itself. It then subtly distorts its activity in such a way as to minimise its own losses and maximise its gains, perhaps by avoiding some of the more costly aspects of the action while emphasising any elements which will bring it rewards. By the time the action comes to be performed, its original nature as a moral act of self-sacrifice has been compromised. It has been assimilated into the agenda of the will-to-power and made to serve its purposes. The act is still carried out under the guise of the original ideal; but its true nature is now egoistic.

This means that there is a distinctive, qualitative difference between the act and the ideal it was originally meant to serve; and it is this which is the shortfall Niebuhr has in mind for his account of the Fall. It is clear, then, that apart from presenting a story to account for the origins of human evil, this has very little to do with the Genesis account. For Niebuhr, 'Original Righteousness' corresponds to the righteousness of the original intention, before it was compromised by the will-to-power's agenda. The Fall itself occurs with each action, as it falls from its original moral perfection into actual sinful self-interest.

> The perfection before the fall is an ideal possibility which men can comprehend but not realise. The perfection before the fall is, in a sense, the perfection before the act. Thus we are able to conceive of a perfectly disinterested justice; but when we act our own achievements will fall short of this standard...Self intrudes itself into every ideal, when thought gives place to action.[253]

> Adam was sinless before he acted and sinful in his first recorded action. His sinlessness, in other words, preceded his first significant action and his sinfulness came to light in that action. This is a symbol for the whole of human history.[254]

The ideal, however, continues to exert its influence on the real. The self remains aware of the ideal it first acted under, and cannot help but realise that the reality of its actions falls far short of the original ideal.[255] The contrast between what is and what should have been, arising from a

---

[253] *BT*, pp. 12-3.
[254] *NDM I*, p. 296.
[255] *NDM II*, pp. 112-3.

consciousness of the real in relation to its ideal, sets up the ethical tension in the person to strive harder to be a better person. The sense of guilt and failure arising from constantly having one's actions judged by the ideal galvanises the person into striving harder to achieve a higher standard of moral behaviour.

This constant shortfall also makes the person aware of the ongoing need for God's grace. It is only by the grace of God that the person and his activities can be seen as righteous in any way. Through this realisation pride is avoided. However, the matter of grace in this context is peculiar. Thelen argues that, for Niebuhr, grace consists of God accepting the original righteousness of the act, under the first inspiration of the ideal, as its true nature rather than the actuality, crediting the person's action with the 'righteousness of Christ' despite its true nature as sinful.[256] If Thelen is correct, then Niebuhr's doctrine raises serious problems in that it seems to imply an act-centred concept of salvation, in which the activity of the person rather than the person himself is accepted by God. Niebuhr hardly mentions this doctrine, and though it warrants further analysis it is not relevant to our discussion at this point.

The main problem with this position, however, is that it consists of a 'Fall into particularity'. The contrast is between perfect transcendence and imperfect immanence. Furthermore, Niebuhr makes clear that *all* human action, from the very beginning, fails to live up to its ideal possibility. If some concept of a historical Fall were incorporated into his theology, this would not be such a problem, since it could be posited that, while this may be the case today, it was not always so, and the ongoing failure of the real occurs not because of the way God made us, but because of human sinfulness. As Niebuhr's theology stands, however, it must be the case that as soon as humanity emerges, with its self-consciousness and will-to-power, so must its failure to conform to the ideal. This means that humanity is effectively created in a state of moral failure and hence sinfulness. However Niebuhr interprets it, asserting an ahistorical Fall inevitably yields a humanity which is created fallen and hence sinful.

A second problem, related to this, is that it leaves the question of the origins of sin completely unanswered, unless Niebuhr takes the unpalatable route of accepting that humanity was made sinful by God. This in turn would open up the difficult issue as to why humanity then deserves eternal punishment for sin. It also questions the status of the Cross of Christ as a gracious gift from God to humanity, and makes it instead the means by which God corrects his own mistakes. It is no coincidence that Niebuhr presents the origins of sin as a 'paradox' – or rather either a total mystery, or a truth with consequences to dire to explicate. Niebuhr's ahistorical Fall

---

[256] Thelen, Mary F., *Man as Sinner in Contemporary American Realistic Theology*, (New York: Kings Crown Press, 1946), p. 107.

pushes him into a dead end here, and proclaiming the origins of sin to be a mystery or paradox is an unacceptable solution.

The third problem, brought up by Meyer (p. 131), is that according to this scenario, the moral quality of the action is determined solely by its relation to the transcendent. Its consequences in relation to the fabric of history and society are absent. Effectively, this means that the action occurs in a vacuum, with no real connection with past or future actions, or the rest of humanity. Maybe this is a good thing, in that it removes the criteria of judgment from society and places it in a transcendent location, thus setting up a mechanism for absolute judgment between act and ideal divorced from cultural norms. The danger, however, is that the action's consequences in this realm can hardly count for anything. If the criteria for judgment lies outside the historical/social sphere, then the effect the action has in that sphere is ultimately irrelevant; and since the action *always* falls short of the ideal, the difference between the relatively good versus the relatively bad action ceases to count. Niebuhr thus stands in danger of undermining one of his most important contributions to theological ethics, namely that historical consequences *do* count and make a difference, and so human activity is significant despite its sinfulness. There are no safeguards in his theology of Fall as act to prevent historical distinctions, and the significance historical action has, being lost.

2. SYMBOL

Symbols work in a similar way to myths, to the extent that Niebuhr often uses these terms synonymously; but unlike myths, symbols are discrete, concrete historical entities. The Cross is a symbol, the Kingdom of God a myth. Symbols, like myths, provide a revelation of transcendent realities which are too different from historical realities to be expressed through the usual historical forms of epistemology. A rational attempt to dissect a symbol and the way it influences history will fail, since its source, its communicatory nature and the will-to-power which it reaches are all, essentially, alien to reason. A symbol will point beyond itself to something in another realm. It exists as itself, but in its manifestation it carries with it the attributes of other orders of existence. In bringing in qualities from other realms, it embodies the eternal in the temporal, the infinite in the finite, the complete in the incomplete, following the pattern of myth. In the limitations of the finite object, the qualities of that which it represents are revealed in a way which defies rational analysis; and, as an expression of the transcendent within the immanent, the potency of the transcendent is channelled through the symbol into the existence of the will-to-power through the self-consciousness, changing its self-understanding, nature and direction.

The most important Christian symbol is Jesus Christ. Christ is the manifestation of the eternal in time, the infinite in the finite.[257] In the finite body and human person of Jesus, God enters history in the form of a man. Christ is therefore both the ideal human being, and God the eternal and infinite Creator. God is revealed in the finiteness of Christ, and Christ points beyond himself to the transcendent God whom he represents.

This means that, on the one hand, Christ is the perfect human: in him, uniquely, the real and ideal merge, showing humanity as it should be. The possibilities of humanity, what humanity is capable of, are therefore revealed in Christ. On the other hand, Christ is the symbol of God, an actual manifestation of the transcendent realm within history.

> Christ is the symbol both of what man ought to be and of what God is beyond man. In Christ we have a revelation of both the human possibilities which are to be fulfilled and the divine power which will fulfil them. [258]

It is through Christ that we come to know who God is, and what humanity, in God, could become. The Cross of Christ is the ultimate symbol, since here the Cross is instigated under the highest of ideals, the law of love, and, most importantly, carried through as selfless love untainted by the will-to-power. This means that no Fall occurs between ideal and act, since the law of love progresses from one to the other without compromise. Christ's total trust in the power and love of God enables him to avoid the selfish grasping at power which characterises the agenda of the will-to-power, and carry through a life of pure ideal-realisation, free from sin. Following the Cross comes the Resurrection, the symbol of God's power overcoming the tragedy of life. While it is Christ's sinlessness which brings him to the Cross, it is God's power which carries him beyond death into Resurrection. The Cross therefore forms the symbol by which the power and workings of God are revealed definitively. Christ and the Cross thus form the most crucial Christian symbols, providing the revelation of transcendence, but also the realisation of humanity's ideal possibility, an inspiring vision of its actuality.

3. PARADOX

The third motif in Niebuhr's epistemology is that of paradox. This is similar to myth and symbol in that it forms a way of holding together complex and profound truths which would be disassembled by rational systematisation; it differs in that, unlike myth and symbol, paradoxes provided no stimulus for change. They are simply forms of revelation for transcendent realities.

---

[257] *BT*, pp. 13-24, 192.
[258] *BT*, pp. 23-4.

It should be noted that Niebuhr uses the term 'paradox' loosely and often with very little consistency.[259] At times he simply means to refer to concepts which could in principle be clearly expressed but only at the price of certain unfortunate consequences.[260] As is the case with the origins of sin, this can be the result of badly formulated ideas which he has not thought through properly. In other cases Niebuhr uses the term 'paradox' for something which might be better described as a mystery, for example the Trinity. In still other cases, he seems to use the word purely for rhetorical reasons: an exciting term to capture attention, where actually he means irony, such as the 'paradox' of the oppressed having to act selfishly to achieve justice.[261]

Perhaps the only genuine paradoxes concern the entry of the infinite into the finite. Some aspects of God's being or activity may correctly be thought of as paradoxical: predestination not precluding human responsibility for sin, perhaps. Niebuhr presents one of the key questions of his thought in terms of paradox, which is the 'prophetic question' of the relation between justice and the mercy of God.[262] For Niebuhr, this matter cannot be solved by rational consistency;[263] and this emerges in his doctrine of the Cross: a symbolic event revealing God's mercy and judgment combined. The clearest case of paradox, though, is the Incarnation, in which two natures, one eternal, infinite and divine, the other finite, temporal and human, exist in the same person. For Niebuhr, this key Christian doctrine can only be expressed in terms which outrage 'all the canons by which truth is usually judged'.[264] Whether in fact this is a 'contribution to doctrinal theology of the first order', as Lehmann states, is open to question, however.[265] First, this only follows Kierkegaard's lead, and therefore cannot strictly be considered an original contribution; second, Lehmann argues that Niebuhr breaks the traditional stalemate regarding the two natures of Christ and how they might relate to each other by his employment of paradox. In fact all Niebuhr has done is re-classify the doctrine, labelling it paradoxical rather than mysterious. This solves nothing and gives no new insight into the content of the doctrine; in fact it simply states it to be essentially irrational, and is no help at all in justifying the doctrine or explaining its meaning.

---

[259] As Tillich points out, 'Reinhold Niebuhr's Doctrine of Knowledge' in *KB*, pp. 35-44 (pp. 38-9).
[260] Cf. Williams in *KB*, pp. 225-8.
[261] *REE*, p. 266.
[262] *NDM I*, p. 152; *NDM II*, p. 219.
[263] *CPP*, pp. 197-8.
[264] *BT*, p. 14.
[265] *KB*, p. 276.

Considerations

Niebuhr's epistemology raises a number of questions. First it must be asked if the epistemology he employs, and the cosmology which underlies it, are strictly Christian. We have already considered the strongly Platonist undercurrents of his hierarchy of being, and the approximation to the Forms to which his transcendent realm corresponds. It seems that his epistemology carries with it similar semi-pagan connotations. The irrationality of being finds little biblical support, and neither do the symbols which are supposed to communicate between different orders of being. Furthermore, if biblically the Logos is the substance of the cosmos, and our world is ordered and consistent enough to be identified with reason to a significant degree, then for Niebuhr's view of reality as non-rational and power-based, and by implication unordered, self-justifying or even self creating (as sin and evil seem to be for him) is at odds with the biblical picture and has dangerously dualist undertones. In particular, his heavy deployment of myth, symbol and paradox as the primary means of revelation sits uneasily with the traditional understanding of revelation in terms of the Word of God. It is necessary to approach this area of his thought with caution. Too many of his commentators accept his use of myth with little, if any, criticism or thought as to whether his use of them is Christian or ought to be accepted.

There is a second matter related to this. Hofmann identifies Niebuhr's use of myth with orthodoxy's concept of Word as the means by which God reveals himself (p. 77). In fact, however, there are substantial differences. Most importantly, myth is impersonal, and describes non-historical situations which can then be interpreted and appropriated personally. They begin impersonally, and become personal. Biblical revelation, however, begins with a person - God - and proceeds through personal interactions - encounter and Word - to bring personal involvement between believer and God. Biblical revelation is personal throughout, a fact reflected in the key biblical concept of covenant: a personal promise given by one person to another. In Niebuhr's theology, though, the personal element only emerges with the believer. 'Transcendence' is not personal. Furthermore it is never clear with Niebuhr whether the transcendence or 'ideal possibility' he is speaking of is God himself (personal), the will of God (still personal to some extent, since it reflects God's desire for the situation) or the ideal possibility of history itself (impersonal). The account of the transcendent force which draws humanity upward towards its ideal possibility gains nothing by adding a force which is personal (God), and loses nothing by removing it. The account given here tends to focus on Niebuhr's early works such as *ICE*, *REE* and *BT* because his epistemology of myth, symbol and paradox emerges there most clearly, and at that stage of his life he was clearly more liberal than later on. However, the same ideas emerge in *NDM I* and *II* and *CPP*.

A third point here is that, if Niebuhr sees myth as the revelation of transcendence, then other myths, apart from Christianity, must reveal truth in the same way, in fact with equal validity and accuracy. Hence the pagan myths of ancient Greece and Rome, or Manichaeism, or Hinduism should also be regarded as the authentic revelations of God. The lack of personhood in his understanding of transcendence threatens the Christian identity of his theology and leaves him open to manipulation by pluralists, who could argue convincingly from his theology that he must regard other forms of religion, likewise expressing their truths in mythical ways, to be of equal validity with the gospel and the personal involvement by God with his chosen people.

A fourth matter concerns the danger of relativism which comes with Niebuhr's approach. As we have seen, Niebuhr's epistemology starts with the impersonal and becomes personal by individual interpretation and appropriation. The problem is that this creates an essentially subjectivist theology, in which truth emerges by each individual interpreting the symbols of faith afresh. This is the opposite of dogma, in that it allows each individual to interpret unchanging truths anew,[266] but while this helps keep faith fresh and relevant, the problem is that it provides no external criteria for assessing truth claims. Truth becomes what the individual perceives it to be. This means that, in theory, *any* personal interpretation must be accepted, however outlandish. Furthermore, faith and interaction with God become matters of (non-rational) personal experience or encounter with some form of supposed transcendence.[267] Ultimately this means that the object of faith can be dismissed as no more than some subjectively-generated idea, imposed on a specially chosen cultural symbol – the substance of Feuerbach's critique of religion. Religious experience becomes nothing more than subjective impressions mediated through myth or symbol: a dangerous position against which Niebuhr has no theological defence.

The final criticism for this section, made by several of his commentators, is that Niebuhr's lack of metaphysics results in his failing to establish or clarify the status and metaphysical structure of myths and symbols.[268] What is the difference between myth and symbol? How do they actually connect different realms of being? Why are they effective? Do all symbols have equal validity? Are some human constructs and others divine, or are all divine (or human)? How can you tell? What is real in them, justifying belief, and what is only perceived?[269] As Calhoun notes in his review of

---

[266] Cf. Rasmussen, pp. 28-9.
[267] Grenz and Olson, p. 111.
[268] Heim, Mark S., 'Prodigal Sons: D. C. Macintosh and the Brothers Niebuhr', *Journal of Religion*, 65 (1985), pp. 336-58 (p. 353); Bennett in Landon, pp. 91-3; Richardson in *KB*, p. 247-8; Tillich in *KB*, pp. 38-9; Thelen, pp. 110-11.
[269] West, *American Evasion*, pp. 156-7.

NDM II,[270] the lack of methodological principles for interpreting them carries the danger of a return to the allegorical method, in which the meaning of the symbol rests entirely with the perceiver, and thence it is only a short step to subjectivism (p. 61).

The result of this significant flaw in his theology is that we are made unsure of the status of so many key Christian doctrines. Sooner or later Niebuhr presents virtually every Christian doctrine in terms of myth or symbol: Creation (*ICE*, pp. 32-7; *BT*, pp. 7-10), Fall (*BT*, pp. 10-13; *NDM I*, pp. 281-5, 293-7), Christ's life, teachings, death and Resurrection (*BT*, pp. 13-18, 290, 304; *REE*, pp. 287-8), Atonement and grace (*BT*, pp. 16-18; *REE*, p. 290), Eschaton (*BT* pp. 182-93, 282; *NDM II*, Chapter X, especially pp. 297-312) and the Kingdom of God (*ICE*, pp. 42, 68, *BT*, Chapter 14). How are we to understand these? Are they all mythological or symbolic, with no real historical substance? Should we take any of them literally (apparently not) or even seriously? With no principle of interpretation, Niebuhr simply leaves these vital questions unanswered. For all its profundity, Niebuhr's use of existential concepts, but without Tillich's or Kierkegaard's dedication to metaphysical clarity, leaves him with dangerous gaps in his theology which undermine too many areas of essential Christian doctrine.

Christian Realism

Introduction

We have shown that Niebuhr's theological agenda consists of providing a Christian answer to the reality of human sin, which he identifies in terms of characteristics of the will-to-power. This task shapes his cosmology, anthropology, doctrines of sin and salvation, his Christology, and epistemology. Up to this point, however, we have considered only his applications of this agenda in terms of the individual. This reflects the fact that his doctrine of sin, and the means of overcoming sin through encounter with God, repentance and faith, revolve around the human personality. It is the individual's self-consciousness which gives rise to anxiety and the power-acquisition which is the will-to-power. It is also through the (individual) self-consciousness that awareness of God arises, bringing the possibility of repentance, which can progress into salvation by the person's surrender to God, and the appropriation of divine power for living. Thus

---

[270] Calhoun, Robert L., 'Review of Niebuhr, Reinhold, The Nature and Destiny of Man, Vol II: Human Destiny, *The Journal of Religion*, 24 (1944), 59-64.

we see that the foundations of Niebuhr's theology revolve around the individual person.

Niebuhr's concept of sin, in terms of a force corresponding to the nature of the will-to-power, remains constant throughout his theology; the means of dealing with the will-to-power, however, changes according to context. While the task of salvation consists of dealing with this force effectively, the nature of the task depends on whether it is an individual who is being dealt with, or a corporate body. Niebuhr's primary mechanism for salvation lies with the individual, with its focus on love, forgiveness and ultimate dependency. An individual will generally respond positively to such an approach, based on the law of love, and so relationships between individual people work well along these lines for the mutual benefit of all concerned. It is Niebuhr's belief, however, expressed radically in his first major work, *MMIS*, that this approach fails to work in areas of life where people operate on a collective basis.[271] This means that corporate relations, concerning groups of people rather than individuals, demand a very different ethical approach. Where corporate bodies such as socio-economic classes, large corporations, races or nations are concerned, the employment of the law of love, consisting essentially of selflessness, is self-defeating. It results not in mutually-beneficent harmony, but ruthless, even vicious exploitation. An alternative is needed, which must remain ultimately accountable to Jesus' commandment to love others, but is effective in dealing with the reality of the will-to-power as it emerges in the field of collective relations.

Niebuhr's position regarding group ethics follows from his (individual) anthropology and concept of sin as the will-to-power. As we have seen, for him a human being consists of a will-to-power with an attached self-consciousness. The self-consciousness has a moderating influence on the will-to-power, curbing its excesses and also providing the means of encounter with God which brings truth, repentance and salvation. The self-consciousness, however, is essentially individual, involved with its own will-to-power and having only a limited influence even there. Where the will-to-power is concerned, on a number of individuals coming together, the quantity and power of the will-to-power grows disproportionately, forming a kind of 'critical mass'. The self-consciousness does not generate in the same way, and so its influence does not grow in proportion to the will-to-power. Where a group forms, self-conscious restraint becomes impotent relative to the force of the combined wills-to-power.

> In every human group there is less reason to guide and to check impulse, less capacity for self-transcendence, less ability to comprehend the needs of others and therefore more unrestrained egoism than the individuals, who compose the group, reveal in their personal relationships.

---

[271] *MMIS*, pp. 257-72.

The inferiority of the morality of groups to that of individuals is due in part to the difficulty of establishing a rational social force which is powerful enough to cope with the natural impulses by which society achieves its cohesion; but in part it is merely the revelation of a collective egoism, compounded of the egoistic impulses of individuals, which achieve a more vivid expression and a more cumulative effect when they are united in a common impulse than when they express themselves separately and discreetly.[272]

It seems that Niebuhr sees the will-to-power working more effectively 'en masse', while the self-consciousness, being personal/individual, only has sufficient effect to influence its own will-to-power which, when united with others, becomes increasingly domineering. So it is that an angry mob, though composed of individuals, will carry out actions which no individual alone would ever consider. This means that, as group size increases, its behaviour as will-to-power becomes progressively less moderated and more unpleasant.[273]

Apart from acting more aggressively, the loss of the influence of self-consciousness also means that the means of salvation effective for individuals ceases to work. The group will-to-power simply lacks the resources of self-consciousness to bring about repentance and salvation and for the law of love to work for the good of those concerned. A different moral approach is needed to overcome the effect of the group will-to-power:[274] one of which is more forceful, even brutal, sufficient to stop collective egoism getting out of hand and marauding against weaker members of society who would otherwise be defenceless against it: the old, the poor, ethnic minorities, even weaker nations. If this different ethical approach works, vulnerable members of society will be protected from stronger aggressors, and a state of justice will be achieved. It is this task, of providing the theological resources to deal effectively with the will-to-power at a corporate level, that is the crux of Niebuhr's 'Christian Realism'.

Christian Realism

1. SOCIAL REALISM

Niebuhr's response to the problem of the will-to-power at a corporate level begins by establishing the precise constitution of society and social relations. This requires setting aside what he considers to be naïve, optimistic expectations of humanity and society, prevalent in liberalism and

---

[272] *MMIS*, pp. xi-xii; see also p. 85.

[273] *MMIS*, xii, xxii-xxiv, 267-70.

[274] The theme of *MMIS*, expressed most concisely in the Introduction; see also p. 257; *CRSW*, p. 64; *CPP*, p. 13; *FH*, pp. 91-2.

humanism, and facing humanity's true nature. Building on the basis of his anthropology and doctrine of sin, Niebuhr makes it clear that the true, unchanging nature of humanity is the will-to-power. The social consequence of this is that the era of peace and goodwill, the Kingdom of God, expected particularly by the liberals he opposed, would only be realised in the transcendent, ideal possibility of the Kingdom of God, and never within history. The constant lust for power which is the will-to-power will continue to emerge in aggressive domination as long as humanity continues in its unredeemed state. This means that conflict in society is inevitable; indeed, the use of force is a constant necessity as aggressive wills-to-power are fought against to prevent their exploitation of others.[275] Violence in society, then, is not to be seen as a temporary phase, an aberration, but on the contrary will always be, in fact should always be, present. Where struggle ceases, it is because one will-to-power has gained unchallengeable ascendancy and can now successfully dominate its rivals; and this is not a state of justice, but the exact opposite.

This means that conflict is to be expected in society and planned for. It also means that force must be used if justice is to be achieved. This is the controversial conclusion Niebuhr first reaches in *MMIS*. For Niebuhr, the reality of the will-to-power, seen most visibly in the corporate realm which is the political arena, results in will *always* seeking to dominate will, and this agenda is intrinsic to human nature. Furthermore, as we have seen, the will-to-power can only be reached and changed effectively in the individual person, where the power of God can replace human power as the means of survival. Reason has a difficult enough task to control the will-to-power on the individual level; on the corporate level it is practically impossible: the most powerful body simply overwhelms its lesser rivals, no matter how good their arguments. Only when it is confronted by an equal or greater force will it alter its course. Coercion, therefore, is necessary to force powerful bodies to change direction, and power is the resource necessary for establishing justice.

> Since reason is always, to some degree, the servant of interest in a social situation, social injustice cannot be resolved by moral and rational suasion alone, as the educator and social scientist usually believes. Conflict is inevitable, and in this conflict power must be challenged by power. [276]

2. HUMAN POSSIBILITIES

The second aspect of Niebuhr's thought directed towards dealing with the will-to-power in society is his agenda of doing justice to the possibilities as

---

[275] *MMIS*, pp. xv, xx, xxiii, 89, 231.
[276] *MMIS*, pp. xiv-xv; see also pp. xvii- xviii.

well as the limits of humanity.[277] His doctrine of sin, soteriology and eschatology make it clear that ultimately it is only by the power of God that we are saved from the will-to-power, not only in the personal realm but also in society. It is by the power of God that history unfolds and society is changed for the better. However, human society will only be made completely righteous at the Eschaton, when it really does become the Kingdom of God, a realm of holy people under the complete and direct authority of God. In the meantime, Niebuhr regards it as humanity's task to carry out its part in the work of making a better world. Niebuhr therefore seeks to give proper respect to the human contribution to be made in the work of maintaining society during this age, particularly the task of establishing justice in society. He is convinced that humanity has an important part to play here, and that human power is essential for standing up against aggressors and protecting the weaker members of society. As we saw in the section on epistemology, important areas of his thought concern generating human vitality by the use of myth and symbol – an energy which can then be used to fight against the evils of society.

This means that, for Niebuhr, the means of overcoming the will-to-power in society actually revolves around redirecting the will-to-power for this task. As Hinze states, 'Sin-tainted power-over is a primary tool for the accomplishment of "social sin," yet, ironically, Niebuhr also views it as the primary weapon for checking that sin.'[278] The person inspired by transcendent ideals retains his nature as a will-to-power, even though he is changed by the encounter with transcendence. It is through ideals such as the Kingdom of God that the will-to-power's nature and agenda are influenced; but a will-to-power it remains and, as such, is a crucial source of power to be employed in the task of fighting evil. Again, this emphasis he lays on human vitality as the means by which evil is overcome is the factor picked up by West and Diggins in their identification of him as a Pragmatist.

An important part of Niebuhr's theological response to the will-to-power, therefore, is his agenda to do justice to the possibilities, as well as the sinful limitations, of humanity. His experiences in Detroit and of the US confronting Hitler showed him that to a large extent it is human action which overcomes the evils in history, not rational arguments, or a misplaced belief in the power of human love, or even a passive expectation of divine intervention. It is when human beings stand up and fight against aggressors that evil is defeated; and Niebuhr, with his strong social conscience and practical ethics, is determined to give full weight to this fact. Within this, he maintains the constant factor of the will-to-power as the basis of his calculations. Christian Realism, therefore, consists neither of asserting the importance of negotiating with the aggressors, who in fact

---

[277] *NDM I*, p. 161; Hofmann, pp. 109-10.
[278] Hinze, p. 86.

are not open to reason, nor of asserting the potency of human love, nor even advocating religious activities such as prayer, but rather understanding the nature of sinful humanity, and making effective use of this knowledge in society. This means employing will-to-power against aggressive will-to-power to counter its own worst effects.

It should be noted here that its ability to do justice to both the possibilities and limits of humanity is a major reason why Niebuhr is convinced of the accuracy and value of Christian doctrine.[279] It is his regular argument that only in Christianity can the correct balance be found which recognises human sinfulness (and therefore the reality of the will-to-power), but also the possibilities humanity has for overcoming evil. This forms the basis of his arguments against all rivals to Christianity (and those within the Christian tradition with whom he disagrees), that they focus either on humanity's limitations, and so lapse into pessimism, or on humanity's possibilities, in which case the will-to-power is not understood, and an unwarranted optimism emerges. Much of Niebuhr's theology, therefore, is centred on revealing his opponents' failings in this matter and establishing his own theology as recognising both humanity's limitations and possibilities, since it is only with such a balance that the will-to-power can be recognised and effectively met.

Power and justice

We have seen that Niebuhr regards power as an essential aspect of human relations, particularly in the corporate sphere. In the cosmology section we saw that he presents two kinds of power at work in the world: the holy power of God, in which power and goodness work together to carry through the divine purposes of God; and human power, which is the will-to-power, power corrupted by anxiety and self-seeking, such that power contradicts goodness. The former consists of the Kingdom of God, under the direct authority of God, the latter the Kingdom of the world, where the will-to-power sets the agenda.

In the human realm, it is the will-to-power which provides Niebuhr with his model of power. To quote Hinze, it is 'power-over' rather than 'power-to' that is at work here: power which is domineering, self-serving and aggressive (pp. 4-5, 64). It is intent on enslaving and exploiting those around it to secure its own well-being. Thus human power has a clear-cut identity such that, when encountering other forces, it is intent on mastering them and making them conform to its nature and purposes. Most importantly, it is antithetical to goodness: as we saw in the section on salvation, Niebuhr presents his interpretation of the Cross and Resurrection in terms of them demonstrating the destruction of goodness when

---

[279] *REE*, pp. 114-6, 203-4; *NDM I*, pp. 140-41.

encountering the will-to-power, but then a consequent reliance upon God for power when goodness is chosen. For Niebuhr, the will-to-power effectively defines human reality, in such a way that, the power of God aside, it is necessary to conform to the will-to-power in order to survive. Standing against the will-to-power and taking the route of selflessness results in destruction.

Niebuhr's understanding of human power, arising from his analysis of human nature in terms of the will-to-power, is therefore largely negative. He quotes Lord Acton's dictum, 'All power corrupts; and absolute power corrupts absolutely', with approval.[280] For him, the influence of human power is destructive. It corrupts goodness, demands conformity to its egoistic nature and destroys those who attempt to resist it. This is the definitive type of power at work in our society, to the exclusion of all alternatives. But this means that only the will-to-power is available to humanity for the vital task of resisting the will-to-power. Since, as we have seen, the will-to-power is opposed to goodness and love, Niebuhr's 'realistic' model for society is not the community of love as presented by his liberal forbears (and also by the Marxists in respect of a post-revolutionary society), but rather a society of justice. For him, this consists of a balance of power in which conflicting organisations are set against each other to ensure that the more aggressive groups are counterbalanced effectively by opposing forces.[281] This situation, however, is essentially unstable, an 'uneasy truce' in which powerful groups, each with its agenda for power-acquisition, grapple for position. With this there is a constant threat of anarchy, even civil war, since the competing wills-to-power will all be attempting to gain ascendancy through the acquisition of power. This means that a powerful force is required to master the competing wills, so that power itself is the means by which society itself is held together.[282]

> [T]he internal justice of a community is never so perfect and the accommodation of interests so complete that any society could dispense with the alloy of coercion in the amalgam of its social peace. Nor is it possible to secure the external peace of a community in the partial, and sometimes total, anarchy of nations, without balancing power against power in times of peace and without setting power against power in times of war.[283]

To counter the disruption of the will-to-power, Niebuhr presents his concept of strong government. An authority is needed which will be

---

[280] *CPP*, p. 163.
[281] *MMIS*, pp. 4-6, 154-5, 231; *REE*, p. 230; *CPP*, pp. 26-7; Schlesinger in *KB*, pp. 136-7.
[282] *MMIS*, pp. 88-9; *CPP*, pp. 14, 124; *SNE*, pp. 31-3.
[283] *CPP*, p. 124.

powerful enough to control even the most aggressive groups within its borders and protect the more vulnerable members of society. Following Augustine, Luther and Hobbes,[284] Niebuhr's analysis of the will-to-power leads him to affirm a power-based doctrine of government, in which the ruling power must use coercion to counter the effects of the will-to-power, particularly in the corporate sphere. In *SNE* he goes so far as to praise Hobbes for his competent analysis of society and his affirmation of the necessity of state domination (p. 51). But Niebuhr is also a modern thinker, living in the age of democratic government; and it is this which saves him from the pessimism of Luther and Hobbes,[285] who wrote in the shadow of great political upheaval. Niebuhr's faith in democracy enables him to present an account of government more positive than mere dictatorship, and this despite his negative attitude to human power. For Niebuhr, the central task of government is to use force, where needed, to check the chaos inherent in a society composed of competing wills-to-power.[286] The problem is, of course, that since the identity of human power consists of the will-to-power, the employment of this power carries with it the danger of corruption, of conforming to the will-to-power's nature as a result of working with it closely. When this happens, the dominion of the government ceases to oppose the nature and means of operation characterising the will-to-power, and begins to fall in with it, finally assuming the tyrannical identity of the will-to-power itself. This is the danger that the (optimistic) Russian revolutionaries failed to identify: unable to see the reality of human nature and the will-to-power, they failed to foresee the effect (human) power would have on their new government, and left themselves completely vulnerable to the tyranny of the will-to-power in the form of the Communist regime.[287]

From what Niebuhr has to say about various governments it is clear that he regards strong government as a necessity for establishing a civilised society. However, at the same time he sees the danger of having a government which is strong enough to carry out the task of restraining the will-to-power of powerful groups. His answer to this situation is modern democracy.[288] Here, the most powerful body in society, the government, is held accountable for its use of power by society as a whole. While the government continues to serve its society by controlling anti-social elements, it has the support of the people it is meant to serve. However, once the influence of power takes effect and the government itself becomes self-serving, aggressive and unnecessarily domineering, the mechanics are in place for its peaceable removal and the election of a new, uncorrupted set

---

[284] Durkin, p. 91.
[285] Bennett in Landon, pp. 67-9.
[286] *NDM II*, pp. 275-9
[287] *MMIS*, pp. 192-6; *NDM I*, pp. 49-50, 110.
[288] *CPP*, pp. 26-7, 85, 93, 104.

of leaders. The new government is selected (in theory) according to its ability to serve the country as a whole. Once this new body becomes corrupted, it can also be removed. Furthermore, in a proper democracy, the government's opponents are also supported by the political system in such a way that they can influence the government and counteract its will-to-power tendencies for as long as possible while it remains in power.

For Niebuhr, therefore, democracy is a political system which arises out of the reality of human power in the form of the will-to-power. Democracy's basic premise is also that 'power corrupts, and absolute power corrupts absolutely'. Therefore it is a system designed to prevent the situation of absolute power ever arising. Even while the democratic government is 'in power', it is held accountable for its actions by the free press, the Opposition, the judiciary, the Church and so on; and its removal from power, should it become aggressive, is guaranteed. This is not to say that Niebuhr is excessively idealistic about democracy, and in fact he is at pains to make its shortcomings apparent.[289] Considering the nature of humanity, however, and the identity of human power, he regards it as the best system of government available.

Love, justice and pacifism

A final matter concerns the question of applying the law of love to the corporate sphere. Niebuhr's hostility towards the notion of pacifism in the corporate sphere becomes clear. He hold that pacifism, with its belief in seeking to overcome evil by loving one's enemies rather than fighting them, is the result of a misapprehension concerning the radical distinction between personal and corporate ethics. He considers the argument of pacifism to be based on the mistaken belief that the law of love, so important for individual relations, is in its undeveloped form, also the correct moral principle for corporate relations.[290] In one sense, Niebuhr actually agrees with the pacifists in that he considers the law of love to be the law for the whole of humanity, including the political sphere; but whereas in the personal realm a simple endeavour to love is reasonably effective for overcoming evil, in the corporate realm this is not the case, due to the very different dynamics which arise from the lack of influence from self-consciousness. For 'Immoral Society', carrying out Jesus' commandment to love does not so much mean acting selflessly, but rather using one's resources in such a way that other, weaker members of society are protected and justice is done; and this means being prepared to carry out actions such as imprisonment, even killing, which would not be considered 'loving' in the normal sense of the word, i.e. in the context of personal relations. However, while justice may work using methods incompatible

---

[289] *REE*, pp. 55-6, 61, 152-7.
[290] *CPP*, p. 4.

with love as it is seen in personal relations, this does not mean that justice itself contradicts love or remains incompatible with it, even when actions which would not normally be considered loving are carried out. As Carnell states, for Niebuhr,

> Justice is never discontinuously related to love, however. Justice is a negative application of love. Whereas love seeks out the needs of others, justice limits freedom to prevent its infringement upon the rights and privileges of others... Justice is a check (by force, if necessary) upon ambitions of individuals seeking to overcome their own insecurity at the expense of others. It is a mistake for the religious mind to disregard degrees of justice in society simply that the social ego cannot accommodate the purity and perfection of the law of love. Justice *is* love's message for the collective mind. (p. 224)

For Niebuhr, therefore, the expression of love in the corporate realm is the work of establishing political justice. It is by the effective use of power by government bodies to limit the effects of the will-to-power that the goals of love, particularly the prevention of domination and exploitation of others, is fulfilled. A simple application of the law of love in this sphere will not result in love's requirements being fulfilled, but rather the opposite: the ruthless domination by others in the will-to-power's agenda to master those around it. Only by the use of force can this be prevented. In that use, though, the demands of the law of love can be directly contradicted.[291] It is hard to see that shooting another person, even if they are part of an brutal invading army, complies with the instruction to 'turn the other cheek'; yet in Niebuhr's view, this is precisely what is required if the command to love others is to be genuinely fulfilled. Keeping one's own hands clean of murder while others are attacked and killed by the people one refused to kill is, for Niebuhr, not a victory for love but actually its negation, an abdication of responsibility towards those one is meant to serve and protect. Thus in considering the Nazi threat, Niebuhr's position is that pacifism is hopelessly naïve,[292] and would result in world domination by Hitler's forces. His work *CPP* is basically aimed at driving this point home. For Niebuhr, pacifism would result in 'peace at any price', a situation which would not only be unjust, consisting of appeasing aggressive wills-to-power while they exterminated their rivals, but also 'no peace at all', since those under Hitler would be at his mercy and constantly harassed by him, helpless to stand up against his aggression.[293] So it is that Niebuhr's understanding of human nature emerges in his Christian Realism, in which tough action is

---

[291] *MMIS*, pp. 257-72.
[292] *CPP*, pp. 167-8.
[293] *CPP*, pp. 14-6, 86-7.

taken against individuals in order to ensure that Christian ethics are genuinely carried out.

Considerations

There are a number of matters relating to Niebuhr's Christian Realism which need to be discussed. First, Niebuhr employs the will-to-power as the basis for understanding of power as a whole, and this results in simplistic 'pre-modern'[294] concept of power. Following the work of Foucault, Arendt and Giddens, the nature of power as complex, relational and intrinsic to human activity has emerged. Niebuhr's focus on the self as a nucleus of energy directed by the self-consciousness results in an view of power as something internalised in the human personality; consequently, he overlooks the relational nature of social power. When this combines with his existential leanings and concept of sin, he emerges with narrow concept of power as something operating from within the person to produce a largely negative effect. This means in turn that his response to power and the will-to-power is focused on shattering the individual self and dealing with the negative consequences of sin. With a broader understanding of power, he might be able to incorporate the effects of social relations into the equation, and be less concerned with the inner self. It also means that he regards society as perhaps less stable than it really is, since, with all the individual, easily-changeable wills-to-power active in their power-seeking agendas, rapid change in society seems more possible than actually occurs. This makes Niebuhr perhaps overly concerned with tackling the will-to-power to prevent it getting out of hand, which emerges in his approval of heavy-handed government. With more recent understandings of power brought to the fore, the effects of wayward individuals can be more realistically assessed, and the need for a whole society to participate in change rather than a few determined individuals recognised. This seems a more accurate understanding of situations like Nazi Germany, where it was

---

[294] 'Pre-modern' as opposed to a 'modern' concept of power such as Foucault's or those following after him. Axel Honneth argues that Foucault developed his confluctial, social and activity-based concept of model of power following the failure of both classical and Marxist political theories which were based on pre-modern power models. She states that a pre-modern model would regard power as a quality or substance, acquired by individuals or groups for their own use and able to be lost or gained through legal means or by force; whereas a modern perspective would understand power to reside in relations existing between active agents, deriving its effects from their activity and interaction. Honneth, Axel, *The Critique of Power: Reflective Stages in a Critical Social Theory*, trans. by Kenneth Baynes (London: MIT Press, 1991), pp. 152-61. See also Barker, Philip, *Michel Foucault: Subversions of the Subject*, (Hemel Hemstead: Harvester Wheatsheaf, 1993), pp. 77-82 and Hinze, pp. 111-26.

through the approval of the populace as a whole that the Nazis were able to carry out their atrocities against the Jews, and not simply a group of thugs operating on the fringes of society. This understanding of power, then, where power lies in relations and through consent and resistance rather than in the will of the individual, can be seen as a more realistic social model; and this in turn requires a model of ethics different from that employed by Niebuhr, which is aimed first and foremost to deal with the will-to-power within individuals.

Niebuhr's preoccupation with the will-to-power also results in an attitude towards power which might be considered unduly pessimistic. In her useful work, Hinze states that, to formulate an adequate Christian social theory, a balanced perspective on power needs to be held, in terms of its ability to bring about good as well is to destroy it (pp. 9-11). In her terms, understanding power as 'power-to', the means to change society for the better, is as important as recognising the dangers of 'power-over', or dominating power, if a positive role for Christian action is to be established. Of course Niebuhr does provide a positive role for power, in terms of its ability to stand up against aggression; but essentially this is employing 'power-over' against itself to achieve a positive result. This remains essentially pessimistic since it sees the only good use of force in terms of overcoming its own properties – a very negative perception. The opportunity power holds for actively building a better society, not just limiting the will-to-power, is generally absent from Niebuhr's account. This may be partly due to his reaction against optimistic social policies which saw power almost exclusively in terms of facilitating power and failed to see its detrimental nature; but it does leave a vacuum in the whole area of Christian social ethics which makes providing a positive, active role for Christians in society difficult to formulate. If political activity consists basically of using evil to combat evil till the power of evil overcomes us, then it is hard to see why Christians should engage in politics. This attitude also results in being too accepting of the violent use of political power for social control. Niebuhr, following Luther and Hobbes, understands the force of sin so well that he is inclined towards social pessimism and perhaps too ready to sanction heavy-handed government intervention when other, less authoritarian solutions might work just as well.

A third point, following from the second, is that, in drawing such a clear line between personal and social ethics, Niebuhr is in danger of collapsing the tension between the ethics of the Sermon on the Mount and the reality of corporate life. Niebuhr's view is not that the law of love is irrelevant to corporate relations, but rather that it needs careful application and modification based on the reality of the political realm. He is forceful regarding the very different natures of the two realms, in places going so far as to assert the incompatibility of ethics between the two realms based on their very different dynamics. The law of love remains relevant to the political sphere, however, in that it is love which must ultimately be the motivation for acting forcibly if true justice, and not domination, is to be achieved. It is in this sense that love fulfils or completes justice: it holds up a higher standard than simple domination of others for gauging whether an action really is selflessly seeking the well-being of others or is in fact a disguised bid for domination. Thus for Niebuhr the law of love is at least relevant, if not directly applicable, to the political sphere.

Even so, it must be questioned whether his position maintains the tension between the law of love and the reality of political life. Clark, a sympathetic reader of Niebuhr, considers him to set up too strong a division between public and private spheres (p. 151). If the two realms really are incompatible and work to such very different rules, then the ethics of love which are relevant to one sphere can easily be dismissed in the other. With such a vague and distant connection between the law of love and the use of force to fight against aggressors, it is to easy to give lip-service to the ideal of love while acting forcefully in a situation when less aggressive and destructive means might be equally effective. Ironically, Niebuhr's Christian Realism can be, and has been, used as the justification for 'Pragmatic politics',[295] in which moral standards are too easily understood to be 'impossible ideals' and therefore need not always be adhered to. If compromise is inevitable, and the use of force expected, then it becomes not the last resort Niebuhr intends it to be, but the first. As the feminist and Liberation theologians point out, Niebuhr's theology is for the powerful; thus, in understanding the critique most relevant to them, the power-wielders become the ones most aware of their inevitable shortfall and the impossibility of overcoming their own egoism. Thus it soon becomes acceptable to unleash their wills-to-power in the work of stopping others from gaining ascendancy.[296] For those in the US government, where Niebuhr's influence has been substantial, this is a most dangerous position to reach.

It must also be questioned whether Niebuhr's position on corporate ethics really does justice to the Christian message. Certainly at present it seems that the principle of the Sermon on the Mount is difficult enough in the personal sphere and impossible in political circles. But is this necessarily the case? According to Niebuhr's position, 'Immoral Society' is a fact, unchanging and beyond serious hope for redemption; but in reality, at the head of each corporate body stand individuals capable of influencing their corporations to act in a Christian fashion. Certainly the principle of 'turning the other cheek' is difficult here; but Jesus makes no corporate versus personal distinction, and is it not possible for those in charge of large corporations to consider the well-being of those around them and seek to act in a way which avoids ruthless exploitation? Using the power at the

---

[295] Clark, pp. 118-20.
[296] Clark, pp. 179-82.

disposal of a large corporation, it *is* possible for that company to act honourably, even selflessly towards its suppliers and creditors, paying on time, striving to provide excellent service without demanding excessive profits in return and responding to criticism with humility. Niebuhr is just too pessimistic regarding the possibilities for corporate bodies acting for the benefit of others, and business itself is criticised far too little by him (and other Christian commentators) for its 'business is business' approach, its all too often greedy, if not ruthless profiteering and its shirking of social responsibilities. A more positive ethic is needed so that the difference which an ethical corporation may make to a large number of people can be recognised and encouraged, and the unacceptable side of business can be seen as such.

A final matter which needs to be mentioned here regards the role of the corporate Christian body in this world, the Church, in implementing Christian ethics. Niebuhr simply fails to provide a doctrine of the Church as the body of Christ: a matter highlighted by numerous commentators.[297] There are two reasons for this substantial oversight in his theology.

The first is the previously-mentioned fact that the nature of God's involvement in the cosmos is never clarified by Niebuhr. It is difficult to determine where the line is to be drawn between human and divine activity, particularly where violence is used to bring about divine purposes, as it was during the Babylonian invasion of Judah. Niebuhr provides no criteria for identifying divine power rather than human power at work, other than the over-simplistic idea of divine power combining power and goodness and human power contradicting it. According to these criteria, the consistently aggressive nature of the political and business spheres exclude, by definition, the power and activity of God, for here, the qualities of the will-to-power determine the nature of the power employed. Niebuhr's whole Christian Realism is based on the idea that the use of coercion is necessary in the corporate realm; yet it is precisely this power which is antithetical to God's activity. Ultimately this must mean that God is excluded from working in the political arena: a wholly unacceptable position, clearly unscriptural and almost certainly not what Niebuhr intends. Without a better understanding of how God works in history, especially in the corporate sphere, it is difficult to decide what type of power is at work in a situation, and therefore what role, if any, God is playing. Unable to identify clearly the activity of God in history, God's action may be overlooked or even excluded from Niebuhr's account of political activity. Niebuhr fails to describe precisely how the Christian lives in relation to God on a daily basis, particularly in terms of what living by the power of God actually consists of; this results in something approximating to a deist perspective,

---

[297] See particularly Fox, p. 215; Hofmann, p. 246; Bennett in Landon, pp. 80-81; Wolf in *KB*, p. 248.

in which God has some vague overall control of the universe but no personal involvement. As Cornelison says, for Niebuhr

> God becomes reduced to a principle of transcendence which "impinges" on the world, not a personal God who acts in the world. The world is effectively closed off from God, and God seemingly remains aloof from it. God's grace does not penetrate the world in any concrete way. (p. 57)

In fact, God can be excluded from Niebuhr's account of Christian political activity with relative ease, so that it is difficult to establish the difference between a Christian political stance and an ethical but atheistic humanism.

The second reason for the absence of a doctrine of the Church emerges from another major theological inadequacy, also related to the problem of God's involvement in history: the absence of a doctrine of the Holy Spirit. Again, this is picked up by various critics.[298] Niebuhr fails to develop a doctrine of the Spirit, to the extent that, as Lehmann notes, his theology could be accurately described as binitarian.[299] Again, what emerges here is the liberal deist view of a detached God involved in history at nothing more than the most abstract level. In Niebuhr's theology, God is too detached from his world, especially his own people, and too impersonal. He says nothing concerning the way in which the Holy Spirit works in a personal way to sanctify and develop the individual Christian; neither does he describe the activity of the Spirit in drawing together a corporate body of believers to form a Christian community of faith. This reflects Niebuhr's general difficulty in defining and explaining the way God works within the historical framework to bring about his redemptive purposes. To quote Cornelison again,

> As has been often stated, one of the greatest flaws in Niebuhr's theology is his lack of a viable doctrine of the Spirit. This omission, it can be contended, is not an accidental one, nor an oversight in Niebuhr's thought, but is necessary for maintaining his understanding of the relationship of God and the world... In fact, the omission of the Holy Spirit seems to be necessary for the consistency of Niebuhr's theology as a whole... Nowhere did he explain how the Spirit works in the world.

---

[298] For example Cornelison (see quote below); Hofmann, p. 246; Plaskow, p. 158; and most vigorously, Rachel Hadley King's *The Omission of the Holy Spirit From Reinhold Niebuhr's Theology*. King contends that the absence of a doctrine of the Spirit is not accidental, but in fact reflects a deep-seated aspect of Niebuhr's worldview. 'His science-conditioned confidence that all events in the created universe have their causes in previous events in the created universe makes it impossible for him to believe in miracle and so rules out a belief in the Holy Spirit, in a genuine Incarnation, and in the continued existence of Jesus Christ after Calvary.' (Foreword).

[299] *KB*, pp. 277-9.

Nor did he adduce any concrete transformation of the world as a result of the activity of the Spirit. (pp. 58-9.)

This matter of God's involvement in history, most crucially through the Spirit, combines with his general pessimism regarding corporate bodies to deprive him of a doctrine of the Church as the body of Christ. With no doctrine of the Holy Spirit, he is unable to distinguish the Church from any other corporate body, with its own sinful power-seeking agenda. For him, the Church is essentially a human institution, and little more. He can give no account of the power of God at work in a unique way in the Christian community since for him there is no indwelling Spirit to differentiate it from another community. This means that the Church must be viewed with the same caution and hostility as any other corporate body. Some might consider this a valid, even important critique; the history of the Church contains its share of abuses. However, the result of Niebuhr's position is that the operation of the Church and the resources it brings to the political, as well as the individual realm, are overlooked. Corporate bodies *are* capable of ethical action and the bringing of 'other-regarding' principles to society as a whole. It is a pity that Niebuhr, fixed in his 'Immoral Society' mindset, fails to see this, and leaves the most important instrument for bringing God's influence to society out of his account of Christian Realism.

CHAPTER 4
Conclusion

Introduction

In this book we have sought to establish a new interpretation of Niebuhr's theology, namely that his work is an attempt to provide a Christian answer to the existence of human evil. The success of this interpretation entails certain consequences, first for the study of Niebuhr, but also for the wider field of theology, particularly the significant theological question of the problem of evil.

Consequences for the study of Niebuhr's theology

Over the last seventy years, commentators have attempted to provide a principle of interpretation for Niebuhr's thought by which his theology can be comprehended. His theology has been presented in various lights: as an attempt to come to terms with his liberal heritage; as a Christian Marxist approach to political analysis or practical ethics; as a Pragmatist effort to generate human vitality in order to overcome evil; and a Neo-orthodox attempt to re-establish the transcendence of God. The consequence of the argument of this book is that none of these accounts can be considered finally satisfactory. While Niebuhr's theology indubitably incorporates each of these factors, none of them can now be regarded as definitive. This is not to say that the work carried out by previous commentators is claimed to be obsolete; it means rather that when the claim is made that Niebuhr is ultimately concerned with political matters, or human vitality, or the transcendence of God, we must disagree. However, when or if we are prepared to acknowledge that Niebuhr is ultimately concerned with providing a Christian response to the will-to-power, a new coherence emerges in his theology.

First, we see how his relationships with the schools of thought discussed in Chapter 2 make sense: his disillusionment with liberal Protestantism and Marxism alike, which both failed to recognise the existence of this evil; his drawing on Kierkegaard's theology, particularly in seeking a psychological explanation for the source of sin; his use of Nietzsche's idea of the will-to-power, whilst recognising the destructiveness of that quality and hence his drawing back from embracing Nietzsche's pessimism; his appreciation of James' Pragmatism, particularly the Pragmatic method which gave him a practical, results-based approach to theology he could employ successfully for his own ends; and his battle with Barth, whom he saw as too negative in his evaluation of humanity's contribution to the fight.

Second, the underlying coherence of his own theology emerges. As we have observed, each area of his thought forms a part of a comprehensive framework by which humanity's sinfulness can be understood and responded to effectively. In his cosmology we discover his perspective regarding humanity's place in Creation, and why the world is such a hostile place in which to live. In his anthropology, and in his closely-connected doctrine of sin, we see how, for Niebuhr, the constitution of human existence gives rise to anxiety, which emerges in the sinful lust for power which is the will-to-power. In turn, this leads on to his doctrine of salvation, which consists of dealing with that anxiety and overcoming the effects of the will-to-power through the grace of God. His Christology also emerges in this context, whereby Christ and his Resurrection provide us with the ultimate demonstration of the power of God, and how we as Christians are to live in relation to that power.

His epistemology also develops according to the agenda set by the will-to-power, first in recognising the limitations of reason when it comes to fighting its effects, second in establishing a different understanding of other, non-rational forms of communication, which he sees as more effective when dealing with the will-to-power. Finally we can see how his Christian Realism emerges as the practical expression of this agenda, aimed most importantly at the realm of corporate relations which he regards as the area of life most in need of his new understanding of humanity. We have, therefore, a new understanding of Niebuhr's thought which can be employed to interpret his theology in a new way and bring out its underlying coherence. On the employment of this new understanding, disparate elements of his thought come together to form a unified whole.

The ability of this understanding to draw together the strands of Niebuhr's thought influences the way we view other studies of his work. Much of what has been written about Niebuhr deals with specific aspects of his thought, and so concentrates on the particular issues they are concerned with: his relationship with liberalism or Marxism; his anthropology, his Christology, and so on. So, for example, Lovin, Harland and Cornelison focus on his Christian Realism; Hofmann on his understanding of sin and salvation; and Clark on the contemporary consequences of Niebuhr's thought. This approach to Niebuhr is at its clearest in the Kegley and Bretall volume, whereby the various aspects of his theology are discussed in turn. The problem, though, is that this method fragments his theology, concentrating on the matter at stake without really demonstrating the coherence of the whole. In the Kegley and Bretall volume, for example, no attempt is made to demonstrate how the area of thought dealt with in each chapter relates to the whole; in fact it is difficult to determine, from that collection of articles, what Niebuhr's theology is really about, since so many different areas of interest are discussed. Elsewhere, there have been attempts to unite the disparate elements of Niebuhr's theology; but this tends to be in terms of his Christian Realism. Other areas of his theology are discussed only in so far as they impinge on this aspect of his thought, and are not therefore discussed and criticised in sufficient depth. Since the argument of this book is that his Christian Realism is an expression of a deeper agenda, that of dealing with the will-to-power, attempts which have been made to interpret his thought comprehensively along this line must finally be considered inadequate. An alternative approach, taken by Fox and Durkin for example, is to provide a summary of his work, either chronologically or by consistent themes in his work. While this provides some level of coherence, the sole connection running throughout the whole account is simply that it is Niebuhr's life and work, and once more this fails to demonstrate the underlying coherence of the work.

What seems to be lacking in the field of Niebuhrian studies is a fundamental interpretation of his thought by which all the various aspects can be united into one cohesive system. Lacking such an interpretation, studies tend to engage piecemeal with his thought, a valuable approach in itself, but frustrating without some means of placing the issue in question within the wider context. One purpose of this book has been to attempt this kind of synthesis. By employing the interpretative principle with regard to the problem of the will-to-power, it has been possible to formulate exactly the kind of over-arching comprehension which has not really emerged before. Even if the argument of the book is ultimately disproved, it is hoped that the interpretation given may prove to be sufficiently thought-provoking to stimulate further discussion, and to provide a starting point for the work of bringing the whole of Niebuhr's theology, unsystematic as it sometimes is, into a more productive cohesiveness.

Niebuhr's method: a Pragmatic approach to theology

We will now turn to another matter raised by our discussion, namely the Pragmatic approach Niebuhr employs for his theology. In Chapter 2, we demonstrated the way in which Niebuhr is to be understood as a Pragmatic thinker. Of particular interest is the question of whether Niebuhr's Pragmatic approach to theology, in which the practical issues of the day are allowed to set the agenda for his theology, could be usefully employed in the field of theology generally. Niebuhr's method is to take contemporary issues and, using Christian doctrine and modern insight, provide a useful theological response both intellectually vigorous and practical in its application. Should this approach be taken up by theology in general?

Positively, there is much to commend it. Niebuhr's method of engaging with relevant issues through books, journals and newspaper articles corresponds well with the traditional task of apologetics. His method of starting with something which is generally recognised to be a problem guarantees the relevance of his thought, at least while the issue remains live. This also makes his thought a matter of general interest, and not just to those within specialist theological circles. One of Niebuhr's greatest qualities was that people outside the Christian tradition found his work valuable. An important consequence of this was to bring Christian influence into the intellectual mainstream, particularly into the area of political analysis.[1] The approach of engaging piecemeal with specific issues as they arose, employing Christian insight to interpret them well and guide society to effective action, proved a valuable contribution to society and one which has helped restore and maintain Christianity's credentials as perceptive and intellectually coherent.

There are, however, a number of difficulties with this approach. The first is that, in taking his cue from world situations and the challenge of thinkers often hostile to Christianity, Niebuhr allows the agenda of his theology to be set by his surroundings rather than by the revelation of God. If theology is to be theology – the study of God – then, while relating that revelation to contemporary society is of crucial importance, to begin with society and its current issues and then seek to fit divine revelation in around it is to 'put the cart before the horse' as it were, and reverse the method of unpacking revelation which theology perhaps ought to employ on taking the revelation of God seriously. Niebuhr begins his theology 'from below' with the problem of evil, and takes Christian (and non-Christian) concepts to make sense of the situation with which he is concerned. He then returns to the world at large to offer his insight, engaging with issues using the arsenal of resources he has accumulated. While this makes his theology relevant, on occasions one must question whether it is strictly a Christian position he holds: as we have already discussed, his Platonist leanings, suspected binitarianism and lack of any substantial doctrine of the Church give cause for concern. By allowing his theological agenda to be set in this way, rather than beginning with biblical analysis, or careful consideration of Christian tradition, his theology develops unsystematically and in a way which some see as being at odds with orthodox theology.[2] This emerges in the way he allows his understanding of sin as will-to-power to dominate his thinking. Focusing on the single major factor he identifies as being responsible for the suffering he observes, his agenda becomes a matter of how to deal with it. This is to the detriment of other concepts of sin, as we have seen, and

---

[1] As Heather Warren points out, Niebuhr was one of a select group of theologians who substantially influenced Western governments as well as the Christian community, particularly before and during the Second World War. Warren, A. Heather, *Theologians of a New World Order: Reinhold Niebuhr and the Christian Realists 1920 - 1948*, (Oxford: OUP, 1997).

[2] This is Edward Carnell's concern in particular.

distorts his understanding of salvation and Christology. The result is a theology which is underdeveloped in the areas of Atonement, divine immanence and the Holy Spirit. These areas of doctrine are too important to be left neglected. The final consequence is that Niebuhr's theology, while relevant and thought-provoking, leaves one unsatisfied, even floundering in areas of great theological importance.

Second, the outcome of Niebuhr's approach is that, for him, theology becomes a matter of ethics. How are we to act, as Christians, in response to the will-to-power? This is his primary question, which emerges in his Christian Realism, his most substantial theological contribution. His Christian Realism continues to inspire monographs, while his doctrines of God, or Christology, or epistemology are rarely mentioned. The question must now be asked whether ethics is what theology, or indeed Christianity, is really about. Evangelism and the fulfilment of the Great Commission of Matthew 28, seen by some as the essential work of the Church, is rarely discussed by Niebuhr. His priority is to provide effective action against the will-to-power. However, this force is an aspect of *this world's* sinfulness – a world which in time will pass away. Where is the eschatological element in Niebuhr's thought, which looks forward to the end of this sin-dominated world and the start of the next one, free (one presumes) of the will-to-power entirely? In substance, it is reduced to ahistorical myth.[3] This means that in Niebuhr's understanding the will-to-power will always be present: there is no end to its dominion since God will not end it, and as a result, fighting it becomes a priority. His theology then becomes a matter of providing an effective response to the perpetual problems the will-to-power throws up. Of course it *is* necessary to provide a Christian ethic in response to humanity's sinfulness; the criticism here is that by presenting the Second Coming and the Kingdom of God in terms of a force *over* ongoing history, rather than the event which ends history, he effectively gives the world as it is a perpetual life-span, and with it, the dominion of the will-to-power. Therefore he loses his perspective that the will-to-power is temporary, provisional, and will ultimately pass away, and so is not necessarily the primary matter with which the Church should be concerned. Perhaps the biblical position is that our priority for this world is to preach the gospel and reap souls for heaven, allowing 'the world' to carry on its own way to ultimate destruction by the power of God at the Eschaton. Overcoming the world's problems, in which we as Christians are to see ourselves as essentially strangers, pilgrims passing through, is not necessarily the Church's first priority; and Niebuhr, by allowing the will-to-power to set

---

[3] Niebuhr's ideas regarding eschatology, particularly the status of the Eschaton, would benefit from further research and analysis. A useful area of further research would consist of unravelling his views, particularly concerning the relation between Eschaton as myth and as (post-) historical event, and how his eschatology influences the rest of his theology.

his theological agenda, becomes side-tracked from the primary task of preaching the gospel.

Our conclusion in this matter of whether to advocate Niebuhr's approach to theology is that it must depend on the field of theology concerned. In terms of forging a systematic, comprehensive theology covering the areas of doctrine necessary for a thorough, Christian understanding of life, this approach must be regarded as inadequate, even detrimental. If theology can be regarded as the unpacking of God's personal revelation, Niebuhr's approach is back-to-front in method and produces fragmented results. However, in certain areas of theology his approach may well be employed fruitfully. Although the primary focus of Christian life must be evangelism and discipleship, apologetics forms a vital part of the Church's duty to present Christian doctrine, including the gospel, as coherent and intellectually defensible. For this to occur, it is necessary to engage properly with the questions which a contemporary society brings forward. For Christians to engage effectively with the world around them, it is necessary to respond to the issues at stake, as Niebuhr did. The criticism made against him is that he allowed his agenda to be set too firmly by the issues confronting him, and that ultimately this had detrimental consequences for his theology. Perhaps Christian theology should start by establishing a biblical perspective on the matter in a bid to ensure that God's priorities for this world are made clear from the start. This can then proceed to considering the challenges of the present time, and again by use of biblical principles, formulating a response to them which, taking our cue from Niebuhr, should be relevant, intellectually rigorous and practical. By employing this method, a systematic form of apologetics might emerge which could avoid the flaws of Niebuhr's own theology while taking up the positive aspects of his approach, particularly his relevance and practical 'realistic' emphasis.

Niebuhr's theology as a response to problem of evil.

Our final area of discussion concerns the possibilities Niebuhr's theology holds for a solution to the long-standing question of the problem of evil. On page 2 of the Introduction to their collection of articles on the matter, Adams and Adams provide us with a concise definition of the problem.

> It is often seen as the *logical* problem whether the theistic belief
> 1) God exists, and is omnipotent, omniscient, and perfectly good, is logically consistent with
> 2) Evils exist. [4]

---

[4] Adams, Marilyn McCord, and Robert Merrihew Adams, eds., *The Problem of Evil*, (Oxford: OUP, 1990).

The argument is that, if God is really able to do anything, and is aware of the evils going on in the world, and is also perfectly good, then he would eliminate evil. However, the sufferings of the world seem to indicate that genuine evils do exist; therefore, it is argued, one of the attributes of God stated – omnipotence, omniscient, or perfect goodness – must be false. Since all of these qualities are taken as essential for the orthodox understanding of God's nature, the Christian conception of God must be false. One possible course is to deny the true evil of evil, claiming for example that evil is necessary for a greater good and therefore not ultimately evil at all. But this seems to dismiss the reality of people's sufferings. The alternative is to try and re-formulate the traditional notion of God, compromising either the divine omnipotence, or omniscience, or God's perfect goodness. None of these approaches has been entirely satisfactory, prompting J. L. Mackie to assert that 'there is no valid solution to the problem which does not modify at least one of the constituent propositions in a way which would seriously affect the essential core of the theistic position'.[5] Does Niebuhr's theology provide an answer to this, one of Christianity's most serious challenges?

When considering Niebuhr's response to the problem of evil, our first point of interest is that Niebuhr's theology reflects the fact that during this century, *human nature* has proved to be the main source of humanity's sufferings. Two world wars, Nazism and the Holocaust, Stalinist Russia, Cambodia, Rwanda, and Bosnia, to name but a few of the most obvious candidates were (and are) situations of appalling horror clearly created by humanity. What else apart from humanity's own destructive character could be blamed for these atrocities? At the same time, advances in scientific knowledge have made substantial inroads into overcoming 'natural evils' such as disease or famine. For the first time in history, humanity has emerged as the prime means by which suffering arises in Creation.

The modern problem of evil must therefore concern the shameful aspect of human nature which causes these problems. It is also this factor which is the focus of Niebuhr's theology, described by him in terms of the will-to-power. Niebuhr's theology, therefore, is directly aimed at dealing with the element in humanity which is to be identified as the real problem underlying the problem of evil. It is possible, then, that Niebuhr provides a theology which recognises the real problem of evil, i.e. as an essentially human matter; and he might also provide a solution. Two aspects of his thought are to be seen as relevant here.

---

[5] J. L. Mackie, 'Evil and Omnipotence', in *The Problem of Evil*, ed. by Adams and Adams, pp. 25-37 (pp. 36-7).

1. NIEBUHR'S PRAGMATIC APPROACH

Having discussed the way in which Niebuhr might be considered a Pragmatist, we can see how this emerges in his approach to the existence of human evil. He begins by allowing the reality of the situation to set the parameters for his discussion. Human evil he sees as a fact, empirically verified and encountered on numerous occasions; therefore its potency, violence and depth cannot, and should not, be doubted. However, God also exists. This is never doubted or discussed by Niebuhr, and simply regarded as a fact, beyond dispute. Given the existence of both God and evil, therefore, what is to be done with the situation in which humanity finds itself? he asks; and this progresses into his practical ethics.

This can be characterised as Pragmatic because as an approach to theology it is very similar to William James' approach to philosophy. Like James, Niebuhr is prepared to accept certain realities as given rather than theorising at length about their ontological status. The test he invokes to find the truth of an idea is then James' method of evaluation, namely assessing the difference made to a situation in which the concept is employed. This impatience Niebuhr has with metaphysics drives him beyond the fruitless, centuries-old debates about the existence of God and of evil, and settles him instead on the matter of what difference these things can, and should make to one's perception of life and the activities involved in living it. He regards the metaphysical debate to be simply irrelevant. Clearly evil exists; so does God, as far as he is concerned; Niebuhr's question then is what these facts together mean in terms of human possibilities of action. Thus the true evil of evil is not questioned, and neither are the important qualities of God. Niebuhr's approach in dealing with the fact of evil as a Christian can therefore be regarded as Pragmatic; dismissing metaphysics, he moves beyond sterile rationalist deliberation to establish a new 'problem of evil': what does evil actually consist of, and how shall we deal with it effectively, given the power, knowledge and goodness of God?

His approach, therefore, really changes the nature of the problem of evil. Unlike the formulation given by Adams and Adams, Niebuhr does not see the matter in terms of logic at all. His Pragmatic approach sidelines the question of logical incompatibility between God and evil and makes the practical issue of how to deal with reality the central problem. The logical element of the equation is reduced to the matter of how evil could have emerged in God's Creation in the first place – a question Niebuhr deliberately avoids answering by declaring it a 'paradox', beyond logical solution. While this might be frustrating, Niebuhr thus avoids becoming embroiled in a fruitless discussion for which centuries of debate have failed to provide a satisfactory answer. He is then able to concentrate on the matter he is really concerned with – dealing effectively with the will-to-power.

This practical focus indicates the second way in which his approach is basically Pragmatic. The result he is seeking is 'difference made', a change in the situation with which he is concerned. He is not seeking an understanding of the situation for its own sake, but rather in order to engage effectively with a real-life situation. The success of his theology, for him, is to be assessed, not in terms of rational coherence, but in whether it provides the means of overcoming the will-to-power. Hence his consistent work of writing on the issues of his time in a way which would enable Christian and non-Christian alike to act towards human aggression in a way he perceived would also maintain moral integrity. In his own Pragmatic terms, then, his theology must be considered at least a partial success if his 'Christian realism' was (and is) effective in facilitating moral action to fight the will-to-power.

Niebuhr's approach also responds well to both Liberation and feminist theologians who insist that it is activity which solves the problem of evil rather than rational discourse and analysis.[6] A major criticism made by Liberation theologians concerning traditional Western theology is that, by making human suffering a matter of abstract discussion, the concrete task of fighting tyranny, which can be bloody, is sidelined and undermined. To help the world's oppressed, action is required, and Niebuhr's theology goes some way to correcting this traditional deficiency. Andrew Kirk identifies five specific failings of 'North Atlantic' theology (*Liberation Theology*, p. 27), which include: language which is 'vague, unrealistic and non-conflictive'; an 'unjustified distinction between ethics and dogmatic theology'; and proponents who 'are not committed in practice to changing society, only to explaining and criticising it'. Clearly Niebuhr's theological approach is in tune with Liberation theology's requirements, due in part perhaps to their common grounding in Marxist political theory.

Similarly, a common perception by feminists is that if the time and energy taken up by debates about the world's evils were ploughed into the events which gave rise to the discussions, then the problems themselves could actually be dealt with and the problem itself would reduce or perhaps

---

[6] Gutiérrez, Gustavo, *A Theology of Liberation: History, Politics and Salvation*, trans. and ed. by Sister Caridad Inda and John Eagleson (London: SCM, 1974), pp. 13-5; Kirk, J. Andrew, *Liberation Theology: An Evangelical View from the Third World*, (Basingstoke: Marshall Morgan & Scott, 1979), pp. 26-7, 35-7. Jantzen, Grace M., *Becoming Divine: Towards a Feminist Philosophy of Religion*, (Manchester: Manchester University Press, 1998), pp. 146-7, 260-64; Dorothy Soelle, discussed in depth by Kenneth Surin in his *Theology and the Problem of Evil*, (Oxford: Blackwell, 1986), pp. 113-7; Johnson, Elizabeth A., *She Who Is: The Mystery of God in Feminist Theological Discourse*, (NY: Crossroads Publishing Co., 1992), pp. 252-71; Beverly Wildung Harrison, 'The Power of Anger in the Work of Love: Christian Ethics for Women and Other Strangers', in Loades, Ann, ed., *Feminist Theology: A Reader*, (London: SPCK, 1990), pp. 194-214 (pp. 201-12).

even disappear. 'By making it an intellectual problem to be solved, concentration on the adequacy or inadequacy of the preferred solution can take up all the time and energy that could otherwise be devoted to doing something about the suffering itself.'[7] Again, Niebuhr's Pragmatic approach helps direct resources away from dry academic discussions into the hard task of making the world a better place.

However, the question is, does this really provide the solution to the problem of evil? Niebuhr's avoidance of metaphysical discussion may allow him to move beyond the boundaries of a debate he (and others) consider pointless; but that does not mean that the debate really *is* pointless. Niebuhr's approach leaves important areas of theology neglected. These include a comprehensive statement of his definition of God and his grounds for believing that such a being exists. He also avoids the key question of how evil originally emerged in a cosmos wholly created by a perfectly good God. In declaring the origin of evil to be a 'paradox', he successfully avoids fruitless metaphysical discussion in an area he is not interested in; but if a coherent account explaining the presence in evil in God's Creation is to be provided (and this is a task with which theodicy must be concerned), then it is inadequate simply to separate off this question and state the matter to be a mystery. Hence while Niebuhr's theology may answer *a* problem of evil, in as much as Niebuhr provides an effective response to the existence of human evil, it may not be the case that he answers *the* problem of evil which has confronted theology at least since Hume wrote his *Dialogues Concerning Natural Religion*.

2. NIEBUHR ESTABLISHES THE PROBLEM OF EVIL AS HUMANITY'S PROBLEM

It appears, then, that employing Niebuhr's Pragmatic method may not solve the traditional problem of evil as defined earlier in this section. Is there another way in which his theology might achieve this task?

We have seen that Niebuhr establishes the problem of evil in terms of it being a *human* problem. It is humanity's sinfulness, the will-to-power, which is to be regarded as the primary source of suffering in the world. How then does this affect the problem of evil we defined earlier?

It must be noted that the understanding of the problem of evil as it emerges in the formulation above makes reference to certain selected qualities of God, and to some concept of evil, but nothing more. On consideration, it is clear that, whilst these two aspects of the situation are indeed crucial, they are by no means the entire picture. One of Niebuhr's primary achievements has been to establish a modern, empirically-based doctrine of human sinfulness. The result of this doctrine of sin is that he identifies humanity as the source of the evil he is concerned with. The traditional formulation, however, makes no mention of the source of evil. It

---

[7] Jantzen, *Becoming Divine*, p. 260.

states that evil exists, but does not consider that humanity itself might be its origin. There is no mention of humanity in the equation. This is the first point.

The second is that, in opposition to the sinfulness of humanity, Niebuhr asserts, amongst other things, the holiness and justice of God. Indeed, his important discussion of the 'prophetic question' of how God's mercy can be reconciled with his justice revolves around these divine qualities. Niebuhr's significant contribution to modern theology includes both his reinterpretation of the doctrine of original sin and a reassertion of the holiness and justice of God. He then acknowledges the dire situation of a sinful humanity before a holy, judging God, and with it the conflict between God's love for humanity and the necessities of divine justice. This creates an impasse which is broken by the Atonement. In Niebuhr's theology, sin is recognised in its full depth of evil, as is the holiness of God; and only by Christ's saving work is humanity spared the consequences of its sin. Thus the whole biblical dynamic of sin, wrath, judgment and grace is established in the modern context in a way which arises from the empirically-discerned existence of human evil.

This means that Niebuhr has established the problem of evil as humanity's problem. It is due to human sin that the suffering of the world arises. Furthermore, it is right for God to judge and condemn humanity for this sinfulness, and even to *increase* our sufferings beyond what would occur naturally, through human activity alone, as the just punishment for our sins. It is humanity's fault, in other words, that evil exists as it does in our world; and God, as the holy Judge, is righteous not only to allow our sufferings to continue (since they are of our doing, not his), but also to actively punish us for the evil we do to others. It is solely by the grace of God that this does not happen more than it does. Therefore our response to the existence of evil should not be to query the existence of God in the light of suffering but to acknowledge the fact that God's grace in Christ spares humanity the full consequences of evil. Niebuhr shifts the whole emphasis away from regarding ourselves as the innocent victims of unjust sufferings, for which we blame God and even dismiss the divine Person altogether, to the guilty perpetrators of endless crimes who deserve to suffer more than we actually do.

Let us consider the traditional problem of evil in this light. There, the qualities of God are listed as omnipotence, omniscience and perfect goodness; and in addition to these, evils exist. This is stated to be the full picture. However, we now know that this definition of God is inadequate. God is certainly these three things; but he is not just these three. Most importantly, he is also holy, and a righteous Judge. Furthermore, evil clearly does exist; but it is *human* evil. To present the existence of evil as discrete, separate from humanity, even self-existent, does not correspond to its true nature as emerging from humanity's sinfulness. This is Niebuhr's great contribution to theodicy. It is a restatement of a key biblical doctrine, the intrinsic sinfulness of humanity which deserves wrath but is ultimately overcome by God's grace. The evil with which the problem of evil grapples, therefore, is to be understood as a human problem.

This means that the view of God which the traditional formulation of the problem of evil presents should not be accepted, since it does not correspond to the Judaic-Christian understanding of God at all. It lacks the key elements of divine holiness and justice. It is closer, perhaps, to Plato's Form of the Good. Furthermore, the concept of evil it employs is inadequate. Evil is a secondary quality arising from human existence and therefore dependent upon humanity. The existence of evil in the cosmos is intrinsically bound up with humanity, to the extent that the elimination of evil would require the destruction of humanity. Again, the justice and holiness of God would emerge in wrath and do just that were it not for the love of God which bears patiently with humanity, proving an alternative to annihilation in the form of the Cross of Christ. It is by the grace of God that he allows evil to continue to exist, based on his love for humanity and his unwillingness to purge Creation of the real source of evil. That is the reason for the continuance of evil in the world, and not some lack of power, knowledge or goodness.

The contribution of Niebuhr's theology, therefore, leads us to redefine the problem of evil. It should now be stated as follows.

1) God is the holy and righteous Judge, omnipotent, omniscient and perfectly good (or better, perfectly loving).
2) Evils exist, arising from human sinfulness, a quality which is intrinsic to all humanity.

The issue which emerges from this formulation is not 'How can there be a God when there is so much evil?', but actually Niebuhr's 'prophetic question' of how a holy but merciful God can maintain his justice without destroying humanity. This establishes a very different perspective on evil and the problems it creates in God's universe. Humanity is no longer the virtuous victim of malevolence and injustice, but actually the source of the problem. It is not God who is put on trial, but ourselves. The real mystery of evil does not concern the existence or goodness of God, but how God can justify sinners while maintaining his justice. This sets the scene for understanding the need for divine grace through Christ's work on the Cross as the means by which evil can be overcome.

This new problem of evil is not based on humanist presuppositions regarding the supposed essential goodness of humanity, together with an insipid, indulgent Deity, but on a Christian position derived from a biblical understanding of sinful humanity and the revealed God. Of particular interest is the fact that Niebuhr's theology has such a strongly empirical basis, formulated from the terrible experiences of the twentieth century. It is more than just abstract doctrine, and carries the weight of empirical substantiation. It is the *reality* of sin which gives rise to Niebuhr's theology, and therefore to this new formulation of the problem of evil, and as such it is not so easily dismissed as dogmatic, obscurantist pessimism. This new formulation of the problem of evil emerges from this century's history, and the actual record of events which substantiate biblical doctrine. It is no longer a question of God having to justify himself to us, but rather the reverse. From here it is but a short step to the gospel of Jesus Christ, who does justify sinners before a holy God. The final solution to the problem of evil, in the light of Niebuhr's theology, is therefore the Cross of Christ. One hopes that Niebuhr would approve of this conclusion.

Appendix 1: The Cosmological Chart

1. Creator and created	God (The Creator)	Creation (the cosmos)	
2. Transcendence and immanence	God (Divine transcen-dence)	Natural transcen-dence; ideals	Physical realm of nature, including humanity (immanent)
3. Power and authority	The power and authority of God; Power and goodness together; Kingdom of God		Human power; Power vs goodness; Kingdom of the world

Bibliography

Published Works By Reinhold Niebuhr

Does Civilisation Need Religion?: A Study in the Social Resources and Limitations of Religion in Modern Life, (New York: Macmillan, 1928)
Leaves from the Notebook of a Tamed Cynic, (New York: Da Capo Press, 1976, reprinted from the 1929 edition)
The Contribution of Religion to Social Work, (New York: Columbia University Press, 1932)
Moral Man and Immoral Society: A Study in Ethics and Politics, (New York: Scribners, 1960, reprinted from the 1932 edition).
Reflections on the End of an Era, (New York: Scribners, 1934)
An Interpretation of Christian Ethics, (London: SCM, 1936)
Beyond Tragedy: Essays on the Christian Interpretation of History, (London: Nisbet, 1938)
Christianity and Power Politics, (New York: Scribners, 1940, reprinted in 1969 in an unaltered and unabridged edition by Archon Books)
The Nature and Destiny of Man: A Christian Interpretation, 2 vols, (London: Nisbet, 1941 – 1943)
The Children of Light and the Children of Darkness: A Vindication of Democracy and a Critique of its Traditional Defenders, (London: Nisbet, 1945)
Discerning the Signs of the Times: Sermons for Today and Tomorrow, (New York: Scribners, 1949)
Faith and History: A Comparison of Christian and Modern Views of History, (New York: Scribners, 1949)
The Irony of American History, (New York: Scribners, 1952)
Christian Realism and Political Problems, (New York: Scribners, 1953)
The Self and the Dramas of History, (New York: Scribners, 1955)
Pious and Secular America, (New York: Scribners, 1958)
The Structure of Nations and Empires: A Study of the Recurring Patterns and Problems of the Political Order in Relation to the Unique Problems of the Nuclear Age, (New York: Scribners, 1959)
Man's Nature and His Communities: Essays on the Dynamics and Enigmas of Man's Personal and Social Existence, (New York: Scribners, 1965)

Collections of Reinhold Niebuhr's shorter writings

Faith and Politics: A Commentary on Religious, Social and Political Thought in a Technological Age, ed. by Ronald H. Stone (New York: George Braziller, 1968)
Justice and Mercy, ed. by Ursula M. Niebuhr (New York: Harper and Row, 1974)

Article by Reinhold Niebuhr Cited in the Thesis

'Ten Years That Shook My World', *The Christian Century*, 56 (26 April 1939), 542-546. Fourteenth article in a series on "How My Mind Has Changed in This Decade".

Secondary Sources on Reinhold Niebuhr

Allen, E.L., *A Guide to the Thought of Reinhold Niebuhr: Christianity and Society*, (London: Hodder and Stoughton, no date)
Bingham, J. *The Courage to Change: An Introduction to the Life and Thought of Reinhold Niebuhr*, (Lanham, Maryland: University Press of America, 1993)
Carnell, Edward J., *The Theology of Reinhold Niebuhr*, (Grand Rapids: Eerdmans, 1951)
Cornelison, Robert T., *The Christian Realism of Reinhold Niebuhr and the Political Realism of Jurgen Moltmann in Dialogue: The Realism of Hope*, (San Francisco: Mellen Research University Press, 1992)
Clark, Henry B., *Serenity, Courage, and Wisdom: The Enduring Legacy of Reinhold Niebuhr*, (Cleveland, Ohio: Pilgrim Press, 1994)
Davies, D. R., *Reinhold Niebuhr: Prophet from America*, (London, James Clark, no date)
Durkin, Kenneth, *Reinhold Niebuhr*, (London: Geoffrey Chapman, 1989)
Fox, Richard W., *Reinhold Niebuhr: A Biography*, (New York: Pantheon, 1985)
Harland, George, *The Thought of Reinhold Niebuhr*, (New York: OUP, 1960)
Harries, Richard, ed., *Reinhold Niebuhr and the Issues of Our Time*, (London: Mowbray, 1986)
Hofmann, Hans, *The Theology of Reinhold Niebuhr*, trans. by Louise Pettibone Smith (New York: Scribners, 1956)
Kegley, Charles W., and Robert W. Bretall, eds., *Reinhold Niebuhr: His Religious, Social, and Political Thought*, Library of Living Theology Series, II (New York: Macmillan, 1956)
King, Rachel Hadley, *The Omission of the Holy Spirit From Reinhold Niebuhr's Theology*, (New York: Philosophical Library, 1964)
Landon, Harold R., *Reinhold Niebuhr: A Prophetic Voice in Our Time*, (Greenwich, Conn.: Seabury Press, 1962)
Lovin, Robin W., *Reinhold Niebuhr and Christian Realism*, (Cambridge: CUP, 1995)
Merkley, Paul, *Reinhold Niebuhr: A Political Account*, (Montreal: McGill-Queen's University Press, 1975)
Plaskow, Judith, *Sex, Sin and Grace: Women's Experience and the Theologies of Reinhold Niebuhr and Paul Tillich*, (Washington D.C.: University Press of America, 1980)

Rasmussen, Larry, ed., *Reinhold Niebuhr: Theologian of Public Life*, (London: Collins, 1988)
Robertson, D. B., *Reinhold Niebuhr's Works: A Bibliography*, (Boston, Mass.: G. K. Hall and Co., 1979)
Scott, Nathan A., ed., *The Legacy of Reinhold Niebuhr*, (Chicago: University of Chicago Press, 1975)
Warren, A. Heather, *Theologians of a New World Order: Reinhold Niebuhr and the Christian Realists 1920 - 1948*, (Oxford: OUP, 1997)

Other works

Adams, Marilyn M., and Robert M. Adams, eds., *The Problem of Evil*, (Oxford: OUP, 1990)
Allen, E. L., *Kierkegaard: His Life and Thought*, (London: Stanley Nott, 1935)
Aristotle, *Poetics*, trans. with an introduction and notes by Malcolm Heath (London: Penguin, 1996)
Balthasar, Hans Urs von, *The Theology of Karl Barth*, trans. by John Drury (New York, Chicago, San Francisco: Holt, Rinehart and Winston, 1971)
Baltzell, E. D., *The Protestant Establishment: Aristocracy and Caste in America*, (New York: Random House, 1964)
Barker, Philip, *Michel Foucault: Subversions of the Subject*, (Hemel Hemstead: Harvester Wheatsheaf, 1993)
Barth, Karl, *Church Dogmatics, II/2, The Doctrine of God, Part 2*, trans. by G.W. Bromiley et al (Edinburgh: T & T Clark, 1957)
-------------, *Church Dogmatics, III/2, The Doctrine of Creation, Part 2*, trans. by G.W. Bromiley et al (Edinburgh: T & T Clark, 1960)
-------------, *Church Dogmatics, III/3, The Doctrine of Creation, Part 3*, trans. by G.W. Bromiley and R. J. Ehrlich (Edinburgh: T & T Clark, 1960)
-------------, *Church Dogmatics, IV/1, The Doctrine of Reconciliation, Part 1*, trans. by G.W. Bromiley (Edinburgh: T & T Clark, 1956)
Bell, Daniel, *The End of Ideology: On the Exhaustion of Political Ideas in the Fifties*, revised edition (New York: The Free Press, 1962)
Berdyaev, N., *Freedom and the Spirit*, trans. from the Russian by O. F. Clarke (London: Bles, 1935)
----------------, *The Meaning of History*, trans. from the Russian by G. Reavey (London: Bles, 1936)
Berkouwer, G. C., *The Triumph of Grace in the Theology of Karl Barth*, (London: Paternoster, 1956)
----------------------, *Sin*, (Grand Rapids: Eerdmans, 1971)
Bernstein, Richard J., *Praxis and Action*, (London: Duckworth, 1972)
Blackham, H.J., *Six Existentialist Thinkers*, (London: Routledge and Kegan Paul, 1961)
Bonhoeffer, D., *Ethics*, ed. by E. Bethge (London: SCM, 1955)

Brereton, G., *Principles of Tragedy: A Rational Examination of the Tragic Concept in Life and Literature*, (Miami: University of Miami Press, 1968)

Brink, G. van den, *Almighty God: A Study of the Doctrine of Divine Omnipotence*, (Kamphen: Pharos, 1993)

Brunner, E., *Dogmatics Vol. II: The Christian Doctrine of Creation and Redemption*, trans. by O. Wyon (London: Westminster, 1952)

Buhle, P., *Marxism in the United States: Remapping the History of the American Left*, (London: Verso, 1991)

Bultmann, R., *Theology of the New Testament*, trans. by K. Goobel (London, SCM, 1952)

Cantor, Milton, *The Divided Left: American Radicalism, 1900 - 1975*, (New York: Hill and Wang, 1978)

Caponigri, A. Robert, *A History of Western Philosophy: Philosophy from the Romantic Age to the Age of Positivism*, (Notre Dame, Indiana: University of Notre Dame Press, 1971)

Cargill Thompson, W. D. J., *The Political Thought of Martin Luther*, (Brighton: Harvester, 1984)

Carver, Terrell, ed., *The Cambridge Companion to Marx*, (Cambridge: CUP, 1991)

Cooper, D. E., *Existentialism: A Reconstruction*, (Oxford: Blackwell, 1990)

Copleston, F., *A History of Philosophy*, 9 vols (London: Burns and Oates, 1946-1975)

----------------, *Friedrich Nietzsche: Philosopher of Culture*, (London: Search, 1975)

----------------, *Arthur Schopenhauer: Philosopher of Pessimism*, (London: Search, 1975)

Corrington, Robert S., *The Community of Interpreters: On the Hermeneutics of Nature and the Bible in the American Philosophical Tradition*, 2nd edn (Macon, Georgia: Mercer University Press, 1995)

Davis, Stephen T., ed., *Encountering Evil: Live Options in Theodicy*, (Edinburgh: T & T Clark, 1981)

Diggins, John P., *The Rise and Fall of the American Left*, (London: Norton, 1992)

--------------------, *The Promise of Pragmatism: Modernism and the Crisis of Knowledge and Authority*, (Chicago: University of Chicago Press, 1994)

Dillenger, J., *Luther: On Secular Authority*, (New York: Doubleday, 1961)

Dodd, C. H., *The Epistle of Paul to the Romans*, (London: Hodder and Stoughton, 1932)

Dunning, W. A., *A History of Political Theories: From Luther to Montesquieu*, (London: Macmillan, 1902)

Dupre, Louis, *The Philosophical Foundations of Marxism*, (New York: Harcourt, Brace and World, 1966)

Egbert, Donald Drew, and Stow Persons, eds., *Socialism and American Life*, 2 vols (Princeton: PUP, 1952)

Fiddes, Paul S., *The Creative Suffering of God*, (Oxford: Clarendon, 1988)
Ford, David F., ed., *The Modern Theologians: An Introduction to Christian Theology in the Twentieth Century*, 2 vols (Oxford: Blackwell, 1989)
Gill, Robin, *Moral Leadership in a Postmodern Age*, (Edinburgh: T & T Clark, 1997)
Grenz, Stanley and Roger Olson, *20th Century Theology: God and the World in a Transitional Age*, (Carlisle: Paternoster, 1992)
Guignon, Charles, ed., *The Cambridge Companion to Heidegger*, (Cambridge: CUP, 1993)
Gutiérrez, Gustavo, *A Theology of Liberation: History, Politics and Salvation*, trans. and ed. by Sister Caridad Inda and John Eagleson (London: SCM, 1974)
Guyer, Paul, ed., *The Cambridge Companion to Kant*, (Cambridge: CUP, 1992)
Halliwell, S., *Aristotle's Poetics*, (London: Duckworth, 1986)
---------------, *The Poetics of Aristotle*, trans. with a commentary (London: Duckworth, 1987)
Handy, Robert T., *The Social Gospel in America, 1870-1920: Gladden, Ely and Rauschenbusch*, (New York: OUP, 1966)
Hauerwas, Stanley, *A Community of Character: Toward a Constructive Christian Social Ethic*, (London: University of Notre Dame Press, 1981)
Heidegger, M., *Being and Time*, trans. by John Macquarrie and Edward Robinson (Oxford: Blackwell, 1962)
Hegel, G. W. F., *The Encyclopaedia of the Philosophical Sciences*, trans. as *The Logic of Hegel* by William Wallace (Oxford: Clarendon, 1892).
Heron, Alasdair, I. C., *A Century of Protestant Theology*, (Cambridge: Lutterworth, 1980)
Hinze, Christine F., *Comprehending Power in Christian Social Ethics*, (Atlanta: Scholars Press, 1995)
Hollingdale, R.J., ed., *A Nietzsche Reader*, (London: Penguin, 1977)
Honneth, Axel, *The Critique of Power: Reflective Stages in a Critical Social Theory*, trans. by Kenneth Baynes (London: MIT Press, 1991)
James, William, *The Will to Believe and Other Essays in Popular Philosophy*, (New York: Longmans Green and Co., 1904)
-------------------, *The Varieties of Religious Experience: A Study in Human Nature*, (New York: Longmans and Green, 1917)
-------------------, *Pragmatism*, (New York: Dover, 1995)
Jantzen, Grace M., *Becoming Divine: Towards a Feminist Philosophy of Religion*, (Manchester: Manchester University Press, 1998)
Johnson, Elizabeth A., *She Who Is: The Mystery of God in Feminist Theological Discourse*, (NY: Crossroads Publishing Co., 1992)
Kant, Immanuel, *Immanuel Kant's Critique of Pure Reason*, trans. by Norman Kemp Smith (Basingstoke: Macmillan, 1929)
Katz, Claudio J., *From Feudalism to Capitalism: Marxian Theories of Class Struggle and Social Change*, (London: Greenwood Press, 1989)

Kaufmann, Walter, *Nietzsche: Philosopher, Psychologist, AntiChrist*, 4th edn (Princeton: Princeton University Press, 1974)
Kegley, C.W., and Bretall, R.W., eds., *The Theology of Paul Tillich*, Library of Living Theology Series, I (New York: Macmillan, 1952)
Kierkegaard, S., *The Concept of Anxiety: A Simple Psychologically Orienting Deliberation on the Dogmatic Issue of Hereditary Sin*, ed. and trans. by R. Thomte and A. Anderson (Princeton: Princeton University Press, 1980)
------------------, *The Sickness Unto Death: A Christian Psychological Exposition for Upbuilding and Awakening*, ed. and trans., with an introduction and notes, by Howard V. Hong and Edna H. Hong (Princeton: Princeton University Press, 1980)
------------------, *Philosophical Fragments*, ed. and trans., with an introduction and notes, by Howard V. Hong and Edna H. Hong (Princeton: Princeton University Press, 1985)
Kirk, J. Andrew, *Liberation Theology: An Evangelical View from the Third World*, (Basingstoke: Marshall Morgan & Scott, 1979)
Lash, Nicholas, *A Matter of Hope: A Theologian's Reflections on the Thought of Karl Marx*, (London: Darton, Longman and Todd, 1981)
Leaman, Oliver, *Evil and Suffering in Jewish Philosophy*, (Cambridge: CUP, 1995)
Livingston, James. C., *Modern Christian Thought: From the Enlightenment to Vatican II*, (New York: Macmillan, 1971)
Loades, Ann, ed., *Feminist Theology: A Reader*, (London: SPCK, 1990)
Lukes, Steven, *Power: A Radical View*, (London: Macmillan, 1974)
Luther's Works, ed. by Jaroslav Pelikane and Helmut T. Lehmann, 55 vols (Philadelphia: Muhlenberg Press, 1952-86)
MacIntyre, Alasdair, *Marxism and Christianity*, (London: Duckworth, 1968)
Mackey, James P., *Power and Christian Ethics*, (Cambridge: CUP, 1994)
Mackintosh, Hugh Ross, *Types of Modern Theology: Schleiermacher to Barth*, (London: Nisbet, 1937)
Malantschuk, G., *Kierkegaard's Thought*, ed. and trans. by H. Hong and E. Hong (Princeton: Princeton University Press, 1971)
Marcell, David W. *Progress and Pragmatism: James, Dewey, Beard and the American Idea of Progress*, (London: Greenwood, 1974)
Marx, Karl, and Friedrich Engels, *The Communist Manifesto*, (London: Penguin, 1967)
--, *Collected Works*, 47 vols (London: Lawrence and Wishart, 1975-1998)
Meyer, D. B., *The Protestant Search for Political Realism, 1919 - 1941*, (Los Angeles: University of California Press, 1960)
McGrath, A. E., *Christian Theology: An Introduction*, (Oxford: Blackwell, 1994)
McLellan, David, *Marx*, (Glasgow: Fontana/Collins, 1975)

——————————, ed., *Karl Marx: Selected Writings*, (Oxford: OUP, 1977)
——————————, *Marxism and Religion: A Description and Assessment of the Marxist Critiques of Christianity*, (Basingstoke: Macmillan, 1987)
Miller, Perry, *Errand into the Wilderness*, (Cambridge, Mass.: Harvard University Press, 1956)
Mills, C. Wright. *Sociology and Pragmatism: The Higher Learning in America*, (New York: OUP, 1966)
Moltmann, J., *How I Have Changed: Reflections on Thirty Years of Theology*, (London: SCM, 1997)
Moore, Edward. C., *American Pragmatism: Peirce, James and Dewey*, (New York: Columbia University Press, 1961)
Niebuhr, H. Richard, *The Kingdom of God in America*, (Hamden, Conn.: Shoe String Press, 1956)
Neill, Stephen, ed., *Twentieth Century Christianity: A Survey of Modern Religious Trends by Leading Churchmen*, (London: Collins, 1961)
Nietzsche, F., *The Complete Works of Friedrich Nietzsche*, ed. by Oscar Levy (London: Allen and Unwin),
——————, Vol. IX: *The Dawn of Day*, trans. by J.M. Kennedy (1924)
——————, Vol. XII *Beyond Good and Evil*, trans. by Helen Zimmern (1923)
——————, Vol. XIII: *The Genealogy of Morals*, (1910)
——————, *The Gay Science*, trans. and with commentary by Walter Kaufmann, (New York: Random House, 1974)
——————, *The Birth of Tragedy*, trans. by S. Whiteside (London: Penguin, 1993)
——————, *Twilight of the Idols; The Anti-Christ*, trans. by R.. J. Hollingdale (London: Penguin, 1990)
——————, *The Will to Power: an Attempted Transvaluation of All Values*, trans. by A.M. Ludovici, 2 vols (London: Foulis, 1914)
O'Connor, D. J., ed., *A Critical History of Western Philosophy*, (New York: Macmillan, 1964)
Ott, H., *Reality and Faith: The Theological Legacy of Dietrich Bonhoeffer*, trans. by A. A. Morrison (London: Lutterworth, 1966)
Pells, Richard H., *Radical Visions and American Dreams: Culture and Social Thought in the Depression Years*, (Middletown, Conn.: Wesleyan University Press, 1973)
Perkins, Robert, ed., *The Concept of Anxiety: Vol. 8 of The International Kierkegaard Commentary*, (Macon: Mercer University Press, 1985)
Putman, Ruth Anna, ed., *The Cambridge Companion to William James*, (Cambridge: CUP, 1997)
Rauschenbusch, Walter, *A Theology for the Social Gospel*, (New York: Macmillan, 1919)
——————————, *Christianity and the Social Crisis*, ed. by Robert D. Cross (New York: Harper and Row, 1964)

Reardon, Bernard M. G., *Religious Thought in the Nineteenth Century: Illustrated from Writers of the Period*, (Cambridge: CUP, 1966)
------------------------------, ed., *Liberal Protestantism*, (London: Adams and Charles Black, 1968)
Robinson, H. Wheeler, *The Christian Doctrine of Man*, (Edinburgh: T&T Clark, 1958)
Roemer, John E., *Free to Lose: An Introduction to Marxist Economic Philosophy*, (London: Century Hutchinson, 1988)
Ross, Ralph, ed., *Makers of American Thought: An Introduction to Seven American Writers*, (Minneapolis: University of Minnesota Press, 1974)
Ruether, Rosemary Radford, *Womanguides: Readings Towards a Feminist Theology*, (Boston: Beacon Press, 1985)
Schopenhauer, A. *The World as Will and Idea*, 6th edition, trans. by R.B. Haldane and J. Kemp, 3 vols (London: Kegan Paul, Trench, Trubner, 1907-1909)
Shannon, David A., *Between the Wars: America, 1919 - 1941*, 2nd edn (Boston: Houghton Mifflin, 1979)
Silk, M. S., and Stern, J.P., *Nietzsche on Tragedy*, (Cambridge: CUP, 1981)
Solomon, Robert C., ed., *Nietzsche: A Collection of Critical Essays*, (New York: Anchor, 1973)
Sophocles, *The Theban Plays: King Oedipus, Oedipus at Colonus, Antigone*, trans. by E. F. Watling (London: Penguin, 1947)
Surin, Kenneth, *Theology and the Problem of Evil*, (Oxford: Blackwell, 1986)
Sweezy, Paul, ed., *The Transition from Feudalism to Capitalism*, with an introduction by Rodney Hilton (London: NLB, 1976)
Sykes, S. W., ed., *Karl Barth: Centenary Essays*, (Cambridge: CUP, 1989)
Tanner, Kathryn, *The Politics of God: Christian Theologies and Social Justice*, (Minneapolis: Fortress Press, 1992)
Thiselton, A. C., *New Horizons in Hermeneutics*, (London: HarperCollins, 1992)
------------------, *Interpreting God and the Postmodern Self: On Meaning, Manipulation and Promise*, (Edinburgh: T&T Clark, 1995)
Tillich, P., *Love, Power and Justice: Ontological Analyses and Ethical Applications*, (London: OUP, 1954)
------------, *On the Boundary: An Autobiographical Sketch*, (London: Collins, 1967)
------------, *Systematic Theology, Vol. II*, (London: Nisbet, 1957))
------------, *The Interpretation of History*, trans. by N. A. Rasetzki and Elsa L. Talmey (London: Scribers, 1936)
Turner, Denys, *Marxism and Christianity*, (Oxford: Blackwell, 1983)
Unamuno, M. de, *The Tragic Sense of Life in Men and Nations*, trans. by A. Kerrigan (London: Routledge & Kegan Paul, 1972)

Wahl, J., *Philosophies of Existence : An Introduction to the Basic Thought of Kierkegaard, Heidegger, Jaspers, Marcel and Sartre*, trans. by F. M. Lory (London: Routledge and Kegan Paul, 1969)

Welch, Claude, *Protestant Thought in the Nineteenth Century*, 2 vols, (New Haven: Yale University Press, 1972, 1985)

West, Charles, *Communism and the Theologians: Study of an Encounter*, (London: SCM, 1958)

West, Cornel, *The American Evasion of Philosophy: A Genealogy of Pragmatism.*, (Basingstoke: Macmillan, 1989)

White, Ronald, and C. Howard Hopkins, *The Social Gospel: Religion and Reform in Changing America*, (Philadelphia: Temple University Press, 1976)

Whiteley, D. E. H., *The Theology of St. Paul*, (Oxford: Blackwell, 1964)

Williams, N. P., *Ideas of the Fall and Original Sin*, (London: Longmans, Green and Co., 1929)

Woelfel, James W., *Bonhoeffer's Theology: Classical and Revolutionary*, (New York: Abingdon, 1970)

Young, Julian, *Nietzsche's Philosophy of Art*, (Cambridge: CUP, 1992)

Journal Articles and Theses

Bradley, M. C., 'Nietzsche's Critique of Pure Reason: With a Nietzschean Critique of Parsifal', *Neophilologus*, 72 (July 1988), pp. 394-403.

Calhoun, Robert L., 'Review of Niebuhr, Reinhold, The Nature and Destiny of Man, Vol I: Human Nature', *The Journal of Religion*, 21 (1941), pp. 473-480.

Calhoun, Robert L., 'Review of Niebuhr, Reinhold, The Nature and Destiny of Man, Vol II: Human Destiny', *The Journal of Religion*, 24 (1944), pp. 59-64.

Gill, Jerry, 'Kant, Kierkegaard and Religious Knowledge', *Philosophy and Phenomenological Research*, 28 (December 1967), pp. 188-204.

Goldstein, Valerie Saiving, 'The Human Situation: A Feminine View', *The Journal of Religion*, 40 (1960), pp. 100-112.

Heim, Mark S., 'Prodigal Sons: D. C. Macintosh and the Brothers Niebuhr', *Journal of Religion*, 65 (1985), pp. 336-358.

Minnema, Theodore, 'Reinhold Niebuhr's Concept of Power', *Christianity Today*, 6 (19 January 1962), pp. 378-380.

McCann, Dennis, 'Reinhold Niebuhr and Jaques Maritain on Marxism: A Comparison of Two Traditional Models of Practical Theology', *Journal of Religion*, 58 (1978), pp. 140-168.

Milmed, Bella K., 'Theories of Religious Knowledge, from Kant to Jaspers', *Philosophy*, 29 (July 1954), pp. 195-215.

Pyong Gap Min, 'A Comparison of Marx's and Dewey's Reactions to Industrialisation', *Educational Theory*, Winter 1979, Vol. 29, No. 1, pp. 41-51.

White, Richard, 'Art and the Individual in Nietzsche's Birth of Tragedy', *British Journal of Aesthetics*, 28 (1988), pp. 59-67.

Yates, K. L., 'An Analysis of the Development of Reinhold Niebuhr's Theological Realism in the Light of the Social, Economic and Political History of the United States from 1910 to 1940' (unpublished MPhil thesis, University of Nottingham, 1979).

Index

A

anthropology, xv, 8, 13, 16, 22, 24, 31, 34, 38, 39, 41, 47, 56, 58, 61, 73, 89-93, 100, 110-112, 142, 145, 151, 170, 171-173, 188

anxiety, 27-30, 32, 34, 58, 94, 95-101, 110, 116, 117, 123, 126, 128, 132, 170, 175, 188
   anxious self, 27, 28, 31, 32, 40, 61, 77, 86, 94, 99, 112, 116, 121, 123, 126, 127, 130, 132, 146

atonement, 85, 119-121, 125, 137, 139-141, 153, 154, 170, 191, 197

B

Barth, Karl, 2, 12, 62-71, 75, 78, 90, 141, 188

C

Christ, xiii, 12, 13, 14, 60, 64-70, 75, 80, 87, 89, 96, 110, 116-125, 131-142, 157, 160, 164-170, 183, 184, 185, 188, 197, 198, 199
   Cross of Christ, 68, 95, 117-125, 137-142, 164-167, 175, 198, 199

Christian Realism, xv, xvii, 2, 42, 48, 54, 73, 74, 100, 110, 112, 113, 118, 141, 144, 150, 156, 170-185, 188, 191

Christology, xv, 73, 100, 117-121, 138, 140, 151, 170, 188, 191

Creation, xvi, 20, 60, 66, 67, 73-91, 93, 108, 114, 153, 158, 161, 162, 170, 188, 193, 194, 196, 198

D

democracy, 3, 8, 9, 21, 23, 48, 177, 178

Detroit, 5, 7, 15, 18, 34, 64, 93, 174

E

epistemology, xv, 5, 6, 15-23, 34, 38, 40, 42, 48, 49, 52, 55, 56, 58, 61, 73, 76, 78, 81, 85, 91, 100, 111, 129, 142, 151-156, 161, 162, 165, 166-170, 174, 188, 191

existentialism, 111
   existential self, 16, 19, 57, 93, 143, 147, 154-155, 170

F

Fall, 6, 7, 9, 21, 22, 28, 29, 30, 45, 78, 82, 99, 153, 162-166, 170

Fascism, 2, 4, 8, 9, 21, 42, 135
   Fascist politics, 31, 84

feminist theology, 106, 151, 182, 195

First World War, 2-7, 63

G

grace, xiii, 33, 42, 63, 67-70, 78, 84, 87, 103, 116, 119, 126-139, 142, 148, 154, 160, 164, 170, 184, 188, 197, 198

H

Holy Spirit, 60, 83, 131, 132, 133, 135, 184, 185, 191

J

James, William, 15-20, 39, 48-63, 91, 94, 101, 112, 143, 145, 187, 194
judgment, 12, 14, 63, 65, 70, 84, 85, 88, 98, 108, 109, 114-116, 119-122, 126, 127, 129-133, 135-140, 154, 155, 162, 165, 167, 197
justice, 2, 4, 5, 7, 13, 16, 18, 22, 49, 50, 54, 60, 65, 68, 70, 79, 83, 84, 88, 90, 100, 104, 106, 110, 111, 114-121, 139, 144, 145, 155, 156, 159, 163, 167, 172, 173-179, 182, 197, 198

K

Kierkegaard, Soren, 9, 19, 24-34, 43, 51, 56, 58, 63, 67, 74, 94, 95, 97, 110, 112, 145, 167, 170, 187

L

liberal Protestantism, 11-15, 16, 18, 24, 104, 159, 187
    liberalism, xv, 2-8, 11-15, 18, 34, 41, 54, 63, 74, 84, 89, 90, 118, 141, 148, 151, 172, 188
Liberation theology, 107, 111, 151, 182, 195

M

Marxism, 7-9, 14-24, 53, 64, 104, 111, 118, 142, 151, 187, 188
    Marxist, 4, 7- 8, 14-23, 47, 146, 157, 187
myth, 19, 20, 40, 76, 81, 82, 85, 108, 117, 140-142, 152, 153, 156, 161-170, 174, 191

N

Neo-orthodoxy, 54, 62, 63, 90, 118, 159
    Neo-orthodox, xv, 12, 62-71, 78, 140, 187
Nietzsche, Friedrich, 35-47, 58, 99, 145, 187

O

original sin, 13, 19, 22, 24, 29-33, 64, 70, 95-97, 101-105, 111, 147, 149, 153, 157, 159, 162, 197

P

pacifism, 7-9, 13, 95, 148, 178-179
    pacifist, 6, 95
paradox, 9, 32, 40, 81, 82, 85, 94, 97, 117, 120, 134, 142, 152, 156, 161, 164, 166-168, 194, 196
Platonism, 77, 81, 85
    Platonic, 80-81
    Platonist, 81, 168, 190
Political theology, xv
Pragmatism, 6, 15-21, 48-61, 86, 95, 142, 152, 156, 187
    Pragmatic, xv, 16, 20, 48-62, 65, 78, 94, 118, 182, 187, 189, 194-196
    Pragmatist, 15, 16, 20, 42, 48, 50, 52, 61, 89, 174, 187, 194
problem of evil, xv, 31, 34, 41, 42, 48, 59, 62-65, 70, 71, 76, 77, 88, 91, 95, 99, 104, 107, 113, 114, 118, 137, 187, 190, 192, 193, 194-198

R

rationalism, 33, 129, 151
    rationalist, 4, 33, 35, 49, 58, 90, 92, 143-152, 194

Rauschenbusch, Walter, 3, 4, 11, 13
Romanticism, 34-47, 58, 99, 108, 152
  Romantic, 34-47

S

salvation, xv, 14, 19, 33, 45, 47, 59, 60, 63, 65-70, 73, 83, 90, 96, 98-103, 110-112, 113-141, 142-151, 153-156, 161, 164, 170-172, 175, 188, 191
Second World War, 2, 4, 8
sin, xv, 6, 8, 12, 14, 24-34, 40-42, 45-47, 58, 63, 64, 66-70, 73, 76-79, 82, 85, 87, 89, 90, 93-112, 113-116, 118-123, 126-129, 131-134, 137-145, 148-151, 153, 156, 158-160, 164-168, 170-174, 181, 187, 188, 190, 191, 196-199
Social Gospel, 2-6, 9, 11-14, 15, 61
symbol, 40, 76, 81, 85, 117, 119, 124, 140-142, 152, 156, 161-170, 174

T

tragedy, 34, 42-47, 97, 98, 108, 109, 118-125, 126, 139, 162, 166
  the tragic, 12, 24, 43-47, 100, 107, 108, 109-110, 115, 118, 123, 126, 132, 137, 157

Paternoster Biblical and Theological Monographs

Joseph Abraham
Eve: Accused or Acquitted?
*A Reconsideration of Feminist Readings
of the Creation Narrative Texts in Genesis 1–3*

Two contrary views dominate contemporary feminist biblical scholarship. One finds in the Bible an unequivocal equality between the sexes from the very creation of humanity, whilst the other sees the biblical text as irredeemably patriarchal and androcentric. Dr. Abraham enters into dialogue with both camps as well as introducing his own method of approach. An invaluable tool for any one who is interested in this contemporary debate.

2002/ 0-85364-971-5 /

Emil Bartos
Deification in Eastern Orthodox Theology
An Evaluation and Critique of the Theology of Dumitru Staniloae

Bartos studies a fundamental yet neglected aspect of Orthodox theology: deification. By examining the doctrines of anthropology, christology, soteriology and ecclesiology as they relate to deification, he provides an important contribution to contemporary dialogue between Eastern and Western theologians.

1999 / 0-85364-956-1 / xi + 370pp

Jonathan F. Bayes
The Weakness of the Law
God's Law and the Christian in New Testament Perspective

A study of the four New Testament books which refer to the law as weak (Acts, Romans, Galatians, Hebrews) leads to a defence of the third use in the Reformed debate about the law in the life of the believer.

2000 / 0-85364-957-X / xi + 243pp

Mark Bonnington
The Antioch Episode of Galatians 2:11–14 in Historical and Cultural Context

The Galatians 2 'incident' in Antioch over table-fellowship suggests significant disagreement between the leading apostles. This book analyses the background to the disagreement by locating the incident within the dynamics of social interaction between Jews and Gentiles. It proposes a new way of understanding the relationship between the individuals and issues involved.

2002 / 1-84227-050-8 /

Mark Bredin
Jesus as a Non-Violent Revolutionary
A Study in the Functional Christology of the Book of Revelation
2003 / 1-84227-153-9 /

Colin J. Bulley
The Priesthood of Some Believers
Developments in the Christian Literature of the First Three Centuries

The first in-depth treatment of early Christian texts on the priesthood of all believers shows that the developing priesthood of the ordained related closely to the division between laity and clergy and had deleterious effects on the practice of the general priesthood.

2000 / 1-84227-034-6 / xii + 336pp

Daniel J-S Chae
Paul as Apostle to the Gentiles
His Apostolic Self-awareness and its Influence on the Soteriological Argument in Romans

Opposing 'the post-Holocaust interpretation of Romans', Daniel Chae competently demonstrates that Paul argues for the equality of Jew and Gentile in Romans. Chae's fresh exegetical interpretation is academically outstanding and spiritually encouraging.

1997 / 0-85364-829-8 / xiv + 378pp

Luke L. Cheung
The Genre, Composition and Hermeneutics of the Epistle of James

The present work examines the employment of wisdom genre with a certain compositional structure and the interpretation of the law through the Jesus' tradition of the double love command by the author of the Epistle of James to serve his purpose in promoting perfection and warning against doubleness among the eschatologically renewed people of God in the Diaspora.

2002 / 1-84227-062-1 /

Andrew C. Clark
Parallel Lives
The Relation of Paul to the Apostles in the Lucan Perspective

This study of the Peter–Paul parallels in Acts argues that their purpose was to emphasize the themes of continuity in salvation history and the unity of the Jewish and Gentile missions. New light is shed on Luke's literary techniques, partly through a comparison with Plutarch.

2001 / 1-84227-035-4 / xviii + 384pp

Sylvia I. Collinson
Discipling as an Educational Strategy
An Enquiry into the Congruence of Discipling with the Objectives of Christian Faith Communities

This study examines the biblical practice of discipling, formulates a definition, and makes comparisons with modern models of education. A recommendation is made for greater attention to its practice today.

2002 / 1-84227-116-4 /

Stephen M. Dunning
The Crisis and the Quest
A Kierkegaardian Reading of Charles Williams

Employing Kierkegaardian categories and analysis, this study investigates both the central crisis in Charles Williams's authorship between hermetism and Christianity (Kierkegaard's Religions A and B), and the quest to resolve this crisis, a quest that ultimately presses the bounds of orthodoxy.

2000 / 0-85364-985-5 / xxiv + 254pp

Keith Ferdinando
The Triumph of Christ in African Perspective
A Study of Demonology and Redemption in the African Context
The book explores the implications of the gospel for traditional African fears of occult aggression. It analyses such traditional approaches to suffering and biblical responses to fears of demonic evil, concluding with an evaluation of African beliefs from the perspective of the gospel.
1999 / 0-85364-830-1 / xvii + 450pp

Andrew Goddard
Living the Word, Resisting the World (Provisional title)
The Life and Thought of Jacques Ellul
This work offers a definitive study of both the life and thought of the French Reformed thinker Jacques Ellul (1912–1994). It will prove an indispensable resource for those interested in this influential theologian and sociologist and for Christian ethics and political thought generally.
2002 / 1-84227-053-2 /

Scott J. Hafemann
Suffering and Ministry in the Spirit
Paul's Defence of His Ministry in 2 Corinthians 2:14 – 3:3
Shedding new light on the way Paul defended his apostleship, the author offers a careful, detailed study of 2 Corinthians 2:14 – 3:3 linked with other key passages throughout 1 and 2 Corinthians. Demonstrating the unity and coherence of Paul's argument in this passage, the author shows that Paul's suffering served as the vehicle for revealing God's power and glory through the Spirit.
2000 / 0-85364-967-7 / xiv + 261pp

John G. Kelly
One God, One People
The Differentiated Unity of the People of God
in the Theology of Jürgen Moltmann
The author expounds and critiques Moltmann's doctrine of God and highlights the systematic connections between it and Moltmann's influential discussion of Israel. He then proposes a fresh approach to Jewish–Christian relations building on Moltmann's work using insights from Habermas and Rawls.
2003 / 0-85346-969-3 /

Mark Lovatt
Confronting the Will-to-Power
A Reconsideration of the Theology of Reinhold Neibuhr
Confronting the Will-to-Power is an analysis of the theology of Reinhold Niebuhr, arguing that his work is an attempt to identify, and provide a practical theological answer to, the existence and nature of human evil.
2001 / 1-84227-054-0 / xvii + 217pp

Neil B. MacDonald
Karl Barth and the Strange New World within the Bible
Barth, Wittgenstein, and the Metadilemmas of the Enlightenment
Barth's discovery of the strange new world within the Bible is examined in the context of Kant, Hume, Overbeck, and, most importantly, Wittgenstein. Covers some fundamental issues in theology today; epistemology, the final form of the text and biblical truth-claims.
2000 / 0-85364-970-7 / xxvi + 373pp

Gillian McCulloch
The Deconstruction of Dualism in Theology
with Special Reference to Ecofeminist Theology and New Age Spirituality
This book challenges eco-theological anti-dualism in Christian theology, arguing that dualism has a twofold function in Christian religious discourse. Firstly, it enables us to express the discontinuities and divisions that are part of the process of reality. Secondly, dualistic language allows us to express the mysteries of divine transcendence/immanence and the survival of the soul without collapsing into monism and materialism, both of which are problematic for Christian epistemology.
2002 / 1-84227-044-3 / xii + 281pp

Leslie McCurdy
Attributes and Atonement
The Holy Love of God in the Theology of P.T. Forsyth
Attributes and Atonement is an intriguing full-length study of P.T. Forsyth's doctrine of the cross as it relates particularly to God's holy love. It includes an unparalleled bibliography of both primary and secondary material relating to Forsyth.
1999 / 0-85364-833-6 / xii + 327pp

Nozomu Miyahira
Towards a Theology of the Concord of God
A Japanese Perspective on the Trinity
This book introduces a new Japanese theology and a unique Trinitarian formula based on the Japanese intellectual climate: three betweennesses and one concord. It also presents a new interpretation of the Trinity, a co-subordinationism, which is in line with orthodox Trinitarianism; each single person of the Trinity is eternally and equally subordinate (or serviceable) to the other persons, so that they retain the mutual dynamic equality.
2000 / 0-85364-863-8 / xiv + 256pp

Stephen Motyer
Your Father the Devil?
A New Approach to John and 'The Jews'
Who are 'the Jews' in John's Gospel? Defending John against the charge of antisemitism, Motyer argues that, far from demonising the Jews, the Gospel seeks to present Jesus as 'Good News for Jews' in a late first-century setting.
1997 / 0-85364-832-8 / xiii + 260pp

Eddy José Muskus
Origins and Early Development of Liberation Theology in Latin America
With Particular Reference to Gustavo Gutiérrez
This work challenges the fundamental premise of Liberation Theology, 'opting for the poor', and its claim that Christ is found in them. It also argues that Liberation Theology emerged as a direct result of the failure of the Roman Catholic Church in Latin America.
2002 / 0-85364-974-X /

Esther Ng
Reconstructing Christian Origins?
The Feminist Theology of Elizabeth Schüssler Fiorenza:
An Evaluation
In a detailed evaluation, the author challenges Elizabeth Schüssler Fiorenza's reconstruction of early Christian origins and her underlying presuppositions. The author also presents her own views on women's role both then and now.
2002 / 1-84227-055-9 /

Ian Paul
Power to See the World Anew
*The Value of Paul Ricoeur's Hermeneutic of Metaphor
in Interpreting the Symbolism of Revelation 12 and 13*
This book is a study of the hermeneutics of metaphor of Paul Ricoeur, one of the most important writers on hermeneutics and metaphor of the last century. It sets out the key points of his theory, important criticisms of his work, and how his approach, modified in the light of these criticisms, offers a methodological framework for reading apocalyptic texts.

2002 / 1-84227-056-7 /

David Powys
'Hell': A Hard Look at a Hard Question
The Fate of the Unrighteous in New Testament Thought
This comprehensive treatment seeks to unlock the original meaning of terms and phrases long thought to support the traditional doctrine of hell. It concludes that there is an alternative – one which is more biblical, and which can positively revive the rationale for Christian mission.

1999 / 0-85364-831-X / xxii + 478pp

Ed Rybarczyk
Beyond Salvation
*An Analysis of the Doctrine of Christian Transformation
Comparing Eastern Orthodoxy and Classical Pentecostalism*
2003 / 1-84227-144-X /

Signe Sandsmark
Is World View Neutral Education Possible and Desirable?
A Christian Response to Liberal Arguments
(Published jointly with The Stapleford Centre)
This thesis discusses reasons for belief in world view neutrality, and argues that 'neutral' education will have a hidden, but strong world view influence. It discusses the place for Christian education in the common school.

2000 / 0-85364-973-1 / xiv + 181pp

Andrew Sloane
On Being a Christian in the Academy
Nicholas Wolterstorff and the Practice of Christian Scholarship
An exposition and critical appraisal of Nicholas Wolterstorff's epistemology in the light of the philosophy of science, and an application of his thought to the practice of Christian scholarship.
2002 / 1-84227-058-3 /

Daniel Strange
The Possibility of Salvation Among the Unevangelised
An Analysis of Inclusivism in Recent Evangelical Theology
For evangelical theologians, the 'fate of the unevangelised' impinges upon fundamental tenets of evangelical identity. The position known as 'inclusivism', defined by the belief that the unevangelised can be ontologically saved by Christ whilst being epistemologically unaware of him, has been defended most vigorously by the Canadian evangelical Clark H. Pinnock. Through a detailed analysis and critique of Pinnock's work, this book examines a cluster of issues surrounding the unevangelised and its implication for Christology, soteriology and the doctrine of revelation.
2001 / 1-84227-047-8 / xviii + 362pp

G. Michael Thomas
The Extent of the Atonement
A Dilemma for Reformed Theology from Calvin to the Consensus
A study of the way Reformed theology addressed the question, 'Did Christ die for all, or for the elect only?', commencing with John Calvin, and including debates with Lutheranism, the Synod of Dort and the teaching of Moïse Amyraut.
1997 / 0-85364-828-X / ix + 277pp

Mark Thompson
A Sure Ground on Which to Stand
The Relation of Authority and Interpretative Method of Luther's Approach to Scripture
2003 / 1-84227-145-8 /

Graham Tomlin
The Power of the Cross
Theology and the Death of Christ in Paul, Luther and Pascal
This book explores the theology of the cross in St Paul, Luther and Pascal. It offers new perspectives on the theology of each, and some implications for the nature of power, apologetics, theology and church life in a postmodern context.
1999 / 0-85364-984-7 / xiv + 343pp

Kevin Walton
Thou Traveller Unknown
The Presence and Absence of God in the Jacob Narrative
The author offers a fresh reading of the story of Jacob in the book of Genesis through the paradox of divine presence and absence. The work also seeks to make a contribution to Pentateuchal studies by bringing together a close reading of the final text with historicalcritical insights, doing justice to the text's historical depth, final form and canonical status.
2002 / 1-84227-059-1 /

Graham J. Watts
Revelation and the Spirit
*A Comparative Study of the Relationship between
the Doctrine of Revelation and Pneumatology in the Theology of
Eberhard Jüngel and of Wolfhart Pannenberg*
The relationship between revelation and pneumatology is relatively unexplored. This approach offers a fresh angle on two important twentieth-century theologians and raises pneumatological questions which are theologically crucial and relevant to mission in a post modern culture.
2002 / 1-84227-104-0 /

Alistair Wilson
Matthew's Portrait of Jesus the Judge, with Special Reference to Matthew 21–25
2003 / 1-84227-146-6 /

Nigel G. Wright
Disavowing Constantine
Mission, Church and the Social Order in the Theologies of John Howard Yoder and Jürgen Moltmann
This book is a timely restatement of a radical theology of church and state in the Anabaptist and Baptist tradition. Dr. Wright constructs his argument in dialogue and debate with Yoder and Moltmann, major contributors to a free church perspective.
2000 / 0-85364-978-2 / xv + 251pp

Stephen Wright
The Voice of Jesus
Studies in the Interpretation of Six Gospel Parables
This literary study considers how the 'voice' of Jesus has been heard in different periods of parable interpretation, and how the categories of figure and trope may help us towards a sensitive reading of the parables today.
2000 / 0-85364-975-8 / xiv + 280pp

The Paternoster Press
P.O. Box 300
Carlisle, Cumbria,
CA3 0QS
United Kingdom

Web: www.paternoster-publishing.com

www.ingramcontent.com/pod-product-compliance
Lightning Source LLC
Chambersburg PA
CBHW070248230426
43664CB00014B/2443